The Flavours of Canada

The Flavours of Canada

A Celebration of the Finest Regional Foods

by Anita Stewart

Photography by Robert Wigington

RAINCOAST BOOKS

Vancouver

A Denise Schon Book

First published in 2000 by
Raincoast Books
8680 Cambie Street
Vancouver, B.C.
V6P 6M9
(604) 323-7100
www.raincoast.com

Canadian Cataloguing in Publication Data
Stewart, Anita.
The Flavours of Canada

Includes index.
ISBN 1-55192-182-0

1. Cookery, Canadian. I. Wigington, Robert. II. Title.
TX715.6.S738 2000   641.5971   C00-910168-3

Produced by: Denise Schon Books Inc.
Design: Adams + Associates Design Consultants Inc.
Editor: Kirsten Hanson/Jennifer Glossop
Copy Editor: Shaun Oakey
Index: Barbara Schon

Studio Photography
Food Stylists: Olga Truchan, Wendy Bowen
Prop Stylist: Maggi Jones
Front jacket: Pan-Seared Port Renfrew Lingcod
with Watercress Sauce, Soybean Croquettes and
Honeyed Local Vegetables (p. 39)

Printed and bound in China
9 8 7 6 5 4 3 2 1

Dedication

For my sons, Jeff, Brad, Mark and Paul.

Thanks for being by my side and constantly reminding
me why life, particularly here in Canada, is such
a treasure. Stay tuned guys...our journey continues.

Contents

Our many-splendoured Canadian cuisine is sometimes described as a multicultural "tossed salad" (as compared to a "melting pot" south of the border). At other times, it's pictured as a gigantic layer cake, or a multi-tiered sandwich that keeps getting bigger and better, with layer upon layer of intriguing flavours and colours and textures.

I prefer the layered, rather than tossed, analogy, but I'd package it a bit differently. Canadian cuisine doesn't present itself conveniently on one plate. It's more like one of those enormous, alluringly wrapped gift boxes that when opened reveals another inside, then another and another until you find something very special at the centre.

This big package of Canadian flavours is not easy to unwrap. To do so requires someone with persistence, patience and passion for the task. Someone like Anita Stewart. Anita understands that Canadian cuisine is much more than surface wrappings (whether that be stylish new restaurant menus or stereotyped traditions like butter tarts and tourtière). She insists on digging more deeply, savouring every new discovery, and finding in each a connection to who we really are as Canadians.

The food ways of every country are a direct reflection of everything else about the country — its geography, history, culture, people. So the long-standing challenge of defining Canadian cooking is understandable: How do you package a cuisine that spans some 8000 kilometres and encompasses a dozen dramatically different regions, three centuries of history and wave after wave of new flavours from all over the world?

I've long maintained that Canadian cuisine is best defined by its diversity, and Anita pulls it all together in this book. She presents a dazzling package of our regional, seasonal, multicultural tapestry of flavours, not only interweaving the past and present but adding an important new dimension — the future. She often uses the words "vision" and "possibilities" — just as she has ever since I've known her.

I first met Anita when she was researching her first book about farmers' markets, and the sparkle was already in her eye. Such awesome bounty, such wonderful people, such amazing stories! The whole world needed to know about this! That passion grew even stronger as she expanded her explorations of Canadian food ways, wrote several more books, and in the early 1990s led the founding of Cuisine Canada, the first national association of food professionals.

Over the years, Anita has often called me to share stories, serious or silly, about her food experiences — from lighthouses and oil rigs to farm kitchens and fabulous inns, or simply after "a long walk on a soft Quadra Island night, with the scent of overripe blackberries filling the air." But whether she's alone or visiting with farmers or fishers, food scientists or artists, historians or futurists, she always gets to "that something very special at the centre" — a connection to our identity as Canadians, our heritage and our future.

Canadians are traditionally self-effacing about such things. Anita says, "Let's get over it." This is the perfect time to rev up our culinary flag-waving, to celebrate and share proudly our rich diversity of traditions, contemporary styles, splendid regional ingredients and visionary food people. Here's to *The Flavours of Canada!*

Carol Ferguson

Left: *Herbs and flowers used in vinegars and preserves at Tangled Garden, Nova Scotia*

Canada overflows with magnificent flavours! Our ingredients, of the land and sea, link us with our past, our present and our future. As a culinary explorer, I have been one of the most privileged people in the nation. I have tasted my land — savoured it deeply. This book chronicles much of that colourful journey. It's been almost two decades in the making and reflects countless meals across tens of thousands of kilometres.

While I was growing up in the countryside near Toronto, food was unsophisticated and fresh. Childhood days were filled with picking raspberries and marvelling at how high the blackcurrant bushes were. I watched the asparagus patch for the first spring shoots and ate sugar-dipped rhubarb stalks and chased the neighbours' geese that ravaged our gardens. In the late 1950s my mother and I moved to Mount Forest, the home of our Irish, English and Prussian ancestors. There, in the centre of Ontario's farming country, we used bottled dressings and packaged cheese slices, but we also tapped our own trees to make maple syrup in the spring and haunted the dusty back roads in the summer for chokecherries and elderberries to make jellies. In August we filled the fruit cellar with pickles, and at Christmas we hand-dipped chocolates and feasted on roast goose.

By the 1970s I had moved to Elora, a proud village in the heart of Wellington County, and was cooking frugally from scratch as my forebears had. I pored over Mennonite cookbooks, scoured the local farms for ingredients from dried beans to maple syrup and became versed in baking, freezing and preserving. At Christmas, my four sons and I gave gifts of gingerbread houses, homemade candy and wild grape jelly. When we started the Elora Co-operative Pre-School with the help of the local United Church, our kick-off project was a hand-assembled cookbook. That was my first foray into publishing.

11

While I was taking a history of food course at the University of Guelph, professor Jo Marie Powers suggested that we collaborate on a book that would explore the foods of Ontario's farmers' markets. Off we went every weekend of the summers of 1982 and 1983. The resulting *Farmers Market Cookbook* (General/Stoddart, 1984) provided the foundation that led to myriad other publishing projects. It was then that I began to recognize the connection between who we are as Canadians and what we eat — how tightly our food and culture are intertwined. Thirteen books and many articles followed, all chronicling the good food of our country.

Those were days of heady adventure. I flew to all of B.C.'s light stations with the coast guard and snowmobiled across northern Quebec; I skied and hiked and scuba dived — all in search of that elusive concept, the real Canadian cuisine. And I found it! In farmhouse kitchens and at church suppers, on coast guard icebreakers and in the galley of an oil rig in the North Atlantic. From the thoughtful meals at fabulous inns like Sooke Harbour House on Vancouver Island and Auberge Hatley in the Eastern Townships of Quebec to the honest cooking of great roadside diners in the Maritimes, I learned that Canadian food is as exotic and sexy as any on earth!

Left: *Heli-hikers gather for lunch in the Bugaboos, British Colombia*
Right: *Dulse dories, Grand Manan, New Brunswick*

From Nootka Sound to Cape Spear, our story is one of great culinary wealth. Canadian cuisine is the shore-shattered iceberg that pops and fizzes in your drink at an inn on Cape Onion on the Great Northern Peninsula of Newfoundland. It's the flax seed and the wild rice that really is wild in Saskatchewan. It's a cranberry bog near Huntsville, Ontario, an orchard of heritage apples on Saltspring Island, British Columbia, and a steaming cabane au sucre in the Laurentian Mountains of Quebec. It's joining with friends in a warm Mennonite farm kitchen in Waterloo County, Ontario, to share platters of smoked pork chops and homemade sauerkraut, glass bowls of summer-stewed fruit and crisp confections known as rosettes. It's fishermen who for centuries have sailed along the rocky shores of Grand Manan in their brightly painted dories pulling dulse, the red, salty seaweed, off slippery intertidal boulders at the base of cliffs where eagles nest. Canadian cuisine is lobster dinners and ceilidhs and roundups. It's surf clams in a thick, steaming chowder and toutons drenched in molasses in an all-night café in St. John's. It's fruit wines, pumpkin ale and cloudberry liqueur. It's the utter glory of foie gras and cave-aged Migneron cheese. It's jugs of maple syrup, a warehouse full of aging prosciutto hanging in perfect rows like giant saffron-coloured teardrops, and huge wheels of golden cheddar cheese. It's the pitch-dark, bitter-cold ice wine harvest.

Canadian cuisine is recipes like those in this book, chosen from every layer of culinary Canada. Some are truly old-fashioned, historic dishes, such as the Pot en Pot "Tante Yvonne" aux Fruits de Mer, Maple Syrup Crème Brûlée, Waterloo County Roasted Pig Tails and Valerie's Version of Lady Ashburnham's Pickles. Some recipes, like *The* Best Butter Tarts and Astorville Cipaille/Sea Pie, have raised thousands of dollars for community organizations and parishes all across the nation. Others are utterly upscale, like the Pan-Seared Arctic Char with Golden Oat and Cheddar Cheese Risotto and Balsam Fir Browned Butter, and Woolwich Dairy Ravioli with Smoked Tomato and Basil Sauce, and reflect not only the scope of our ingredients but the tremendous talent of our chefs. But above and beyond all else Canadian cuisine is about celebrating our magnificent differences, our roots and our ethnicity. It's about possibilities and how we as a people continue to welcome immigrants from all over the earth and in doing so permanently enrich our food ways. It's about creating the best from our local ingredients, then selling it to the world. It's about branding ourselves Canadian and giving our producers an unmistakable edge that no other nation can emulate. It's about proudly joining together as a people at a national table to share the flavours of Canada.

13

Anita Stewart
January 2000

Left: *Salmonberries*
Right: *Farm tractor, British Colombia*

Chapter 1
British Columbia

British Columbia is a magical place. I head there whenever my spirit needs recharging. Over the millennia, the area has fed countless other souls — spiritually and physically. Coastal British Columbia was the first region on the continent to be settled. About 10,000 years ago, small bands of people crossed the Bering land bridge and settled along the Pacific coast. They became the people of the salmon, for the fish was their most important food. The chiselled multi-thousand-year-old fish images on the boulders that line many of the Gulf Islands not only honour the salmon's presence, they are testament to the faith these people had in the spirits to bring fish to them in plentiful schools.

These early settlers caught the first salmon of the season as part of a First Salmon Ceremony. This springtime ritual was a time for the band to celebrate and give thanks. That first fish was sacrificed so that his brothers and sisters would come. And they came! Silvery blue coho, powerful chinook and later school upon school of pinks and chum. They were trapped in weirs at the mouths of rivers and speared or netted or simply caught on hooks with kelp or cedar lines. The eagles fed well during those salmon summers.

Salmon are so elemental to British Columbia that Roderick Haig-Brown, a fisher and environmentalist, stated unequivocally in *The Salmon:* "If there is ever a time when the salmon no longer return, man will know he has failed again and has moved one stage nearer his own disappearance." Salmon are still central to B.C. cooking.

On the islands and coast of British Columbia, the First Nations people also developed a system of commerce called potlatching. During an extended period of fasting and feasting, the Natives redistributed wealth in a sensible and generous fashion. The theory was that the waters and the forests were so rich they had to be shared. The person who gave away the most, often impoverishing himself in the process, was the richest in terms of prestige. Although now mere shadows of the previous extravagant events, potlatches still take place.

Without question, eulachon oil, or grease as it is commonly called, is the most treasured and valuable potlatch gift from the waters of British Columbia. Honey-coloured, the fermented fish oil was once so widely traded that the trade routes were called grease trails. Alexander Mackenzie, the first European explorer to cross the continent of North America and reach the Pacific, followed one such trail from the Interior to the coast in 1793, arriving in Bella Coola, still considered home of the best grease.

Left: *Shucking oysters, Cortes Island*
Above: *View of Bugaboo Glacier from Bugaboo Lodge*

Canada's only indigenous cooking method, bentwood box cookery, was developed during the ancient times, long before European contact. It was women's work, a ritual completed with pride. Handmade cedar boxes were filled with water to soak and tighten for three or four days. A fire was lit and potato-sized beach rocks were placed in it to heat. The hot rocks were then picked out of the fire with a split alder branch, washed briefly in one box, then placed in a second filled with water and salmonberry shoots. In moments the water foamed and boiled. Seafood was added — prawns, scallops, clams, chunks of halibut or salmon — and a woven mat was placed over top to hold the steam. Within minutes the pure, sweet tastes of the sea were retrieved from the box and the feast began.

In the days before Confederation, the Canadian Pacific Railway (CPR) played a formidable role in defining the culinary West. With the railway in 1858 came the first Chinese labourers, men who'd already toiled for a decade in California. Two years later the flood of Chinese immigrants — mostly male — began to fill in gaps in the frontier economy. They ran laundries and restaurants, but most of all they did dangerous work that few Europeans would tackle. When the Gold Rush ended and the railway was completed, many took jobs in the coastal canneries; others started market gardens. But most founded businesses and lived on the shores of False Creek in the heart of what is now Chinatown in Vancouver. Their wives soon joined them and helped transform the city into the culinary maze we know today. Mangosteens and rambutans, Black Dragon tea and hair fungus: shop after shop spills its array of Asian foods onto Pender and Main and Keefer streets. Fresh durians hang from slings over a pyramid of crisp, green-stemmed gai lohn from the Fraser River delta. Clerks haul well-iced bins of live geoduck clams onto the sidewalk to entice customers, while Dungeness crabs wriggle crossly, and prickly rockfish stare from their tanks.

Today, British Columbian cuisine is characterized by youthful bravado and a drive to break all rules, cast away traditions, experiment, and change the taste of food in Canada. In the 1960s and 1970s, when British Columbia was a haven for the flower children, vegetarianism took hold here. Fusion cooking, an ever-changing blend of Asian flavours with British Columbian ingredients, began here in earnest. Hothouse growing is big business, and British Columbia sets the North American standard for hydroponically grown tomatoes and peppers.

Left: *Centuries-old petroglyph and bentwood box, Quadra Island*
Above: *Greens in market, Chinatown, Vancouver*

Many of B.C.'s restaurants are trend-setters. Sooke Harbour House in the town of Sooke on Vancouver Island is a tiny inn whose owners set out to define local cuisine. There Canadians first tasted edible flowers and gooseneck barnacles and geoduck clams. And Chef Hidekazu Tojo introduced Vancouverites to the wonders of sushi and sashimi and all foods Japanese long before it was fashionable anywhere else in North America.

Vancouver takes its restaurants seriously. The Vancouver Magazine Restaurant Awards fills a ballroom with chefs and restaurateurs and critics. The energy in this competitive culinary community is palpable. The Vancouver Playhouse Wine Festival is widely known and prestigious, and the wine industry is booming and replete with vocal renegades who refuse to comply with the rules. This is feisty B.C., after all. Granville Island Market bustles, and new areas outside the city are filled with fabulous food experiences.

Travellers and commuters switch gears when they ferry from Vancouver to Vancouver Island. Even the climate is gentler. Disembarking at Swartz Bay, en route to the city of Victoria, you drive through the Saanich Peninsula, a region of small, often organic farms. Here you can buy kiwifruit and fresh figs. Rosemary bushes and roses bloom all year round.

Victoria has less rain than the mainland, and residents garden for eleven months of the year. In February, Victorians thumb their noses at the rest of Canada and count their flowers. The British influence is obvious there. Victorians love tea — all aspects of it. A multitude of blends are available — some custom-made — and throughout the city, small cafés and large hotels like The Empress make a ritual of taking tea in the afternoon. Murchie's is probably the most famous tea shop in Canada, and Rogers' Chocolates just across the street is equally well known.

Victorians have also appreciated great handcrafted beer since the city's earliest days. Victoria had the first commercial brewery in western Canada. Even before they had a lighthouse to guide ships into the harbour — the Fisgard light, the first in B.C., was constructed in 1860 — William Steinberger of the Victoria Brewery was supplying settlers with tankards of suds. And today Victoria still can claim the most innovative brew pub

Above: *Geoduck clams*

in the nation, Spinnakers. Whenever I'm in town I stop for a pint and a bowl of steamers, fresh shellfish simmering in its own delicious broth.

Throughout British Columbia there are lush growing regions, each with its own special flavours. The Okanagan and Similkameen valleys are among the great fruit-growing regions on the continent. The first apples were planted near Kelowna in 1862 by an Oblate priest, Father Charles Pandozy. For generations, orchards and fruit groves have stretched for kilometres over the valleys' sun-soaked slopes.

Father Pandozy also planted grapes, and today the valleys' wine-growing potential is being recognized around the world. Two of the original wineries, Gehringer Brothers Estate Winery at Oliver and Gray Monk Cellars near Vernon, bracket the long, slender Okanagan region. New ones are springing up on most arable hillsides, and in the Similkameen Valley, which pokes westward toward Keremeos, growers are beginning to plant in earnest. The L-shaped territory is the northernmost desert viticultural area in the world. It's a bit warmer than Burgundy in France and compares favourably to Sonoma in northern California. Dry breezes blow away pests and discourage disease, allowing many vintners to be certified organic. During the intense, hot summers, sugar levels in the grapes soar, and lack of rainfall ensures that the flavours remain concentrated. Some wineries receive sunlight not only from overhead but also reflected from the lake. The region is also blessed with deep winter freezes, absolutely perfect for making ice wine.

In the Shuswap/Thompson region north of the Okanagan, where the summers are hot and long, the vegetables have incredible flavour. The wild harvest from the rocky slopes and the high mountain meadows includes some of the most exotic ingredients British Columbia has to offer. Pine mushrooms, which flourish in the evergreen forests, are so treasured that buyers, often with prices boldly posted, camp on the roads near where pickers are foraging. The carrots are so sweet they taste as if they have been injected with sugar.

From the Fraser River Valley with its hazelnuts to the Pemberton-Lillooet area with its potatoes and ginseng and huckleberries; from the handcrafted balsamic vinegar of Marilyn and Giordano Venturi-Schulze on Vancouver Island to the rare vetch-flower honey found only in the foothills of the Monashee Mountains, British Columbia is a land of abundance and promise. Indeed, as in the potlatching tradition, this land is so rich that it must be shared.

Above: *Vigneti Zanatta vineyard, Vancouver Island*

Oyster Jim's Clayoquot Roasting Oysters

Oyster Jim (Jim Martin) is a local character and grower of the most flavour-filled mollusks that I've ever eaten. Mind you, the experience was enhanced by standing on a beach in the wilds of Clayoquot Sound on Vancouver Island as we shucked and slurped and savoured.

These recipes, created by Rob Butters while he was chef at the Wickaninnish Inn, are best made with large Pacific oysters like Jim's.

Oysters Topped with Ucluelet's Goat Cheese and Basil

This recipe was tested with goat's milk cheese made on a remote farm near Ucluelet, a small town on the north side of Barkley Sound near Tofino.

1 cup (250 mL)	lightly packed fresh basil leaves
2 tbsp. (25 mL)	canola oil
4 oz. (125 g)	plain goat's milk cheese
12	opened oysters in the shell

✦ Place basil and oil in a food processor and process to a coarse purée, scraping down the sides once. Add goat cheese and process until well blended. Spoon cheese mixture onto the oysters and place in a shallow roasting pan. Use coarse salt or crumpled foil in the pan to keep the shells level. Broil for 5 minutes or until cheese begins to melt. **Makes 4 servings.**

Oysters Topped with Tomato Compote with Parmesan Bread Crust

1 tsp. (5 mL)	canola oil
1/2 cup (125 mL)	finely chopped onion
1/2 cup (125 mL)	finely chopped fennel
2	tomatoes, seeded and chopped
1 tbsp. (15 mL)	chopped fresh thyme
1/4 cup (50 mL)	fresh bread crumbs
1/4 cup (50 mL)	freshly grated Parmesan cheese
2 tbsp. (25 mL)	chopped fresh parsley
12	opened oysters in the shell

✦ Heat oil in a skillet over medium heat. Cook onion and fennel for 5 minutes or until softened. Stir in tomatoes and thyme; cook for 4 to 5 minutes longer until all liquid has evaporated.

✦ In a small bowl, stir together bread crumbs, Parmesan and parsley. Spoon tomato compote onto the oysters. Top with bread crumb mixture. Arrange oysters in a shallow roasting pan. Use coarse salt or crumpled foil in the pan to keep the shells level. Broil for 5 minutes or until golden and heated through. **Makes 4 servings.**

To open oysters. Before using roasting oysters they must be cooked to open. Cook until firm and moist by using any of the methods below. The higher the cooking temperature, the easier the oysters are to open.

✦ In a large pot with 1 inch (2.5 cm) water, steam oysters, covered, for 8 to 10 minutes.

✦ Barbecue oysters for 10 minutes over medium-hot coals or medium gas setting.

✦ Bake for 25 minutes in preheated 425°F (220°C) oven.

Cooked oysters will open about 1/2 inch (1 cm). Place on a firm base with cupped side down. Hold oyster firmly with a towel and gently push oyster knife or strong butter knife between shells along the seam dividing the two halves. Move the knife back and forth to loosen the muscle from the shell, cutting at the hinge. Remove top shell. Loosen the flesh, saving as much of the juice as possible. Discard any oysters that do not open.

The "Wick"

Soft, round notes of a hidden flute rise as the sun sets over the Pacific. As the most westerly shores of Vancouver Island become shadowy, frogs take over, singing their hearts out. Offshore, a line of breakers surges onto a reef connecting the islands. This is Tofino on the west coast of Vancouver Island. More specifically, it is the Wickaninnish Inn, the long-time dream of the McDiarmid family, located in an area that is under consideration as a UNESCO World Biosphere Zone. On three sides of the inn there is the ocean; behind the inn is old-growth forest. When I think of the "Wick," I think of whales and storms and fabulous food. At night on the beach the only lights are from the masses of stars, the lighthouse that flashes rhythmically and a few flickering campfires.

Flash-Grilled Spot Prawns with Garlic Crisps and Roasted Hazelnut Vinaigrette

A dish served at Piccolo Mondo, an Italian restaurant in Vancouver, inspired this unusual recipe. Choose a variety of fresh greens, but if you wish to be true to the innovative tradition of British Columbia, include pea shoots, miner's lettuce and the blossoms of scarlet runner beans. Or mix and match your own mesclun from the list of greens and flowers on page 25.

If you're lucky enough to have Marilyn and Giordano's Venturi-Schulze's precious balsamic vinegar (see above), use a splash of it around the plate rim for a pungent contrast.

Roasted Hazelnut Vinaigrette

This versatile dressing showcases the great hazelnuts grown in British Columbia's southern mainland.

1/2 cup (125 mL)	hazelnuts, roasted and skinned
1	clove garlic
3 tbsp. (45 mL)	apple cider vinegar, preferably organic
2 tsp. (10 mL)	fireweed or other wild British Columbia honey
1 tsp. (5 mL)	dry mustard
1/2 tsp. (2 mL)	salt
1/2 tsp. (2 mL)	freshly ground black pepper
1/2 cup (125 mL)	hazelnut oil
1/2 cup (125 mL)	canola oil

✦ *In a food processor or blender, combine hazelnuts, garlic, vinegar, honey, mustard, salt and pepper. Process for 15 to 30 seconds or until smooth. Add hazelnut and canola oils. Process to blend thoroughly. Refrigerate till needed or for up to 1 week.* **Makes about 1 1/2 cups (375 mL).**

21

> **To roast hazelnuts,** *spread shelled hazelnuts in a single layer on a large cookie sheet. Bake in a preheated 325°F (160°C) oven, shaking and stirring every 5 to 7 minutes until the skins begin to crack and turn dark brown. Transfer nuts to a tea towel. Fold the edges to cover the nuts completely and let cool. Rub vigorously to loosen skins. Unfold the towel and, with your hands, continue to rub off any skins that still cling to the hazelnuts. Store nuts in a tightly covered container.*

(continued)

Garlic Crisps

1 tbsp. (15 mL)	soft unsalted butter
2 tbsp. (25 mL)	sugar
1 1/2 tbsp. (20 mL)	corn syrup
1 1/2 tbsp. (20 mL)	whipping cream (35%)
1 tsp. (5 mL)	all-purpose flour
1/4 cup (50 mL)	minced garlic

✦ Lightly oil 2 baking sheets and line them with parchment paper.

✦ In a small, heavy saucepan, blend butter, sugar, corn syrup, cream and flour. Bring to a boil; reduce heat to low and cook, stirring, for 5 minutes. Stir in garlic; remove from heat.

✦ Spoon batter into 12 rounds on the baking sheets, allowing room for spreading. Bake in a preheated 400°F (200°C) oven for 5 to 6 minutes or until completely golden. If crisps touch each other during baking, cut apart with a very sharp knife while warm. Note that the speed with which they bake varies with the thickness of the baking sheet. Watch carefully, as they must be totally golden but can burn quickly. Let cool on sheets and store in tightly covered container till needed or up to 1 day. **Makes 12 crisps.**

Flash-Grilled Spot Prawns

1 tbsp. (15 mL)	canola oil
1 lb. (500 g)	fresh spot prawns with shells on
	Salt and freshly ground pepper, to taste

✦ Moments before serving, heat the oil in a large skillet over medium-high heat. Sauté the prawns quickly. Add salt and pepper.

To Serve

Fresh salad greens
Balsamic vinegar (optional)

✦ Assemble the salad by placing a layer of greens on each of 6 chilled salad plates. Drizzle with a little Roasted Hazelnut Vinaigrette. Top each with 2 Garlic Crisps, the prawns, a final spoonful of the vinaigrette, and a decorative splash of balsamic vinegar, if using. Serve immediately. **Makes 6 servings.**

Tofino Smoked Salmon, Spartan Apple Potato Cakes, Poached Free-Range Eggs on Fig Anise Toast with Minted Chili Hollandaise

This dish, adapted from the morning menu at the Wickaninnish Inn, has many components, each of which could be used in some other fabulous way. The Fig Anise Bread is incredible with a cheese course, and the Minted Chili Hollandaise could be used over grilled fish. Try the Spartan Apple Potato Cakes with fresh applesauce and sour cream. Or combine them in this magnificent brunch!

Fig Anise Bread

Vancouver Island can now lay claim to a handful of fig growers. The wide-leafed vines grow on the Saanich Peninsula, and the fruit is sold fresh at the small markets around the southern part of the island.

2 tbsp. (25 mL)	active dry yeast
2 cups (500 mL)	warm water
2 tbsp. (25 mL)	butter, melted
1 tbsp. (15 mL)	molasses
2 1/2 cups (625 mL)	whole-wheat flour
2 cups (500 mL)	white bread flour
1 tbsp. (15 mL)	ground anise
1 tsp. (5 mL)	salt
1 cup (250 mL)	chopped dried figs
	Eggwash as needed

✦ Lightly grease two 8" x 4" (1.5 L) loaf pans. In a large bowl, sprinkle yeast over water and let stand for 10 minutes or until frothy. Whisk in butter and molasses.

✦ In another bowl, stir together whole-wheat and bread flours, anise, salt and figs. Stir flour mixture into yeast until a soft dough is formed. Turn out onto floured work surface and knead for 5 minutes or until smooth and elastic, adding up to 1/2 cup (125 mL) additional bread flour if dough is too sticky.

✦ Place dough in an oiled bowl, turning to coat with oil, and cover with plastic wrap. Let rise until doubled, 45 to 60 minutes. Punch dough down, and divide in half. Shape each half into an 8" x 7" (20 x 18 cm) rectangle. Tightly roll dough jelly-roll style, pinching seams to seal. Place in prepared pans. Let loaves rise in a warm place, covered, until 1 1/2 times the original size, about 45 minutes. Brush with eggwash. Bake in a preheated 400°F (200°C) oven for 30 minutes or until golden and loaves sound hollow when tapped on the bottom. Cool on wire racks. **Makes 2 loaves.**

Spartan Apple Potato Cakes

2	Spartan apples, peeled and shredded
1 lb. (500 g)	russet potatoes, peeled, boiled and shredded
2 tbsp. (25 mL)	chopped fresh chives
3 tbsp. (45 mL)	canola oil
	Salt and freshly ground pepper

✦ Mound shredded apples in the centre of a clean kitchen towel, fold over towel to enclose apples completely, and twist ends to squeeze as much liquid from apples as possible. In a large bowl, stir together apples, potatoes, chives, 1 tbsp. (15 mL) of the oil, and salt and pepper to taste. Shape apple mixture into 8 patties.

✦ Heat remaining 2 tbsp. (25 mL) oil in a non-stick skillet over medium heat. Add patties to skillet, in batches if necessary, and cook for 3 to 4 minutes on each side until golden. Remove from skillet and keep warm. **Makes 8 patties.**

Minted Chili Hollandaise

4	egg yolks
2 tbsp. (25 mL)	lemon juice
2 tsp. (10 mL)	water
2 tbsp. (25 mL)	chopped fresh mint
1	jalapeno pepper, seeded and minced
1/2 tsp. (2 mL)	salt
3/4 cup (175 mL)	unsalted butter

✦ In a food processor combine egg yolks, lemon juice, water, mint, jalapeno and salt. Pulse and process until mint and pepper are thoroughly chopped and the yolks are frothy.

✦ In a small saucepan, over medium heat, melt butter until bubbling but not brown. While motor is running, pour butter in a thin stream into egg mixture, and process until sauce is smooth and slightly thickened. Keep warm over a pan of hot water if not immediately serving. **Makes 1 1/4 cups (300 mL).**

Poached Eggs

4	free-range eggs

✦ In a skillet of simmering water, poach eggs 2 to 3 minutes or until desired doneness is reached. Drain.

To Serve

4	toasted slices Fig Anise Bread
4	slices smoked salmon
4	slices smoked salmon jerky (optional)
4	whole fresh chives

✦ Place 1 slice of toast on each of 4 serving plates and top each with smoked salmon. Place poached eggs on top, and spoon Minted Chili Hollandaise over the eggs. Place two Spartan Apple Potato Cakes on each plate, and garnish with smoked salmon jerky and chives. **Makes 4 servings.**

To make eggwash, mix 1 beaten egg with 1 to 2 tsp. (5 to 10 mL) water or milk.

23

Salmon

In their gravelly nest, called a redd, little salmon fry dally for a time, absorbing their egg sac and gaining strength before breaking out to gorge on a watery smorgasbord of mayfly nymphs and chironomid larvae. Eventually, they are drawn to the ocean. Coastal bays and coves are full of these feisty fish, now called smolt. They frolic in the kelp beds, becoming voracious feeders, often overshooting their surface-skimming bug-snack to sail through the air like so many tiny, silvery missiles. As they mature to their "sea run" stage, they begin the fabulous feeding trek that takes some species thousands of kilometres into the Pacific, only to loop back home when gripped by sexual maturity. As they near fresh water, they pause and stop eating. All their energy is directed into that final upstream surge. Away from the salty ocean, they change both shape and colour. In enormous scarlet schools, they power over rapids and around fallen logs, dodging bears and humans, leaping waterfalls — all in order to get home in time to spawn and die.

Northwest Coast Salad

Although this wild, foraged and cultivated green salad mix can be found in many incarnations across Canada, it began in British Columbia, specifically at Sooke Harbour House in Sooke. Then, very quickly, other adventurous restaurants — supplied by the Glorious Garnishes and Seasonal Salad Company — hopped on the culinary bandwagon. However, nowhere was there as true a rendition as there was at Sooke Harbour House, where Dr. Nancy Turner, Canada's expert on coastal plant foods of the First Nations, identified the plants many of us now take for granted.

Since this salad can be prepared in different seasons, the flavour of the dressing should vary to suit the greens. Try Michael Noble's classic vinaigrette (p. 29) for light spring greens or Roasted Hazelnut Vinaigrette (p. 21) for the heartier late-season varieties. Use any or all of the following greens and flowers with wild abandon.

Wild Greens

Select the tender shoots, flower petals and even tiny flower buds of these "weeds":

amaranth	chicory
chickweed	dandelion
lamb's quarters	miner's lettuce
purslane	sorrel

Cultivated Greens

Seeds for these and several dozen more can be obtained from Richters Herbs, Goodwood, Ontario (see p. 107):

mâche (cornsalad)	mizuna
tatsoi	pak choi
gai lohn	red and purple shiso
flowering kale	salad burnet
shungiku	arugula
radicchio	(Italian chicory)

Edible Flowers

These are just a few of my favourites. Remember that they must be organically grown, and you should never experiment without first checking the toxicity of a plant. African violets and lily of the valley are beautiful but not in the least edible. The following list is tried and true:

tuberous begonias	fuchsia
pineapple sage	scented geraniums
Johnny-jump-ups	nasturtiums
herb flowers	scarlet runner bean blossoms
violas	lilacs
daylilies	true lilies
pansies	tulips
old-fashioned roses	

25

Sooke Harbour House

At Sooke Harbour House the beauty is close to overwhelming. Across the Strait of Juan de Fuca, the Olympic Mountains are awash in pink and blue and purple. Seals lie on boulders in a bed of kelp that fills the bay below the inn. The evening air is filled with the smell of wood smoke, the sea and the kitchen. The Sooke Harbour House philosophy has had a huge influence. In a country so young in culinary terms, the inn and its owners, Sinclair and Frederique Philip, are legendary. They believe in harvesting locally, supporting their neighbouring producers and telling the world about it. Gourmet magazine, in its "Rooms at the Top" compilation, gave Sooke the number-one position for Authentic Local Cuisine — not in Canada, not in North America, but in the world!

Left: *Sooke Harbour House*

Salad of Warm Smoked Black Cod, New Potatoes, Leeks and Arugula with Horseradish Vinaigrette

This recipe was developed by Chef Rob Feenie of Lumière, a culinary hot spot in Vancouver. Black cod, or sable fish, is one of the finest fish caught on the coast.

3/4 lb. (375 g)	small new potatoes
3	leeks, white and
	pale green parts only, sliced
4 cups (1 L)	milk
3	sprigs fresh thyme
2	cloves garlic, skins on and crushed
1 lb. (500 g)	smoked black cod
1	shallot, finely chopped
4	radishes, thinly sliced
4 cups (1 L)	arugula, washed and dried
	Edible flowers (p.25) for garnish

✦ In a small saucepan, cover potatoes with salted water. Bring to a boil, reduce heat and simmer, covered, for 15 minutes or just until tender. Remove potatoes from saucepan with a slotted spoon and set aside until cool enough to handle; slice potatoes and place in a large serving bowl. Return water to a boil. Add leeks and simmer for 2 minutes or until tender. Drain well and add to the serving bowl.

✦ In a large saucepan, combine milk, thyme and garlic. Bring to a boil. Add cod and simmer for 5 minutes or until heated through. Using a slotted spoon, remove fish to a plate and flake with a fork. Discard milk. Add cod, shallot, radishes and arugula to serving bowl. Drizzle Horseradish Vinaigrette over salad and toss gently to combine. Scatter with flowers. *Makes 4 to 6 servings.*

Horseradish Vinaigrette

2 tbsp. (25 mL)	cider vinegar
2 tsp. (10 mL)	grated fresh horseradish
1/2 tsp. (2 mL)	dry mustard
1/4 tsp. (1 mL)	salt
1/4 tsp. (1 mL)	freshly ground black pepper
1/2 cup (125 mL)	canola oil
1 tbsp. (15 mL)	finely chopped fresh chives

✦ Place vinegar, horseradish, mustard, salt and pepper in a bowl. Whisk to combine. Whisking continuously, slowly add oil in a thin steady stream until a smooth dressing forms. Stir in chives just before serving. *Makes 3/4 cup (175 mL).*

Warm Salad of Free-Range Chicken, Grilled Vegetables and Red Pepper Coulis

Michael Noble from Diva at the Met in Vancouver raises B.C. cuisine to new and extraordinarily delicious levels. It's the freshness of his ingredients combined with his huge talent that has cemented his reputation.

Popcorn sprouts, which are the sprouted seeds of sweet corn, are becoming more widely available. You can substitute home-sprouted buckwheat, which is exceedingly easy to grow, or alfalfa sprouts.

Michael often serves this in the restaurant with deep-fried shoestring potatoes.

Grilled Vegetables

1	sweet red pepper, quartered and seeded
1	sweet yellow pepper, quartered and seeded
1	medium zucchini, cut in 1/2-inch (1 cm) slices
1	Japanese eggplant, cut in 1/2-inch (1 cm) cubes
10	leaves fresh basil, chopped
2 tbsp. (25 mL)	chopped fresh oregano
2	cloves garlic, minced
1/4 cup (50 mL)	canola oil

✦ In a large bowl, toss together red and yellow peppers, zucchini, eggplant, basil, oregano, garlic and oil. Heat grill to medium-high. Place vegetables on greased grill and barbecue for 2 to 3 minutes on each side or until tender and brown with grill marks. Remove from grill and let cool to room temperature.

Red Pepper Coulis

2	sweet red peppers
1 tsp. (5 mL)	canola oil
	Salt and freshly ground pepper to taste

✦ Place red peppers in a roasting pan and drizzle with oil. Sprinkle with salt and pepper. Broil peppers until skin is blackened, about 2 minutes per side. Remove peppers to a container with a lid and let stand, covered, until cool enough to handle. Peel and seed roasted peppers and place in blender. Blend until smooth. **Makes 1 cup (250 mL).**

Vinaigrette

2 tsp. (10 mL)	white wine vinegar
1 tsp. (5 mL)	grainy mustard
1	shallot, minced
1	clove garlic, minced
1/4 cup (50 mL)	canola oil
	Salt and freshly ground pepper to taste

✦ In a small bowl, whisk together vinegar, mustard, shallot and garlic. Gradually whisk in oil. Season with salt and pepper.

Chicken Salad

4	boneless chicken breasts, with skin
3 tbsp. (45 mL)	canola oil
1 tsp. (5 mL)	chopped fresh thyme
1/2 tsp. (2 mL)	salt
1/2 tsp. (2 mL)	freshly ground pepper
1	small bunch watercress
1 cup (250 mL)	popcorn sprouts
4 cups (1 L)	mesclun greens
4 oz. (125 g)	goat's milk feta cheese, cubed
1 cup (250 mL)	Zucchini Pickles (p. 55)

✦ Drizzle chicken breasts with 2 tbsp. (25 mL) of the oil; sprinkle with thyme, salt and pepper. Heat remaining 1 tbsp. (15 mL) oil in a non-stick skillet over medium-high heat. Cook chicken, skin side down, for 3 minutes or until skin is golden and crispy. Transfer chicken to a preheated 375°F (190°C) oven and roast for 10 to 15 minutes or until chicken is no longer pink. Remove from oven and keep warm.

✦ In a large bowl, combine watercress, sprouts, greens, feta, Zucchini Pickles and Vinaigrette.

To Serve

✦ Divide salad among 4 dinner plates. Arrange Grilled Vegetables around salad and drizzle some Red Pepper Coulis around plate. Slice each chicken breast and place on each salad; serve immediately. **Makes 4 servings.**

29

Cape Mudge Halibut Chowder

The Cape Mudge Lightstation on Quadra Island off Vancouver Island is one of the last manned stations on the coast. Its keepers, Wendy and Jim Abram, have been leaders in the fight against the automation that threatens a pioneering way of life that has survived on the coast for well over a century.

2 tbsp. (25 mL)	canola oil
5	medium carrots, peeled and cut in 1/4-inch (5 mm) slices
3	large stalks celery, cut in 1/2-inch (1 cm) slices
2	large onions, coarsely chopped
4	large cloves garlic, minced
5 cups (1.25 L)	water or fish stock (p. 189)
1	28-oz. (796 mL) can crushed tomatoes
1 tsp. (5 mL)	dried oregano
1/4 tsp. (1 mL)	sea salt
1/4 tsp. (1 mL)	coarsely ground black pepper
1	bay leaf
1	sweet red pepper, coarsely chopped
1	sweet green pepper, coarsely chopped
1 1/2 lb. (750 g)	halibut, boned and cut in 1-inch (2.5 cm) cubes

✦ Heat oil in a large saucepan over medium heat. Sauté carrots, celery, onion and garlic for 10 minutes or until softened. Stir in water, tomatoes, oregano, salt, pepper and bay leaf. Bring to a boil, cover and simmer for 1 hour or until vegetables are very tender. Add red and green peppers; cook, covered, for 15 minutes. Gently stir in fish and simmer 5 to 8 minutes or until fish is cooked through and just beginning to flake. Discard bay leaf.

✦ Ladle into warmed soup bowls. Serve with Cape Mudge Cheese Scones (p. 42). **Makes 6 to 8 servings.**

Potlatching

A potlatch takes years to prepare. Masks must be carved; dances must be learned; the fabulous button blankets worn at the ceremony must be designed and sewn; and the traditional foods of both the land and the sea must be gathered and stored away. Harvesting begins a full year in advance. In the spring, hemlock boughs are suspended in the surf. Herring will coat the boughs with their foamy masses of eggs, and the boughs are then hung to dry. Narrow ribbons of roe-covered kelp are collected and dried. Specially selected seaweed is harvested and dried on cedar racks on village rooftops. Schools of spawning eulachon fish are netted and processed for their rich oil. Berries are picked and frozen.

Most of the village cooks take part in the preparations for guests, who sometimes number in the hundreds. There are many meals and many dishes: kettles of brothy moose stew, roasted venison, baked salmon, fried halibut, battered and fried eulachon, razor and butter clam fritters, fish soup in a light seaweed broth and bowls filled with preserved huckleberries, blackberries and small wild blueberries. Each table has bowls of salty dried seaweed to dip into the pungent eulachon grease.

Seaweed plays a prominent role in the cuisines of many nations, particularly Japan. Canada has the longest coastline on Earth, yet the only seaweeds we eat are carrageen, or Irish moss, and dulse in Atlantic Canada. Now, however, in Bamfield — a remote village on the south side of Barkley Sound on Vancouver Island's western shore — kelp is being harvested, dried (which is no mean feat in this damp climate) and sold around Canada and internationally. Canadian Kelp Resources, a company founded in 1981, processes and packages a variety of kelp, from alaria (Alaria marginata) and bull kelp (Nereocystis leutkeana), to laminaria (kambu) and macrocystis. It is used in soups, sushi and to flavour rice.

Pan-Seared Arctic Char with Golden Oat and Cheddar Cheese Risotto and Balsam Fir Browned Butter

Down Dinner Bay Road, on Mayne Island's southern shore, is Oceanwood, a nearly picture-perfect inn. This recipe is an example of the kitchen's attentiveness to local cuisine. Balsam fir shoots are infused into a pungent, foresty syrup. If you can't find them, substitute fresh rosemary.

Golden Oat and Cheddar Cheese Risotto

3 tbsp. (45 mL)	canola oil
1 tbsp. (15 mL)	unsalted butter
3/4 cup (175 mL)	large-flake (old-fashioned) oats
1	small onion, finely chopped
1	clove garlic, minced
1/2 tsp. (2 mL)	minced fresh ginger
1	bay leaf
1 1/2 cups (375 mL)	vegetable (p. 103) or fish (p. 189) stock
1/2 cup (125 mL)	whipping cream (35%)
1 cup (250 mL)	shredded cheddar cheese
1 tbsp. (15 mL)	chopped fresh tarragon
1 tbsp. (15 mL)	chopped fresh parsley
	Salt and freshly ground pepper

✦ *In a heavy-bottomed saucepan, heat oil and butter over medium heat. Add oats, onion, garlic, ginger and bay leaf. Cook, stirring, for 8 minutes or until oats are golden and fragrant. Add stock, 1/2 cup (125 mL) at a time, cooking each addition until all the liquid is absorbed before adding more stock. Stir in the whipping cream, cheese, tarragon and parsley. Season with salt and pepper to taste; discard bay leaf. Remove from heat and let stand for 10 minutes before serving.*

Balsam Fir Syrup

1 cup (250 mL)	sugar
1/2 cup (125 mL)	balsam fir shoots (or rosemary leaves), cleaned and towel dried
1 cup (250 mL)	water

✦ *Combine sugar, balsam fir shoots and water in a small saucepan. Bring to a boil, reduce heat and simmer for 10 minutes or until reduced by half. Strain syrup through a fine sieve and set aside.*

Pan-Seared Arctic Char

4	boneless, skinless Arctic char fillets (about 4 oz./125 g each)
	Salt and freshly ground pepper to taste
1 tsp. (5 mL)	chopped fresh tarragon
1 tsp. (5 mL)	chopped fresh parsley
2 tbsp. (25 mL)	canola oil
3 tbsp. (45 mL)	unsalted butter
	Balsam Fir Syrup (recipe above)

✦ *Season fillets with salt and pepper and sprinkle with tarragon and parsley. Heat oil in a non-stick skillet over medium-high heat. Add fillets and cook for 3 minutes on each side or until fish is golden and flakes easily with a fork. Remove fish from the skillet and keep warm. Melt butter in skillet and add syrup, allowing it to foam and brown. Remove from heat and season to taste with salt and pepper.*

To Serve

✦ *Divide Golden Oat and Cheddar Cheese Risotto among 4 warm dinner plates. Place Arctic char fillet on top and drizzle with a spoonful of Balsam Fir Syrup.* **Makes 4 servings.**

Whole Crab Pot with
Green Onions and Ginger

John Bishop is one of Canada's foremost and best-loved restaurateurs. He is the epitome of hospitality. Bishop's, his small, near-perfect restaurant on West 4th Street in Vancouver, is the place to which everyone seems to return after trying out the latest culinary hot spots. And John never disappoints.

Enjoy this casual communal recipe of John's with some close friends. Tie big napkins around your necks and spend a couple of hours cracking and eating the crabs. The Chinese hot pots in which the crabs are cooked and served are ceramic with tight-fitting lids. They can be found at Chinese cooking shops.

Fully cooked crab legs may be substituted for the Dungeness crabs. Use 8 whole legs and add to the hot pots along with the tomato sauce and green onions.

4	Dungeness crabs
1 tbsp. (15 mL)	canola oil
1 tsp. (5 mL)	sesame oil
1/2 cup (125 mL)	finely diced red onion
1	large clove garlic, minced
1 tbsp. (15 mL)	minced fresh ginger
1	jalapeno pepper, minced (optional)
1 1/2 cups (375 mL)	diced fresh tomatoes
2 cups (500 mL)	fish stock (p. 189)
1 cup (250 mL)	sliced green onions

✦ Bring a large pot of water to a boil. Add crabs and bring to a simmer. Do not boil. Cook for 8 minutes per pound (500 g) of crab. Remove crabs from pot and let cool. To clean the crabs, pry off the top shell, rinse clean and set aside. Under cold running water, remove all of the innards, including the triangular plate located on the underside of the body.

✦ Heat canola and sesame oils in a large shallow saucepan over medium heat. Add onion and cook for 3 minutes or until tender. Add garlic, ginger and jalapeno; cook for 2 to 3 minutes longer or until fragrant. Stir in the tomatoes and stock. Reduce heat to low and cook, covered, for 30 minutes.

✦ Place each cleaned crab in a hot pot, ladle some of the tomato stock over the crab and sprinkle with green onions. Place each hot pot on its own stove burner and bring to a simmer over medium-high heat. Simmer for 5 minutes. Serve immediately. **Makes 4 servings.**

Above: *Tojo's famous cherry blossom scallops*

Alder-Grilled Salmon with Caramelized Leek and Brie Sauce

This meal is the stuff of memories. One summer day, my son Mark, a west coast salmon-fishing guide and graduate of the Stratford Chefs School in Ontario, loaded his boat with provisions, and we headed to Cortes Island with its rock-strewn beaches. This barbecue is old hat for Mark — his guests have often had the option of such a feast — but for photographer Bob Wigington and me, it was a marvellous baptism into the glories of a "shore lunch."

First, Mark hollowed out a 24- to 36-inch (60 to 90 cm) wide depression in the rocks, ringing it with those rocks removed from the centre. He then placed a bag of charcoal in the pit and lit it. As the coals burned and turned grey, he prepared the rest of the meal. While we walked, we drank Pinot Blanc, the most widely accepted wine pairing with salmon, and slurped back a few chilled fresh oysters that Mark had harvested the day before. From nearby hedgerows, Mark slashed off a few pieces of alder, a tree that grows like a weed in British Columbia. He placed the green branches and leaves directly on the charcoal, then set the grill (an essential part of his guiding equipment) in place. (A shelf scrounged from an old refrigerator can double in this role.)

When the grill was hot, Mark placed the two fillets from a 12 lb. (5.5 kg) chinook directly on top, tail away from the fire so that the flesh cooked evenly. Then he used an old cast-iron skillet as a lid to enclose the salmon in smoke and heat. It was done to perfection in 12 to 15 minutes.

Meanwhile, he transferred the sauce to a small non-stick skillet and placed it on the open side of the grill. As it began to bubble, he added the peppercorns and the cheese, allowing it to melt gently. A few stir-fried B.C. hothouse peppers, a gathered salad from Joyce Farm on nearby Quadra Island and a wild huckleberry crisp (see p. 49) completed the meal set on the old log he'd used as a table.

Caramelized Leek and Brie Sauce

2 tbsp. (25 mL)	unsalted butter
3	medium leeks, white part only, thinly sliced
1/3 cup (75 mL)	fish (p. 189) or chicken (p. 66) stock
1/4 cup (50 mL)	dry white wine
1/3 cup (75 mL)	whipping cream (35%)
1 tsp. (5 mL)	pink peppercorns, crushed
4	3-oz. (90 g) piece Chase Sheep's Milk Brie, chopped, or an equal amount of domestic surface-ripened cheese such as camembert
	Salt

◆ Melt butter in a non-stick skillet over medium-low heat. Add leeks and sauté 3-5 minutes or until soft and just beginning to turn golden. Add stock and wine, increase heat to medium and cook 2 to 3 minutes or until sauce just begins to thicken. Stir in cream, cooking till thickened, 1 to 2 minutes.

◆ Just before serving, stir in peppercorns and cheese, allowing cheese to melt slowly. Season to taste with salt. Spoon a little sauce onto each of 8 plates before topping with salmon. *Makes 8 servings.*

Salmon Species — A Quick Primer

There are five varieties of Pacific salmon. The magnificent chinook (Oncorhynchus tshawytscha) is also known as spring, king and tyee. Feisty and beautiful with their black mouths and spotted blue-green backs, they are the most sought after of the Pacific species because of their large size and rarity. The sleek coho (Oncorhynchus kisutch) was the second most popular sport fish until the recent ban. When caught in the spring they are called bluebacks because of their bright, blue-tinged skin. Sockeye (Oncorhynchus nerka) have the reddest and leanest flesh of all wild salmon. They are the most challenging to cook perfectly. Milder-flavoured chum (Oncorhynchus keta) and pink (Oncorhynchus gorbuscha) are viewed as less desirable as game fish but make up a large portion of the commercial harvest.

Crystal Malt–Crusted Pacific Halibut on a Raspberry Ale– Basil Sauce

Crystal malt is an unusual recipe ingredient to say the least. It is a malted barley roasted until slightly darker than normal and used to give beer its reddish brown colour. It becomes sweeter in the process. You can purchase it at almost any brew-your-own store. At Spinnakers in Victoria the cooks simply head into the brewhouse with a measuring cup. That's how they created this recipe.

2 cups (500 mL)	raspberries (fresh or thawed frozen)
12	fresh basil leaves, coarsely chopped
2 tbsp. (25 mL)	brown sugar
1/4 cup (50 mL)	vegetable stock
1	473 mL bottle raspberry ale
	Salt and freshly ground pepper to taste
2 cups (500 mL)	crystal malt, finely ground in spice grinder
2 tsp. (10 mL)	chopped fresh dill
2 tsp. (10 mL)	chopped fresh basil
1 tsp. (5 mL)	salt
1 tsp. (5 mL)	freshly ground pepper
2 lb. (1 kg)	Pacific halibut, cut into 6 fillets
2 tbsp. (25 mL)	canola oil
	Fresh raspberries, in season

✦ In a saucepan, combine raspberries, basil, brown sugar, stock and raspberry ale. Bring to a boil, then simmer until reduced by one-third. Transfer mixture to the bowl of a food processor and process until smooth. Return to saucepan, and season with salt and pepper. Keep warm.

✦ In a medium bowl, combine crystal malt, dill, basil, salt and pepper. Coat halibut fillets with mixture. Heat oil in a skillet over medium-high heat. Sauté fillets for 5 minutes on each side or until fish is firm.

✦ Spoon a pool of sauce onto each of 4 warmed serving plates, top with the halibut and garnish with additional raspberries. Makes 4 servings.

A Brew Pub

Spinnakers, whose motto is "Our beers feel local," is so local that on Friday nights at least some of the staff of most of the other breweries in Victoria take part in the traditional 4 p.m. ritual of cracking the "firkin" (a 40 L cask of the finest). Spinnakers was one of Canada's first brew pubs and is still, without question, on that proverbial leading edge. Certainly, no one else carts barrels into the Saanich Peninsula fields to catch wild yeasts to make Lambic-style beer. Spinnakers also makes a Scotch ale, a lightly hopped beer with a fabulous peated malt that has overtones of whisky. This brew also forms the basis for Canada's first all-natural malt vinegar, made in a jerry-built contraption behind Spinnakers' elegant Victorian bed and breakfast just up the street. The pub's hot and sour soup using this vinegar is outstanding. Some years, Spinnakers also brews blackberry ale. One year they made raspberry ale from Meeker raspberries, grown organically on the Saanich Peninsula. Merridale cider, one of British Columbia's best ciders, provides the base for an apple-honey ale, sweetened ever so slightly with honey from Preston in the province's interior. Naturally, since British Columbia is the cranberry capital of Canada, there's a cranberry ale for Christmas — reason enough to book the holidays in Victoria. But the other reason is Mary Jameson's preserves. As a kid she sold them beside the road and now, spread on Spinnakers' hemp seed bread (toasted lightly, please), her plum jam is as good as it gets!

Pan-Seared Port Renfrew Lingcod with Watercress Sauce, Soybean Croquettes and Honeyed Local Vegetables

The secret to the flavours for which Sooke Harbour House is famous is found in the freshness of the ingredients. Vegetables, salad greens, fish and herbs are all used within hours of harvesting. Many of the dishes are garnished with edible flowers.

Watercress Sauce

2 tbsp. (25 mL)	unsalted butter
1/4 cup (50 mL)	finely chopped shallots
1/2 cup (125 mL)	fish stock (p. 189)
1/2 cup (125 mL)	B.C. white wine,
	preferably Sauvignon Blanc
1/3 cup (75 mL)	whipping cream (35%)
1 cup (250 mL)	watercress leaves
	Salt and pepper to taste

◆ In a saucepan over medium heat, melt butter. Add shallots and cook until softened but not brown. Add stock, wine and cream. Bring to a boil and simmer until reduced by half. Place liquid in the bowl of a food processor. Add watercress and purée until smooth. Strain sauce through a fine sieve back into the saucepan. Season with salt and pepper. Keep warm.

Soybean Croquettes

Soybeans need to simmer longer than most other beans. Soak them overnight, drain, and then cook them for about 60 minutes in unsalted water. Canned soybeans are also becoming more widely available.

1 tbsp. (15 mL)	unsalted butter
2	shallots, finely chopped
2	cloves garlic, finely chopped
2 cups (500 mL)	cooked or canned soybeans
2 tbsp. (25 mL)	water
1 tbsp. (15 mL)	chopped parsley
1 tsp. (5 mL)	salt
1 tsp. (5 mL)	freshly ground pepper
1	egg, lightly beaten
1 cup (250 mL)	dry bread crumbs
	Canola oil for deep-frying

◆ In a skillet over medium heat, melt butter. Add shallots and garlic and cook, stirring, until softened; remove from heat. In a food processor, purée soybeans with water. Transfer to a bowl and add shallots and garlic, parsley, salt and pepper. Chill for 1 hour.

◆ Form mixture into 8 cylinders. Dip cylinders into beaten egg and coat with bread crumbs. Deep-fry at 325°F (160°C) for 5 minutes or until golden brown. Remove with a slotted spoon; drain on paper towels and serve.

(continued)

39

Honeyed Local Vegetables

2 tbsp. (25 mL)	unsalted butter
1/2 cup (125 mL)	chopped cooked beets
1/2 cup (125 mL)	chopped green onion
1/2 cup (125 mL)	chopped cooked asparagus
1/2 cup (125 mL)	cooked snow peas
2 tsp. (10 mL)	local honey
1/4 cup (50 mL)	water

✦ Melt butter in a skillet over medium-high heat. Add beets,
green onion, asparagus, snow peas, honey and water. Simmer
about 4 minutes or until liquid reduces to form a glaze and
coats the vegetables.

Pan-Seared Lingcod

1 1/2 lb. (750 g)	lingcod or cod fillets
	Salt and pepper to taste
1/4 cup (50 mL)	canola oil

✦ Season lingcod fillets on both sides with salt and pepper.
Heat oil in a large oven-proof skillet over high heat until almost
smoking. Cook fish for 1 minute, then flip over and place in a
preheated 450°F (230°C) oven. Bake about 5 minutes or until
fish leaches milky liquid.

To Serve
✦ Pool the Watercress Sauce on 4 serving plates, top each with 2
Soybean Croquettes, surround with Honeyed Local Vegetables
and place lingcod beside or on the croquettes. **Makes 4 servings.**

Above: *Sooke Harbour House crew at Feast of Fields*

40

Loin of Lamb with Millet Crust, Pinot Reduction and Wild Mushroom and Bulgur Flan

Few chefs are as respected as Bernard Casavant. Good-natured and highly skilled, he has been a vocal advocate of B.C. food for as long as I've known him. After opening and heading up the kitchens of Château Whistler, he and his wife, Bonnie, started a series of successful ventures in the village of Whistler that range from a takeout food café (Chef Bernard's Cuisine to Go — Naturally) to a small bar specializing in B.C. micro-brews (Phil's Lounge).

One of the most prolific wild harvests in the Whistler area is mushrooms. In this recipe they lend the flan an earthy, woodsy aroma.

Wild Mushroom and Bulgur Flan

2 tbsp. (25 mL)	canola oil
1/2 cup (125 mL)	thinly sliced shallots
1/2 cup (125 mL)	thinly sliced wild mushrooms (chanterelles, morels, king boletus, shiitake, oyster)
1/2 cup (125 mL)	thinly sliced leeks, white part only
1/4 tsp. (1 mL)	finely chopped jalapeno pepper
1 cup (250 mL)	bulgur
2 cups (500 mL)	vegetable stock (p. 103)
1/4 cup (50 mL)	chopped fresh lovage or celery leaves
1/2 tsp. (2 mL)	chopped fresh marjoram
1/2 tsp. (2 mL)	chopped fresh lemon thyme or thyme
1/2 tsp. (2 mL)	chopped fresh savory
	Salt and freshly ground pepper

✦ Heat oil in a skillet over medium-high heat; cook shallots 10 minutes or until golden brown. Add mushrooms, leeks and jalapeno and cook for 2 minutes. Add bulgur, stirring to coat vegetable mixture. Add stock and lovage. Bring to a simmer and cook, covered, for 30 minutes or until bulgur is tender. Remove pot from heat and add marjoram, thyme and savory. Fluff bulgur with a fork. Add salt and pepper to taste.

✦ Lightly grease 4 ramekins and fill with bulgur mixture. Tap ramekins lightly on table to compact mixture. Keep warm while preparing lamb.

Loin of Lamb with Millet Crust

2 tbsp. (25 mL)	canola oil
2 lb. (1 kg)	boneless lamb loin
8	cloves purple garlic, peeled
	Salt to taste
1/4 cup (50 mL)	Dijon mustard
1/4 cup (50 mL)	millet, lightly toasted and coarsely ground in a spice grinder
1 1/2 cups (375 mL)	Pinot Noir
1/4 cup (50 mL)	minced fresh herbs (such as rosemary, parsley, oregano, marjoram, thyme)
	Salt and freshly ground pepper

✦ In a large oven-proof skillet, heat oil over medium-high heat. Add lamb and garlic and cook, turning to brown lamb on all sides. Remove from heat. Remove lamb from pan. Sprinkle with salt and coat with Dijon mustard. Roll lamb in ground millet until evenly coated; return to skillet. Bake in a preheated 400°F (200°C) oven 8 to 10 minutes or until meat thermometer registers 160°F (70°C).

✦ Remove lamb and garlic from skillet and keep warm, loosely covered with foil. Place skillet over medium heat. Add Pinot Noir and deglaze by scraping up any brown bits stuck to the pan. Bring to a boil, add the herbs and cook until the liquid is reduced by half. Season to taste with salt and pepper.

To Serve

✦ Unmould flans on 4 serving plates. Carve the loin into uniform slices and arrange on top. Place 2 cloves of garlic on each plate and carefully spoon the sauce around the flan. **Makes 4 servings.**

> **To toast millet,** spread grain in a dry heavy skillet. Place over medium heat and cook, shaking frequently, till it gives off a nutty aroma and just begins to turn golden.

Liquid Gold

Eulachon, a small smeltlike fish (Thaleichthys pacificus) *is so rich in oil that when dried it can be stuck into the sand and lit; hence its other name, candlestick fish. The mid-March eulachon runs are so thick that the fish were originally harvested by simply raking them in. Today dip nets are used. The fish are aged in large bins or pits. The longer they "season," the stronger the taste. The fish are then boiled in the open air on the banks of the river. The precious oil rises to the surface and is skimmed and strained through cedar mats or cotton cloth into pails or jars.*

Huckleberries

Since honeybees are not indigenous to British Columbia, berries were the sole natural sweetener for the First Nations people. Huckleberries were so important to them that the Bella Coola name for huckleberries meant simply "berry." Huckleberries are members of the heather family. There are several varieties. The black mountain huckleberry (Vaccinium membranaceum) *is also known as mountain bilberry. The evergreen huckleberry* (Vaccinium ovatum), *which hangs on to the bushes till after the first snowfall, is also called winter huckleberry. The deliciously tart red huckleberry* (Vaccinium parvifolium) *ripens in late summer. According to ethnobotanist Dr. Nancy Turner, "The Kwakiutl boiled them in high cedar boxes, mixed in red salmon spawn, covered them with heated skunk cabbage leaves, and sealed the tops with eulachon grease and strips of heated skunk cabbage leaf. During the winter ceremonials, they were eaten at feasts with the usual additive of eulachon grease."*

Cape Mudge Cheese Scones

Wendy Abram of the Cape Mudge Lighthouse says that any type of cheddar cheese will work in these scones, including mild, but she prefers medium or old.

2 cups (500 mL)	unbleached all-purpose flour
2 tbsp. (25 mL)	sugar
1 tbsp. (15 mL)	baking powder
1/4 tsp. (1 mL)	salt
1/4 cup (50 mL)	cold unsalted butter
2/3 cup (150 mL)	coarsely shredded cheddar cheese
2	eggs, lightly beaten
1/3 cup (75 mL)	milk

✦ *In a large bowl, stir or sift together flour, sugar, baking powder and salt. Cut in butter finely until mixture resembles coarse crumbs. Stir in cheese.*

✦ *Reserve 1 tbsp. (15 mL) of the beaten eggs. Blend remaining eggs and milk; stir into dry ingredients, mixing only until combined and the dough is not sticky. Turn out onto a lightly floured surface, gathering up into a ball and kneading 6 to 8 times. Divide dough in half and roll each portion into a 6-inch (15 cm) circle about 1 inch (2.5 cm) thick. With a sharp knife, cut each round into quarters and place on lightly oiled baking sheet. Brush with eggwash. Bake in a preheated 400°F (200°C) oven for 12 to 15 minutes or until evenly browned.* **Makes 8 scones.**

Thyme-Scented Apple Focaccia

Terra Breads in Vancouver continues to be one of the best and most innovative bakeries in Canada. This focaccia recipe has been adapted from one developed by baker Mary Mackay using some of the province's great organic apples. She suggests any tart B.C. variety that is crisp and will hold its shape.

Sponge

1/2 cup (125 mL)	warm water
1/8 tsp. (0.5 mL)	active dry yeast
1/2 cup (125 mL)	bread flour

Focaccia

1 cup + 2 tbsp. (275 mL)	water, at room temperature
5 tbsp. (75 mL)	canola oil or hazelnut oil
1 1/2 tsp. (7 mL)	salt
1/2 tsp. (2 mL)	active dry yeast
3 cups (750 mL)	bread flour
2	tart British Columbia apples, unpeeled, each cut in 16 wedges
1 tsp. (5 mL)	minced fresh thyme
1 tbsp. (15 mL)	finely chopped roasted hazelnuts (p. 21)
3 tbsp. (45 mL)	sugar

✦ *In a small warm mixing bowl, make a sponge by stirring together water, yeast and flour. Cover with a tea towel; let stand for 2 to 3 hours at room temperature or until bubbly.*

✦ *To make the focaccia, transfer sponge to a large mixing bowl; stir in water, 4 tbsp. (50 mL) of the oil, salt, yeast and flour. Mix till dough comes together. Turn out onto a floured surface. Knead for 10 to 15 minutes or until very smooth and elastic. Place in a well-oiled bowl, turning to coat with oil, cover and let rise at room temperature until doubled in bulk, about 1 1/2 hours.*

✦ *Divide dough in half. Roll each piece into a 1/2-inch (1 cm) thick oval. Place on a large lightly oiled baking sheet. Brush tops with remaining oil. Loosely cover with plastic wrap; let rise for 45 minutes in a warm place.*

✦ *Place an empty baking pan on the bottom rack of a 450°F (230°C) oven. Meanwhile, press apple wedges evenly into each piece of dough. Sprinkle with thyme, hazelnuts and sugar. Mist the tops with water and ladle 1/4 cup (50 mL) water into hot baking pan to create a burst of steam. Bake focaccias 15 to 20 minutes or until golden brown. Cool on racks before serving.*
Makes 16 servings.

43

Chocolate

At Chocolate Arts on West 4th Avenue in Vancouver, owner and chocomeister Greg Hook creates some of the most delicious and seasonal sweets many of us will ever taste. His is the only rhubarb truffle in existence. Why? It's just too difficult for most chocolatiers to make. He dries and dips organic pears and blueberries. His pumpkin truffles are a chocoholic's version of pumpkin pie — exquisite — and he roasts B.C. hazelnuts to make fabulous nut pralines. His signature chocolates are formed in moulds originally carved by Haida artist Robert Davidson. However, the chocolate that made my day and doused my tastebuds with flavour was a little gem filled with lemon and basil. Unbelievable!

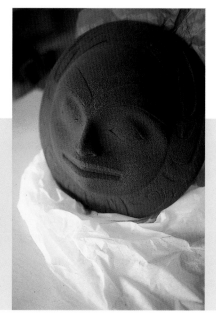

Above: *Terra Breads*
Right: *Chocolate Arts*

Pinot Poached Plums with Hazelnut Shortcakes and Crème Fraîche Ice Cream

This wonderful dessert recipe was developed by Chef David Forestell of Amphora, the bistro at Hainle Vineyards, a winery near Peachland.

Pinot Poached Plums

3 cups (750 mL)	Hainle Vineyards Pinot Noir
3/4 cup (175 mL)	sugar
1	3-inch (8 cm) cinnamon stick
1/2	vanilla bean, split lengthwise
3	whole star anise
5	whole cloves
12	black peppercorns
4 cups (1 L)	purple plums (2 lb./1 kg), pitted and quartered

✦ Combine Pinot Noir, sugar and spices in a medium saucepan. Bring to a boil, reduce heat and simmer, uncovered, until reduced to 2 cups (500 mL). Strain and return liquid to saucepan. Add plums, bring to a boil and simmer, covered, just until skins begin to loosen, about 5 minutes. Pour into glass bowl; cover and chill overnight.

To make crème fraîche, combine 1 1/2 cups (375 mL) whipping cream with 1/2 cup (125 mL) buttermilk or sour cream and refrigerate, covered, for 24 hours.

(continued)

Hainle Wines

Hainle Vineyards in Peachland is one of the few in the world that is fully organic and was the first in the province to be granted a "J" licence, which allows it to prepare and serve food on-site. In the bistro, Sandra Hainle prepares light lunches — which she calls "small snapshots of local food" — in appetizer-sized portions to enjoy with a glass of wine. There is usually only one special item each day, and it might vary from a fresh baguette with smoked British Columbia salmon and her homemade apple chutney to Shuswap sheep's milk brie-style cheese baked with a sun-dried tomato topping.

Throughout the year, the winery restaurant has a busy social schedule with guest chefs and celebrities such as Jurgen Gothe, Carol Ferguson, Murray McMillan and James Barber.

The late Walter Hainle, on arriving in Canada in 1973, brought with him a winemaking tradition that dates from the fifteenth century. He went on to become the first vintner in Canada to grow, harvest and vinify the liquid gold we know as ice wine. His son, Tilman, is true to the heritage. "You can accuse me of many things," he says, "but not of making boring wines." His wines are as individual as he is, varying as great wine does from year to year. Pinot Blanc from Elisabeth's Vineyard may one year be light and have aromas of apple, butter, and melon, while the next vintage will be fuller and have overtones of citrus and caramel.

Hazelnut Shortcakes

2 cups (500 mL)	all-purpose flour
1/4 cup (50 mL)	sugar
4 tsp. (20 mL)	baking powder
1/4 tsp. (1 mL)	salt
1/2 cup (125 mL)	finely ground toasted hazelnuts (p. 21)
1/2 cup (125 mL)	coarsely chopped toasted hazelnuts
1/2 cup (125 mL)	cold butter, cut in cubes
1 1/4 cups (300 mL)	whipping cream (35%)
2 tbsp. (25 mL)	sugar
1 tsp. (5 mL)	cinnamon

✦ In a large bowl, blend flour, sugar, baking powder and salt. Stir in all of the hazelnuts. Using pastry blender, cut in butter until mixture resembles coarse crumbs.

✦ Reserve 2 tbsp. (25 mL) of the cream; stir remaining cream into flour mixture until it begins to clump, eventually using your hands to gently knead into a stiff dough.

✦ On a clean work surface, roll dough to 1/2-inch (1 cm) thickness. Using 2-inch (5 cm) cookie cutter, cut into at least 16 rounds. Transfer to a parchment-lined baking sheet and refrigerate 15 minutes or until firm. Brush tops with reserved cream. In a small bowl, combine sugar and cinnamon; sprinkle over cakes. Bake in a preheated 400°F (200°C) oven until golden, about 15 minutes. Cool on rack.

Crème Fraîche Ice Cream

1/2 cup (125 mL)	sugar
1/4 cup (50 mL)	water
6	egg yolks
2 cups (500 mL)	crème fraîche (p. 45)
2 cups (500 mL)	whipping cream (35%), whipped into stiff peaks

✦ In a small saucepan, combine sugar and water. Bring to a boil and simmer, stirring, 2 minutes or until sugar is dissolved. Place egg yolks in a double boiler over simmering water. Gradually whisk in sugar syrup and continue whisking about 8 minutes or until mixture is frothy and very thick. Pour into a clean bowl. Whisk in crème fraîche. Cool completely. Fold in whipped cream. Freeze in ice-cream maker according to manufacturer's instructions, or simply cover and freeze, as is, in the bowl.

To Serve

Icing sugar
Blackberries
Freeform caramel decorations (optional)

✦ Gently reheat plums and place in 8 individual serving bowls or on dessert plates. Split shortcakes in half. Scoop a small spoonful of ice cream onto one half and top with other half, making two ice-cream cakes per serving. Place on top of plums; sprinkle with icing sugar. Garnish with blackberries and freeform caramel decorations. **Makes 8 servings.**

To make freeform caramel decorations. Line several baking sheets with baking parchment. In a small heavy saucepan, over medium-high heat melt 1 cup (250 mL) sugar, stirring constantly to dissolve. Sugar will become lumpy then a golden liquid. Remove from heat. Pour and swirl in a thin stream onto the parchment to make 8 freeform decorations. Let harden. Can be stored in an airtight container for several weeks.

Fireweed Honey Lavender Ice Cream

Dried lavender flowers are available at health and whole food stores. To dry your own, pick lavender stems just before the flowers have quite opened. Tie them together and let dry at room temperature for about 7 days. Strip flowers off stems and store in an airtight jar. When fully dried, the flowers will keep up to 1 year.

4 cups (1 L)	half & half cream (10%)
1/2	vanilla bean, split lengthwise
1/4 cup (50 mL)	dried lavender flowers
1/3 cup (75 mL)	boiling water
8	egg yolks
3/4 cup (175 mL)	fireweed or other mild honey

✦ In a heavy saucepan, combine cream and vanilla bean. Heat to scalding point (when bubbles form around edge of pan). Remove from heat, cover and let stand for 10 minutes. Meanwhile, in a small bowl, cover lavender flowers with boiling water and steep for 5 minutes. Strain and discard flowers. Set aside lavender infusion.

✦ In a large bowl, whisk together egg yolks and honey. Gradually pour warm cream and vanilla bean into egg yolk mixture, stirring constantly. Return to saucepan and cook over medium-high heat, stirring constantly, for about 10 minutes or until mixture is thick enough to coat the back of a wooden spoon; do not let boil. Strain mixture into a bowl. Stir in lavender infusion. Let custard cool to room temperature; cover and refrigerate at least 4 hours or overnight. Freeze in an ice-cream maker according to manufacturer's instructions. **Makes 4 cups (1 L).**

Ruby and golden salmonberries (Rubus spectabilis) *ripen as early as late May. The trailing wild blackberry* (Rubus ursinus) *is probably the most delicious and the most painful berry to pick. The dark navy berries grow in clusters guarded by vicious thorns. Coastal Native peoples dried the popular salal berry* (Gaultheria shallon) *beside the fire in cedar frames to create thick, leathery rectangles. This was feast food of the first order! The crimson-red soapberry* (Shepherdia canadensis) *can be whipped with a salal branch into a somewhat bitter froth known in every B.C. coastal settlement as Indian ice cream.*

Above: *Vigneti Zanatta Winery, Vancouver Island*

Mark's Huckleberry Crisp

My son, Mark, uses the wild red huckleberries that flourish all over the summertime Gulf Islands. He freezes them in plastic bags and when needed bakes them into this perfect crisp. Because it's easier to transport for his shore lunches, he uses disposable aluminum pans.

4 cups (1 L)	wild red huckleberries
1 cup (250 mL)	sugar

Topping

1 cup (250 mL)	rolled oats
1/2 cup (125 mL)	whole-wheat flour
1/4 cup (50 mL)	brown sugar
1/2 tsp. (2 mL)	cinnamon
1/3 cup (75 mL)	unsalted butter

✦ *Toss berries with sugar and transfer to lightly oiled or buttered 8-inch (20 cm) square aluminum baking pan. In a medium bowl, stir together oats, flour, sugar and cinnamon. Finely cut in the butter. Spoon topping over berries. Bake in a preheated 325°F (160°C) oven for 40 to 45 minutes or until bubbling and browned.* **Makes 6 to 8 servings.**

Rhubarb and Anise Hyssop Pot au Crème with Compote

Davide Feys, the Victoria caterer who shared this recipe, was working at Sooke Harbour House when we first met. The spirit of innovation he absorbed there is obvious.

Anise hyssop deserves a much wider audience. It is one of the most delicious and fragrant of edible flowers. The intensity of its flavour changes throughout the growing season. As a result, in the springtime, when rhubarb is at its best, 6 sprigs — the upper flowering portion of the stem — will perfume this dessert, but by autumn between 10 and 12 are needed.

1 lb. (500 g)	rhubarb, cut in 1/2-inch (1 cm) pieces
1/2 cup (125 mL)	cranberry or clear apple juice
1/3 – 1/2 cup (75 – 125 mL)	whipping cream (35%)
1 cup (250 mL)	coarsely chopped anise hyssop leaves, stems and flowers
4	egg yolks
1/3 cup (75 mL)	sugar
1/2 tsp. (2 mL)	vanilla

✦ *In a small saucepan over medium heat, combine rhubarb and juice. Bring to a boil, reduce heat and simmer, covered, without stirring, 10 minutes or until rhubarb is very tender. Pour into a sieve placed over a 2-cup (500 mL) measuring cup and collect liquid. Do not press down on rhubarb, as this will make liquid cloudy. Discard rhubarb.*

✦ *When rhubarb liquid is cool, add whipping cream to make 1 1/2 cups (375 mL) liquid. Gently stir in the anise hyssop; cover with plastic wrap and allow flavours to infuse overnight in the refrigerator. Then bring to room temperature.*

✦ *In a bowl, using a wooden spoon, gently stir together egg yolks, sugar and vanilla just until sugar dissolves. Strain cream mixture into yolk mixture, pressing on herbs to release all the flavour. Pour into four 1/2-cup (125 mL) ramekins. Place ramekins in a baking dish and pour boiling water into baking dish to come halfway up the sides of ramekins. Bake in preheated 325°F (160°C) oven 25 minutes or until just set. Remove custards from water bath and cool on rack. Refrigerate till serving.*

49

(continued)

Tea at The Empress

Taking tea at the gracious old Empress Hotel is pure ceremony — British and proud of it. Even the china is significant. Presented to King George V in 1914, it was first used at The Empress in 1939 for the royal visit of King George VI and Queen Elizabeth, now the Queen Mother. On these elegant plates you'll be served fruit scones and Jersey cream with strawberry preserves, rich pastries and, of course, tiny sandwiches on white bread. Down the street at Murchie's is the original log book filled with recipes for the tea blends that graced the pots and the parlours of ladies of another era. Held in the utmost security, The Empress Tea Blend is among the guarded secrets.

Rhubarb Compote

1/2 cup (125 mL)	cranberry or raspberry juice
1/4 cup (50 mL)	sugar
3	6-inch (15 cm) stalks rhubarb, cut in three and then sliced lengthwise in 1/2-inch (1 cm) sticks

✦ *Combine juice and sugar in a small saucepan. Stir over medium heat to dissolve sugar. Add rhubarb, cover and simmer 2 to 3 minutes or until barely tender. Remove from heat and set aside to cool. Refrigerate till needed.*

To Serve

1/3 cup (75 mL)	shaved bitter or white chocolate
	Anise hyssop sprigs

✦ *Garnish custards with shavings of chocolate and sprigs of anise hyssop and spoonfuls of Rhubarb Compote. **Makes 4 servings.***

Brown's Bay Marina Ginger Cookies

Perfect on a misty island day, this recipe is a variation on the one found in the diner's handwritten book kept in a magazine rack at Brown's Bay Marina.

1 1/2 cups (375 mL)	softened unsalted butter
2 cups (500 mL)	sugar
1/2 cup (125 mL)	molasses
2	eggs
4 cups (1 L)	all-purpose flour
4 tsp. (20 mL)	baking soda
2 tsp. (10 mL)	cinnamon
2 tsp. (10 mL)	ground cloves
2 tsp. (10 mL)	ground ginger
1/2 tsp. (2 mL)	salt
1/3 cup (75 mL)	finely chopped candied ginger
	Sugar

✦ In a large bowl, cream butter with sugar, molasses and eggs until light and fluffy. Sift or stir together flour, baking soda, cinnamon, cloves, ground ginger, salt and candied ginger. Combine with creamed mixture to form a soft dough.

✦ Using a dessert spoon, scoop out batter and shape into balls between the palms of your hands. Roll in sugar and place 2 inches (5 cm) apart on a lightly greased baking sheet. Flatten slightly with a wet fork. Bake in a preheated 375°F (190°C) oven for 12 to 14 minutes or until well browned. Cool on rack before storing in an airtight container. **Makes about 18 large cookies.**

Where the mountainous British Columbia mainland almost touches Vancouver Island, the surging Pacific forces its way through Seymour Narrows. Once considered impassable, it's now merely an adrenaline-charged challenge for ships of every description, from small motorboats to Class II icebreakers. The narrows are on the route to Brown's Bay, where sailors can stop in at a floating diner sheltered behind a seawall of partially submerged railway tanker cars and a Petro-Canada marina. For fishers who have spent the morning on the water, the diner's breakfasts are generous and real. Later in the day, chowder or oyster burgers and hand-cut fries are worth a fuelling stop.

51

Left: *Tea at The Empress*
Above: *Brown's Bay, Vancouver Island*

Okanagan Pear and Red Fife Sourdough Coffeecake

Use ripe late-harvest pears for this great cake. Toss in dried B.C. cranberries and perhaps a few roasted hazelnuts. Serve at breakfast or as a full-fledged dessert with a scoop of Fireweed Honey Lavender Ice Cream (p. 47).

Sourdough was the main source of leavening in most of early Canada. Originally, a slurry of flour and water was set outdoors to catch wild yeast, then kept, carefully, to make batch after batch of great bread. Today, a fast starter such as this one is the easiest way to achieve similar, if not identical, results. If Red Fife flour is not available, replace it with any good-quality all-purpose flour or two-thirds all-purpose and one-third stone-ground whole-wheat.

Easy Sourdough Starter

3 tbsp. (45 mL)	sugar
2 cups (500 mL)	warm water
1 tbsp. (15 mL)	active dry yeast
3 cups (750 mL)	all-purpose flour
1 cup (250 mL)	milk
1/2 cup (125 mL)	sugar (second amount)

After Each Use

1 cup (250 mL)	all-purpose flour
1 cup (250 mL)	milk
1/2 cup (125 mL)	sugar

✦ Stir 3 tbsp. (45 mL) sugar and water together in a large bowl. Stir in yeast until dissolved. Beat in 2 cups (500 mL) of the flour. Cover with plastic wrap and allow to sit at room temperature 2 to 3 days, stirring down each day, until it has a distinct sour odour. Whisk in remaining flour, milk and 1/2 cup (125 mL) sugar. Refrigerate for 1 day before using.

✦ After every use, beat in flour, milk and sugar till the batter is smooth. Refrigerate 12 to 24 hours before using again.

Pear Coffeecake

2 cups (500 mL)	Red Fife flour
1 cup (250 mL)	sugar
1 tsp. (5 mL)	cinnamon
1/2 tsp. (2 mL)	salt
1/2 tsp. (2 mL)	baking soda
2 cups (500 mL)	Easy Sourdough Starter
2	eggs
2/3 cup (150 mL)	canola oil
2 cups (500 mL)	chopped late-harvest pears

Topping

3/4 cup (175 mL)	brown sugar
1/4 cup (50 mL)	Red Fife flour
1/4 cup (50 mL)	softened unsalted butter
2 tsp. (10 mL)	cinnamon
1/2 tsp. (2 mL)	nutmeg

✦ In a large bowl, stir together flour, sugar, cinnamon, salt and baking soda. In a separate bowl, thoroughly combine Easy Sourdough Starter, eggs and oil. Add to dry ingredients, stirring till no dry spots remain. Fold in pears and transfer to a 9" x 13" (4 L) baking pan.

✦ Make the topping by blending the brown sugar, flour, butter, cinnamon and nutmeg. Spread it evenly over the batter. Bake in a preheated 350°F (180°C) oven for 55 to 60 minutes or until a tester inserted in the centre comes out clean. Let cool in the pan 1 to 2 hours before cutting. Store in a tightly covered container. *Makes 12 to 16 servings.*

As the largest public grain garden in Canada, the Grist Mill preserves old wheat varieties such as Marquis, Red Fife, Thatcher, Ladoga, Stanley, Bishop, Hard Red Calcutta, Park, Cypress and Black Einkorn. Among the thirty varieties of heritage apples grown there are the Richter Banana, developed by the Similkameen pioneer Frank Richter, and Dr. R.C. Palmer's magnificent Spartan, grown first at the Summerland Research Station in 1926. The heavyweight Zucca melon, once grown by the tonne in southern British Columbia for candied peel, flourishes again in the Grist Mill garden. Site manager Cuyler Page cultivates it "for the simple wonder of growing an eighty-pound vegetable." Heritage plants of all sorts are sold; others are returned to the national gene bank. In the case of wheat, though, the cracked-wheat porridge and the whole-wheat flour, ground from the Grist Mill's harvest of legendary Red Fife wheat, are bagged and both used in the tea room and sold in the gift shop.

In Vancouver, near British Columbia's oldest-known yew tree, beside a full-fledged salmon hatchery on the Capilano River, Olympic chef and dedicated outdoorsman Manfred Scholermann spreads a springtime picnic brunch consisting of new potato and asparagus salad, tiny hand-peeled local shrimp with brandied chili sauce, roasted well-herbed chicken breasts with hazelnut chutney, Savary Pie Company's amazing blueberry scones, and Saltspring Island cheese with fresh strawberries. Glasses of Cipes Brut are topped with fresh orange juice. Rockwood Adventures, his hiking company, guides gourmands who want to be able to justify such feasts through virgin rain forests, past magnificent seascapes, up mountains (including the "Grouse Grind," a punishing dash up Grouse Mountain) and even through Vancouver's Chinatown.

Mrs. Peterson's Cinnamon Sticky Buns

Since the mid-1940s, April Point Lodge on Quadra Island was synonymous with great fishing and great food. The late Phyllis Peterson, who was in charge of that famous kitchen until the late eighties, was known for her sticky buns. Recreating her recipe took weeks. I'd bake a batch, then let her grown children and her niece Heidi test them. After about six attempts, we got it right. This is a taste of old British Columbia — from a glorious island in the middle of the Inside Passage.

1/4 cup (50 mL)	warm water
1 tsp. (5 mL)	sugar
2 tbsp. (25 mL)	active dry yeast
3	eggs, well-beaten
1/2 cup (125 mL)	sugar (second amount)
1/2 cup (125 mL)	melted shortening
2 tsp. (10 mL)	salt
1 1/4 cups (300 mL)	warm milk
6 – 7 cups (1.5 – 1.75 L)	all-purpose or bread flour
2 tbsp. (25 mL)	softened unsalted butter
2/3 cup (150 mL)	brown sugar
1 – 2 tsp. (5 – 10 mL)	cinnamon
2/3 cup (150 mL)	raisins
	Melted unsalted butter
	Almond Butter Icing (recipe follows)

✦ In a small bowl, stir together warm water and 1 tsp. (5 mL) sugar in a small bowl; sprinkle with yeast. Set aside for 10 minutes or until foamy.

✦ In a large bowl, whisk together eggs, sugar, shortening, salt and milk. Stir in yeast mixture. Add flour, a cupful at a time, beating well after each addition, until a soft dough is formed. Turn out onto a floured surface and knead 5 to 7 minutes or until smooth and elastic, adding additional flour as required. Return to well-oiled bowl, cover and let rise until doubled in bulk, about 1 1/2 hours. Punch down, turn out onto a floured surface and divide dough in half.

✦ Roll each half into an 8" x 14" (20 x 35 cm) rectangle. Spread with butter and sprinkle with brown sugar, cinnamon and raisins. Roll up from the widest side and slice each roll into 12 pieces. Place no more than 1 inch (2.5 cm) apart on well-greased or parchment-lined baking sheets. Cover and allow to rise till doubled, about 1 hour. Bake in a preheated 350°F (180°C) oven for 12 to 15 minutes or until golden brown. Brush with melted butter; let cool before icing.

Almond Butter Icing

1/4 cup (50 mL)	softened unsalted butter
2 cups (500 mL)	icing sugar
1 tsp. (5 mL)	almond extract
1/2 tsp. (2 mL)	vanilla
	Milk or table cream (18%)

✦ In a medium mixing bowl, combine butter, sugar and almond and vanilla extracts. Beat in enough milk to make a thin frosting. Drizzle over cooled Cinnamon Sticky Buns. **Makes 24 buns.**

53

Left: *Cuyler Page with red fife, Keremeos*
Above: *Rockwood Adventures*

Saltspring Island

The Saltspring Island Fall Fair is the event of the year on this Gulf island. No midway rides here — after all, it is laid-back Saltspring Island. It's pure, do-it-yourself fun. The local baseball team, the S.S. Slugs, sell slug-burgers. The Women's Institute (whose members' average age is eighty and who are also known as The Pie Ladies) stand in a shaded booth, slicing and dishing out fifteen varieties of pie — from cascade blackberry and old-fashioned raisin to loganberry and ginger-pear. Members of Tuned Air, the island's mixed choir, barbecue fresh salmon. The preschool class, or rather their parents, press apples and pears into cider. Local musicians, most of whom are also known off the island, take turns onstage. Sheep-shearing demonstrations are in full swing in one barn while crowds mill through the produce displays. Saltspring has more than forty apiaries, so honey products are everywhere. There's even a home-made-wine competition for islanders who ferment local berries, fruits and, yes, vegetables.

Without doubt, the most popular concession at the Saltspring Island Fall Fair is operated by the Canadian Coast Guard Auxiliary. They have the best imaginable barbecued lamb on a bun. Whole lambs are cut in half, boned and rolled before being skewered and placed over an open alder-wood fire. Members of the auxiliary baste the roasts with equal parts whisky, brown sugar and soy sauce. The line of hungry islanders begins almost as soon as the fragrance of the roasting meat fills the fairground.

54 Saltspring Island Pastry

Evelyn Lee, the matron of the Saltspring Island Women's Institute (a.k.a. The Pie Ladies) dictated this recipe as I gobbled a piece of loganberry pie, then another slice of lemon. Too bad the recipe took so little time to write or I would've been able to justify a sliver of island-grown apple pie.

3 cups (750 mL)	all-purpose flour
1 tsp. (5 mL)	salt
1/2 lb. (225 g)	chilled lard
1	egg, beaten
2 tsp. (10 mL)	white vinegar
1/2 cup (125 mL)	ice water

✦ In a large bowl, blend flour and salt. Cut in lard till mixture is crumbly. Make a well in the centre. Place egg and vinegar in a measuring cup. Add ice water; mix well. Pour into the dry ingredients, combining with a fork until dough holds together. Gather dough into a ball and divide into 3 pieces. Roll out each piece on a floured surface and either use immediately or wrap with plastic wrap and freeze until needed. Before using a frozen shell, let it stand at room temperature for 5 to 10 minutes. *Makes 3 single 8-inch (20 cm) crusts.*

Above: *Heritage apples at Saltspring Island fall fair*

Zucchini Pickles

Michael Noble makes these all year round. They're a
nineties version of the old-fashioned bread and butter pickles that many of our grandmothers made.

2	medium zucchini, thinly sliced
1/2	white onion, thinly sliced
1/2	sweet red pepper, thinly sliced
1/4 cup (50 mL)	coarse pickling salt
1 cup (250 mL)	white wine vinegar
1/2 cup (125 mL)	sugar
1/2 tsp. (2 mL)	turmeric
1/4 tsp. (1 mL)	mustard seed

✦ *Place zucchini, onion and pepper in a large bowl; sprinkle with
salt and add just enough water to cover the vegetables. Let
stand for 1 hour or until soft; drain well. In a large saucepan,
stir together vinegar, sugar, turmeric and mustard seed. Bring
to a boil and add vegetables. Return to a boil and cook for 3
minutes. Remove from the heat and ladle into a clean jar. Seal
and let cool to room temperature. Refrigerate for up to 2 weeks.
Makes 3 1/2 cups (875 mL).*

55

One of the most exciting food happenings in British Columbia in the 1990s was the creation of FarmFolk/CityFolk, an organization that
draws together chefs and producers, consumers and gardeners, academics and media, vintners and government in a dynamic coalition. It
forms a conduit for communication among people interested in food, agriculture and the environment. It has also become a resource centre
for community-assisted agricultural programs that pair consumers and producers prior to the growing season. A real partnership develops
when farmers produce predetermined crops and ensure a consistent supply of fresh foods for their consumers.

Chapter 2
The Prairies

The summer fields are misted with blue flax and deep yellow canola flowers. Golden grain flows sensuously to the horizon. This is Canada's heartland — Alberta, Saskatchewan and Manitoba. It's a land of dramatic contrast. In the south, summer heat visibly bounces heavenward from the dry, painted gulches and parched alkaline flats. In the north, a vast region of fish-filled lakes and forests gives way to tundra, sparse and cold, oftentimes permanently frozen.

Until the late 1800s, from Lake Winnipeg in Manitoba to the foothills of the Rocky Mountains, bison thundered some 60 million strong. They were *the* major food source for the peoples of the First Nations, and their slaughter was surrounded by ritual. With bone knives, the women skinned the huge beasts. Some of the warm blood was consumed by the men in the belief that they would become brave in battle. The medicine men took possession of the tongues to ensure the safety of the next hunt. Then came the task of preserving the meat. The hump, with its fatty tissue, the shoulder and the heart were the prized cuts. Thin sheets of the lean meat were dried until brittle and dark, then pounded and mixed with dried wild berries and rendered fat to make pemmican, the original "trail mix."

The first European settlers in these vast lands were French and British fur traders, the voyageurs who paddled through the continent's maze of rivers in search of furs and a way to the Pacific. Hudson's Bay posts became the centres of activity for much of the West. Then came homesteaders, many travelling thousands of miles to make their way into this harsh environment. They were plagued by fires, dust storms, grasshopper infestations and the most Canadianizing season of all, winter. All their energy was devoted to farming and building a new land.

It's little wonder that the earliest European settlers saw the rolling prairie grasslands and thought of cattle. About two-thirds of today's farms in Alberta raise cattle. These farms are in reality sprawling ranches, where beef cattle graze on many thousands of hectares before being either shipped east to be finished in the feed-lots of Ontario and Quebec or slaughtered, producing what most Canadians claim is the best beef in the world.

During the era of the massive cattle drives, the chuckwagon cook was king. These rolling kitchens, rattling along on high wheels and wide-gauge axles, were portable pantries full of staples such as beans, flour, sugar, coffee and tea. Dried fruits came by the case. Wooden kegs held syrup and molasses. There in the middle of the grassy wilderness, the chuckwagon cook would bake iron kettles full of beans with molasses and salt pork;

57

Left: *At Post Hotel, Lake Louise, Alberta (see recipe p.62)*
Above: *Bison farming at Buffalo Horn Ranch, Eagle Hill, north of Calgary, Alberta*

roast fresh meat; fry up pans of prairie oysters (the testicles of calves); steam puddings; and bake great pies, the undisputed sign of a good Prairie cook.

After Confederation, one million European settlers poured into western Canada by train. At that time as well, a giant step forward was made in wheat production. In the 1800s, wheat required a relatively long growing season. Red Fife, a popular strain in Ontario, froze in prairie fields. At the Central Experimental Farm in Ottawa, William Saunders, its first director, and his son, Sir Charles Saunders, developed a strain of wheat they named Marquis. This superb hard spring wheat had an early-maturing quality that meant the grain could be cultivated in the prairies. Marquis made Canadian wheat famous. By the closing years of the 1920s Marquis accounted for 90 percent of the hard red spring production on the prairies and 60 percent of that in the American heartland.

The most recent Canadian "Cinderella crop" is canola. Each tiny seed is 40 percent oil — and a healthy and delicious oil it is!

From the canola fields come another recent Canadian delicacy, canola blossom honey, light in flavour with a flowery aroma. Most of the honey from Saskatchewan and Manitoba is canola, but other honeys are well represented in the Prairies as well. From Manitoba comes dark, mineral-rich buckwheat honey and lightly perfumed sunflower honey. Bees in Alberta enjoy sweet clover in the lush Peace River Valley. Prairie Gold, an extraordinary "limited edition" honey harvested from borage flowers, is found only in Saskatchewan. The delicate herb grows well there because of the pristine environment.

The fur traders noted that the northern Natives harvested wild rice. In fact, explorer David Thompson wrote that one winter his partner in the North West Company survived on a diet of wild rice and maple sugar. Originally, canoes were paddled or poled through the shallow water in which wild rice grows. Sometimes, earlier in the season, the green stalks were tied together for more even ripening and to keep the heavy stalks from falling into the water or being devoured by birds. Whole families would go "ricing," holding the stems over the canoe and beating the rice into the bottom of the boat.

Top: *Rosthern, Saskatchewan*
Above: *Canola field north of Saskatoon, Saskatchewan*

Across the Prairies, fishing is a sport and a business. Many commercial fishers fish all year round, setting their gill nets under the thick ice. Northern pike, pickerel, tullibee (freshwater herring), whitefish, lake trout, goldeye and lesser-known species such as burbot, mullet and carp are sold on the world market.

To complete the gastronomic prairie landscape, it's necessary to explore some of the farmers' markets scattered from Winnipeg to Edmonton. Not only are they sources of wild rice, canola honey, great beef and prairie breads, they also mirror the growing multicultural community. And look at the variety! Beans are big, with names like Tongue of Fire, Swedish Brown, Black Cocoa, Squaw Yellow and Jacob's Cap. Potatoes aren't far behind beans in popularity. Bintje and waxy yellow fingerlings are piled high in cardboard boxes beside Yukon Golds and russets. From time to time there are even a few baskets of Jerusalem artichokes. There may be newly dug parsnips and fresh spinach, saskatoon berry jams and golden strudels plump with Spartan apples or honey-sweetened poppyseeds. There may even be bison, fed on grain and hay until in April they ignore their mangers of food and stare longingly at the delectable green spring pastures.

Ukrainian families at these markets sell far more than great kolach (braided Easter bread) and holubtsi (cabbage rolls); they share their heritage. When Ukrainian farming families immigrated, mostly at the turn of the century, they brought with them their legendary skills of land husbandry and their Easter and Christmas traditions, which they observe today as they did a century ago in Russia. Ukrainians have a great respect for bread. For them intricately designed bread is central to many religious celebrations.

Russian Mennonites made their way through Ontario to settle from the Red River Valley westward across Saskatchewan and Alberta. With them came the same Eastern European love of good baking. To sample the foods of Manitoba's Mennonite community, all you have to do is head to Steinbach, south of Winnipeg, where, at the Mennonite Village Museum, there's an annual Pioneer Days festival with hearty, homespun foods. Cottage cheese dumplings are boiled and doused with cream gravy; rhubarb is made into platz or "pie by the yard"; wheat is ground at the windmill and baked outdoors into loaves of brown bread. There's cabbage soup and smoked baked farmers' sausage and pluma moos, a fruit soup.

Wonderful food isn't just found at fairs and in homes. At scattered truck stops — you can usually tell by the number of rigs and pick-ups in the parking lot — there are fabulous treats like real borscht, enormous cinnamon buns, matrimonial squares and homemade pies.

Off the main roads, there are foods you'll never find in a supermarket! In the north, especially, pickup trucks are regularly parked, occupants scouring the shoulders for wild berries (strawberries, saskatoons, red currants, raspberries and blueberries). Unlike in Newfoundland, here the pickers don't have to navigate bogs. Rather, they have to fight the mosquitoes and even the odd black bear also intent on filling his belly.

In the Prairies, freshwater fish and wild game are not a delicacy, they are a way of life. It is an area where people still harvest the land. Some still use cattails, dandelions, fireweed shoots, Labrador tea, wild onions, wild mushrooms, licorice root and lamb's quarters. The sourdough here is kept for months, and the riper it gets, the better it is for starting breads and biscuits. Here is the land of wild mushrooms and berries; specialty lentils and pulses; wild boar and rabbit and free-range veal; rosehips and fiddleheads; antelope, prairie chickens and wild ducks; specialty organic flours such as oat, millet, rye and spelt. And the story is just beginning.

Right: *Alberta beef tenderloin*

Bison Carpaccio

Commercially raised bison meat is becoming more and more available across the Prairies. This recipe was created by a 1998 team of Northern Alberta Institute of Technology Culinary Arts students.

2/3 cup (150 mL)	dark ale
1/4 cup (50 mL)	chopped onion
1 tbsp. (15 mL)	chopped garlic
1/4 cup (50 mL)	canola oil
1/4 cup (50 mL)	dry red wine
1 lb. (500 g)	bison (or beef) tenderloin or sirloin tip
2 tbsp. (25 mL)	dry mustard
2 tbsp. (25 mL)	chopped fresh parsley
2 tbsp. (25 mL)	chopped fresh coriander
2 tbsp. (25 mL)	crushed black peppercorns
2 cups (500 mL)	mixed baby lettuces
	Canola oil or Flavoured Canola Oil (p. 89)

◆ In a saucepan, combine ale, onion, garlic and 2 tbsp. (25 mL) each of the oil and the wine; bring to a simmer, remove from heat and let cool. Place bison and ale mixture in a bowl. Cover and refrigerate for 24 hours.

◆ Remove bison from marinade and pat dry. In a skillet over high heat, heat remaining 2 tbsp. (25 mL) oil and brown meat on all sides. Remove from pan, cover loosely and let cool.

◆ In a small bowl, mix together remaining 2 tbsp. (25 mL) wine and dry mustard; brush over the meat to coat it completely. Mix together parsley, coriander and peppercorns. Roll meat in herb mixture. Wrap meat tightly in plastic wrap and freeze for 2 hours or until almost frozen.

◆ Slice meat paper thin and arrange over mixed greens on 4 salad plates. Drizzle with canola oil. **Makes 4 servings.**

Cold-Pressed Canola Oil

At Highwood Crossing Farm, near Aldersyde, just outside Calgary, Tony and Penny Marshall are pioneering a new product — cold-pressed canola oil. Golden and nutty, the organic oil is created slowly with the only heat produced by the friction of the grains themselves. The Marshalls also produce flax seed oil, a product that Tony says is even more heat sensitive. The dark amber bottles can be purchased in health food stores across Alberta and may be frozen for up to one year to preserve the oil's delicate freshness.

61

Above: *Cold-pressed canola and flax oil*

Wild Mushroom Salad with
Grilled Venison Filet

The Post Hotel, a stylish mountain inn on the
Pipestone River at Lake Louise, Alberta, is owned
and lovingly operated by two Swiss brothers, André
and George Schwarz. It has had a reputation for
being one of the finest regional dining rooms for as
long as I have known it. From the inn, guests can
explore the Rockies on horseback, or hike and ski
some of the most beautiful slopes in Canada. Never
go to the Post in the winter without your skis.

2 tbsp. (25 mL)	raspberry vinegar
1/4 cup (50 mL)	canola oil
2 tbsp. (25 mL)	chicken stock (p. 66)
	Salt and freshly ground pepper to taste
4	venison or caribou loin filets
	(about 2 oz./50 g each)
1 tbsp. (15 mL)	unsalted butter
1/2 lb. (250 g)	small fresh wild mushrooms (chanterelle,
	porcini, morel, shiitake), thinly sliced
2	small heads frisée or mâche lettuce

✦ *In a small bowl, whisk together vinegar, 2 tbsp. (25 mL) of the
oil and stock; season with salt and pepper and set aside.*

✦ *Season venison filets with salt and pepper. Heat remaining 2
tbsp. (25 mL) oil in a skillet over medium-high heat. Add venison
and cook 3 minutes on each side or until medium-rare. Remove
from skillet and set aside. Reduce heat to medium and melt
butter in the skillet. Add mushrooms and cook 5 to 7 minutes
or until tender; season with salt and pepper to taste. Remove
skillet from heat and transfer mushrooms to a heated plate to
keep warm. Stir vinaigrette into skillet, stirring to scrape up any
brown bits from the bottom of the pan.*

✦ *Arrange lettuce on each of 4 serving plates. Arrange sautéed
mushrooms over lettuce and top with a venison filet. Drizzle
some warm vinaigrette over each salad and serve immediately.*
Makes 4 servings.

Wild Mushrooms

*The area near Prince Albert and points north is prime mushrooming country. From the precious pine mushrooms so relished in Japan to
chanterelles, morels and boletus, this wild harvest is distributed around the world.*

Warm Chèvre and Apple Rings with Hemp Seed Oil Vinaigrette

Hemp seed oil is a new crop in much of Canada. The bright green oil is created with hemp seed from Manitoba. Its earthy, nutty flavour combines beautifully with the tartness of both the apples and the chèvre. Use it where you would other heavily flavoured oils.

2	apples, cored
1 tbsp. (15 mL)	unsalted butter
8 oz. (250 g)	soft unripened chèvre
2 tbsp. (25 mL)	chopped fresh thyme
1 tsp. (5 mL)	freshly ground pepper

✦ *Slice each apple crosswise into 4 thick apple rings. Melt butter in a skillet over medium-high heat and cook apple rings on one side 7 to 8 minutes or until golden brown and starting to soften. Turn apples over and continue cooking 4 to 5 minutes or until apples are softened. Transfer apple rings to a baking sheet.*

✦ *Divide chèvre into 4 portions and flatten into discs the diameter of the apple rings. Coat with thyme and sprinkle with pepper. Place chèvre discs on top of apple rings. Broil for 3 minutes or until tops are golden brown and bubbling.*

Hemp Seed Oil Vinaigrette

1/4 cup (50 mL)	hemp seed oil
1 tbsp. (15 mL)	apple cider vinegar
1 tbsp. (15 mL)	apple juice
Pinch	salt and freshly ground pepper

✦ *In a small bowl, whisk together all ingredients. Set aside.*

To Serve

2 cups (500 mL)	mixed baby lettuces

✦ *In bowl, toss baby lettuces with half of the Hemp Seed Oil Vinaigrette and divide among 4 plates. Top with warm chèvre and apple rings and drizzle remaining Hemp Seed Oil Vinaigrette over chèvre. **Makes 4 servings.***

Golden Potato Salad with Dill, Radish and Sweet Onion

Potato salad is a staple at Prairie feasts. This recipe, one of the best and most flavourful you'll taste, is laden with fresh dill, a plant that although cultivated in most of Canada has escaped and become wild in the Ukrainian community of Yorkton, Saskatchewan.

2 1/2 – 3 lb. (1.1 – 1.3 kg)	Yukon Gold potatoes
1	Spanish onion, minced
1 1/4 cups (300 mL)	mayonnaise
2/3 cup (150 mL)	light sour cream
1/3 cup (75 mL)	minced fresh dill
2 tbsp. (25 mL)	cider vinegar
1 tbsp. (15 mL)	sugar
	Salt and freshly ground pepper
6 – 8	radishes, thinly sliced

✦ *Peel potatoes and cook in lightly salted water about 25 minutes or until tender. Let cool; cut into 1/2-inch (1 cm) cubes. In a large bowl, toss potatoes with onion. In a separate bowl, whisk together mayonnaise, sour cream, dill, vinegar and sugar. Season to taste with salt and pepper. Toss with potato mixture. Chill thoroughly for at least 3 hours. Before serving, scatter with radish slices. Refrigerate any leftover salad. **Makes 8 to 10 servings.***

63

Smoked Prairie Trout on Green Onion and Corn Pancakes with Cold-pressed Canola Mousseline and Watercress Salad

If I could create a Canadian culinary dream team, a group of chefs with huge talents and matching hearts, Michael Allemeier would be on it. We've crossed career paths many times, meeting originally at Sooke Harbour House in the mid-1980s and then when he was chef at John Bishop's great Vancouver restaurant, Bishop's. When he joined Canadian Pacific Hotels at Whistler, I once again caught up with his talent. My scribbled notes from a meal he treated me to still make my mouth water – right from the first salmon spring roll on a shaved fennel salad to his classic sugar pumpkin crème brûlée.

Now he's put both personal and culinary roots down in Calgary, incorporating the ingredients of southern Alberta in his interpretation of a new Prairie cuisine – fresh, full of flavour and honouring the producers of the province.

This is a great summer appetizer or a light luncheon. Michael uses an excellent cold-smoked trout from a local smokehouse (Classic Smokers) and Highwood Crossing Farm's cold-pressed canola oil (p. 61).

Green Onion and Corn Pancakes

1	egg, lightly beaten
2/3 cup (150 mL)	milk
3/4 cup (175 mL)	all-purpose flour
3/4 tsp. (4 mL)	baking powder
2 tbsp. (25 mL)	butter, melted
2	ears corn, shucked and blanched
2	green onions, chopped
	Salt and freshly ground pepper

✦ In a bowl beat egg and milk together. Combine flour and baking powder; stir into egg mixture until smooth. Stir in melted butter, corn and green onions. Lightly season with salt and pepper (but don't add too much salt; the smoked trout is salty). Lightly oil a large skillet and heat over medium-high heat. Drop tablespoons of batter into skillet and sauté 1 to 1 1/2 minutes or till golden on both sides, turning once. As pancakes are done, remove to a plate; cover loosely with foil to keep warm. **Makes at least 18 pancakes.**

Cold-pressed Canola Mousseline

1 cup (250 mL)	whipping cream (35%)
1	egg yolk
2 tbsp. (25 mL)	grainy Dijon mustard
	Juice of 1 lemon
2/3 cup (150 mL)	cold-pressed canola oil
1/3 cup (75 mL)	canola oil
	Salt and freshly ground pepper
2 tsp. (10 mL)	minced chives

✦ Whip cream to soft peaks and refrigerate. In a large bowl whisk together egg yolk, mustard and lemon juice. Whisk in the oils in a thin stream to make a mayonnaise. Carefully fold whipped cream into mayonnaise. Season with salt and pepper. Fold in chives. Refrigerate until serving.

To Serve

30	slices cold-smoked rainbow trout (about 1 1/2 lb./750 g)
	Trout or salmon roe
1	bunch watercress
	Chive blossoms

✦ Place 1 pancake in the middle of each of 6 serving plates. Place a tablespoon of mousseline on the pancake and top with a slice of smoked trout. Repeat twice, ending with the trout. Wrap the remaining smoked trout around the tower. Place a dollop of mousseline on the top trout and top with roe. Arrange the watercress around the pancake tower and garnish with chive blossoms. **Makes 6 servings.**

64

Tender Spinach Leaves Served with Beet, Celeriac and Apple Salad with Creamy Feta Cheese Dressing

For this recipe Michael Allemeier uses the excellent sheep's milk feta made by Shepherd Gourmet Dairy. This is a great salad for late summer when all the vegetables are available in our famous farmers' markets. Try crumbling the cheese on the salad as well.

6	medium beets
4 cups (1 L)	water
1/2 cup (125 mL)	sugar
1/2 cup (125 mL)	apple cider vinegar
1 cup (250 mL)	peeled and grated celeriac
1 cup (250 mL)	peeled, cored and grated apple
1/2 cup (250 mL)	high-quality mayonnaise
1 tbsp. (15 mL)	lemon juice

✦ In a large pot combine beets, water, sugar and vinegar. Bring to a boil, reduce heat and simmer, covered, for 45 to 50 minutes or until the beets are tender. Drain beets and peel under cold running water. Slice thinly and set aside (refrigerate if not using immediately).

✦ In a bowl stir together celeriac, apple, mayonnaise and lemon juice. Refrigerate till needed.

Feta Cheese Dressing

1	egg
1 tsp. (5 mL)	Dijon mustard
1/3 cup (75 mL)	table cream (18%)
2 tbsp. (25 mL)	lemon juice
1/4 tsp.	cayenne
2/3 cup (150 mL)	canola oil
1/3 cup (75 mL)	hazelnut oil
2 oz. (50 g)	feta cheese
	Salt and freshly ground pepper

✦ In a food processor blend egg and mustard. Add cream, lemon juice and cayenne. Pulse to combine well. With the motor running, slowly add canola oil and hazelnut oil. When a light mayonnaise forms, add feta cheese and pulse a few seconds longer. Season with salt and pepper.

To Serve

1/2 lb. (250 g)	spinach leaves
1/4 cup (50 mL)	roasted hazelnuts (p. 21)
	Crumbled feta cheese (optional)

✦ Arrange spinach leaves like the spokes of a wheel on 6 salad plates.

✦ Overlap beets in the centre and top with celeriac salad. Drizzle the spinach with the Feta Cheese Dressing and scatter with toasted hazelnuts and additional feta if desired.
Makes 6 servings.

65

Amy's Wild Rice Soup

Amy Hadley from the restaurant Amy's on Second in Prince Albert, Saskatchewan, makes the creamiest wild rice soup ever. In a small, art-filled café, she serves up innovative, delicious food. Her chefs grind wild rice to a coarse powder to make savoury Yorkshire puddings to accompany marinated bison tenderloin. Although here, as in most places in the province, real local food only dots the menu, the ingredients that do make it on are treated with real respect — Saskatchewan lamb, golden pickerel from the amazingly fresh water of the northern lakes and lots of beef framed in various ways, from spring rolls to the most traditional and most delicious steak.

1/4 cup (50 mL)	unsalted butter
2 cups (500 mL)	thinly sliced mushrooms
1/2 cup (125 mL)	chopped onion
1/2 cup (125 mL)	chopped celery
1/4 cup (50 mL)	chopped sweet green pepper
1/4 cup (50 mL)	chopped sweet red pepper
1/4 cup (50 mL)	all-purpose flour
2 cups (500 mL)	warm chicken stock
2 cups (500 mL)	cooked wild rice
1 cup (250 mL)	milk
1 cup (250 mL)	half & half cream (10%)
	Salt and pepper to taste

✦ *In a heavy saucepan, melt butter over medium-high heat. Cook mushrooms, onion, celery, green pepper and red pepper 6 to 8 minutes or until softened. Stir in flour; cook 5 minutes, stirring. Add chicken stock, stirring constantly to remove any lumps. Stir in rice, milk and cream. Reduce heat to medium and cook, stirring, till thickened and bubbling. Season with salt and pepper.* **Makes 8 servings.**

Chicken Stock

This basic recipe produces a rich, delicious stock that can be frozen for several months or refrigerated for up to 1 week. The chicken you purchase determines the flavour of the stock. An older stewing hen with yellow fat is perfect. This stock may be used in other recipes, or by adding the reserved meat, a chopped carrot or two, a minced onion and a handful of Perfect Pasta (p. 73), you can create a great chicken soup.

1	large stewing hen (5 – 6 lb./2.2 – 2.5 kg)
8 – 10 cups (2 – 2.5 L)	cold water
3	onions, unpeeled and cut in chunks
4	stalks celery, coarsely chopped
6	sprigs fresh parsley
2	bay leaves

✦ *Place chicken in a large stock pot. Cover with cold water and bring to a boil. Reduce heat and skim scum and fat from the surface. Add onions, celery, parsley and bay leaves. Cover and simmer 4 to 6 hours, without stirring. Remove chicken with slotted spoon and reserve meat for another use. Strain liquid, discarding solids. Chill stock. Skim fat from surface and refrigerate until needed.* **Makes about 6 cups (1.5 L).**

Wild Rice

In the wilds of Saskatchewan where the granite of the Canadian Shield outlines hundreds of lakes, wild rice flourishes. There, outside the town of La Ronge, about 140 miles (225 kilometres) north of Saskatoon, the crop is seeded by hand in sheltered bays on leased Crown land. The competition here is not human but thousands upon thousands of ducks and snowy white pelicans that fly in yearly for a feast. Not a rice but rather a grass, wild rice looks much like wide blades of grass until, in late August and September, the heavy seed heads droop down, making them easily accessible to the airboats that pass back and forth and are used as harvesters. If you visit the La Ronge processing plant of Riese's Canadian Lake Wild Rice during mid-September, you will see long, knee-deep rows of the grain outside awaiting drying. When the wild rice is dried over burners, the air becomes filled with an almost indescribably delicious nutty aroma. Some of the rice is sold in whole grain form, while some is ground into flour, a particularly special product used in baking and pasta.

Strathcona Market

In old Strathcona, once a separate city, now part of Edmonton, in a high-ceilinged former bus garage, one of the great Prairie markets takes place. Founded in 1983, it has flourished. Shoppers can purchase a real taste of Alberta, from Hutterite beans and Bintje potatoes to plum kuchen and buckwheat cabbage rolls.

Prairie Beef Stock

Real beef stock, rich and fragrant, flavours some of the best soups in any prairie kitchen. The secret is long, slow simmering and the best beef in the world. Lamb bones may be substituted in this recipe.

3 – 5 lb. (1.5 – 2.2 kg)	beef bones
1	5 1/2 oz. (156 mL) can tomato paste
4	carrots, cut in chunks
3	onions, coarsely chopped
3	stalks celery, coarsely chopped
1	head garlic, unpeeled but broken apart
1 tsp. (5 mL)	juniper berries
1 tsp. (5 mL)	whole black peppercorns
1 tbsp. (15 mL)	dried or chopped fresh thyme
1 tbsp. (15 mL)	dried or chopped fresh rosemary
1 tsp. (5 mL)	dried sage
1 cup (250 mL)	dry red wine
8 cups (2 L)	cold water

✦ Smear bones with tomato paste and place in single layer in a large roasting pan. Roast at 375°F (190°C), turning the bones from time to time, 45 minutes or until bones are well browned. Transfer bones to a large stock pot. Add carrots, onions, celery, garlic, juniper berries, peppercorns, thyme, rosemary, sage, wine and water. Bring to a boil; reduce heat and simmer, covered, for 8 hours. Cool. Strain stock and discard solids. Return stock to pot; bring to a boil and simmer, uncovered, until reduced by half. Refrigerate until needed. Skim fat from surface before using. *Makes 6 cups (1.5 L).*

Light Dilled Cucumber Soup with Borage Blossoms

This soup is similar to one we had on a steaming-hot summer evening in Rosthern, Saskatchewan, at the Station Arts Centre, located in the old CN station where hundreds of families disembarked to begin their new lives on the Prairies. That evening they were staging a play called Spirit Wrestler, which chronicled the story of the Doukhobors, a Russian Christian sect, in the area. The menu reflected this heritage with its emphasis on vegetarian cookery, cold soups, grain salads and Doukhobor cheese-filled crepes called nalesnyky.

1/2	large English cucumber, peeled and coarsely chopped
1 1/2 cups (375 mL)	plain yogurt
1 cup (250 mL)	chicken stock (p. 66)
1/4 cup (50 mL)	minced green onions or chives
1 – 2 tbsp. (15 – 25 mL)	chopped fresh dill
	Salt and freshly ground pepper to taste
	Borage blossoms and fresh dill sprigs as garnish

✦ In a food processor, purée cucumber, yogurt, stock, green onions and dill. Transfer to a large glass bowl. Season with salt and pepper. Cover and refrigerate at least 4 hours or overnight. Ladle into chilled soup bowls and garnish with borage blossoms and dill sprigs. *Makes 6 to 8 servings.*

Northern Pike with Wheat Berry Tabbouleh

As the name implies, Calories Desserts in Saskatoon creates some of the richest and most delicious desserts on the Prairies. However, this tiny restaurant also offers one of the finest casual dining experiences in the region. Here's a real Prairie specialty.

Wheat Berry Tabbouleh

1 cup (250 mL)	wheat berries or barley
3 cups (750 mL)	water
1	English cucumber, finely chopped
2	tomatoes, chopped
5	green onions, chopped
1/2 cup (125 mL)	chopped fresh parsley
1/4 cup (50 mL)	chopped fresh mint
2 tbsp. (25 mL)	lemon juice
2 tbsp. (25 mL)	cider vinegar
2	cloves garlic, minced
1/4 tsp. (1 mL)	salt
1/4 tsp. (1 mL)	freshly ground pepper
1/4 cup (50 mL)	canola oil

✦ In a small saucepan, bring wheat berries and water to a boil. Reduce heat and simmer, covered, for 45 minutes or until tender. Rinse under cold water and drain. Place wheat berries in a large bowl and add cucumber, tomatoes, green onions, parsley and mint.

✦ In a small bowl, whisk together lemon juice, vinegar, garlic, salt and pepper. Whisking constantly, add oil in a thin stream until well combined. Pour dressing over wheat berry mixture and toss to combine.

Northern Pike

4	northern pike fillets (about 4 oz./125 g each), skinned and boned
	Salt and freshly ground pepper to taste
2 tbsp. (25 mL)	unsalted butter

✦ Season pike fillets with salt and pepper. Melt butter in a non-stick skillet over medium-high heat. Cook pike 3 minutes on each side or until fish is golden and flakes easily with a fork. Remove fish from skillet.

To Serve

✦ Place tabbouleh in the skillet over medium-high heat, stirring to gently heat through. Divide tabbouleh among 4 serving plates and top with pike fillets. **Makes 4 servings.**

Saskatoon

The Saskatoon Farmers' Market is one of the best in Canada. Here, you can taste the seasonal bounty of southern Saskatchewan. All year round, vendors sell the traditional seasonal veggies (snap beans, newly dug potatoes, gorgeous lettuces and fresh herbs) along with truly regional specialties like saskatoon berry jam and pies, homemade egg noodles and locally grown organic grain.

Spring Creek Market in Saskatoon is a small, casual grocery store that specializes in the foods of the province. Their ads say they sell 99 percent Saskatchewan product. Here you'll find local fruits and berries, Prairie Gold borage honey, a variety of perogies, berry syrups, chocolate wheat bark and Grundeen ice cream.

Mike's Beer-Battered Fish

It is meals like this that cause me to love fishing
in the North. I first tasted this fabulous crispy fish
when guide Mike Reimer of North Knife Lake Lodge
made it with the pike I caught. He built a great big
campfire on a beach, somewhere west of Churchill,
Manitoba, on about the 58th parallel. The big old
cast-iron frying pan was full of golden fillets. We ate
them with fresh bread and coleslaw and baked beans.

    The recipe should really begin, "First catch a
pike," but since most cooks are rarely blessed with
such a privilege, use any white-fleshed fish. Pickerel
is great. You can serve it as is, with a mayonnaise
that you've mixed with a handful of fresh dill, or with
the Dill Hollandaise (p. 187) from Hibernia.

	Canola oil for deep-frying
1 1/2 cups (375 mL)	all-purpose flour
1	12-oz. (355 mL) can beer
1	egg
2 tsp. (10 mL)	chopped fresh dill
1 tsp. (5 mL)	salt
1	tsp. (5 mL) pepper
2 lb. (1 kg)	fish fillets, cut in serving pieces

✦ *Heat 3 inches (8 cm) of oil in a deep-fryer or large heavy Dutch
oven to 375°F (190°C). In a bowl, whisk together flour, beer, egg,
dill, salt and pepper until smooth. Drop fish pieces into the batter
and turn until entirely coated. Place fish in hot oil and fry, turning
once, 5 to 7 minutes or until deep golden brown on both sides.
Drain on a wire rack placed over a cookie sheet.* **Makes 6 servings.**

69

Venison Sausage Patties

In the Far North, wild game is a staple. Freezers are filled in the autumn for use all year round. This recipe, adapted from one by Mike Boll, a guide at North Knife Lake Lodge in northern Manitoba, can be used for moose or caribou meat as well. The sausage can be piped into casings or shaped into patties and frozen or used immediately. Since wild meat is very lean, the pork must contain some fat.

2 lb. (1 kg)	venison, cubed
2 lb. (1 kg)	pork shoulder, cubed
1/4 cup (50 mL)	water
2	cloves garlic, finely chopped
1 tbsp. (15 mL)	brown sugar
1 tbsp. (15 mL)	salt
2 tsp. (10 mL)	pepper

✦ In a food processor, combine venison, pork and water; process until finely chopped. Transfer mixture to a large mixing bowl. Add garlic, brown sugar, salt and pepper. Knead until well blended. Divide mixture into quarters and then divide each quarter into quarters again. Flatten each portion into a patty.

✦ Broil patties 5 minutes on each side or until meat is slightly pink in centre. (Alternatively, to pan-fry patties, heat 1 tbsp./ 15 mL canola oil in a skillet and fry 6 to 7 minutes on each side or until slightly pink in centre.) **Makes 8 servings or 16 patties.**

North Knife Lake Lodge

My friends and I, a few other fishers and the pilot, are flying towards the horizon in a tiny plane packed with fishing gear, over sun-dappled tundra, lakes of many colours and spruce trees that at first are thick, then merely seem to outline streams or fault lines. The destination? North Knife Lake Lodge, a one-hour flight from Thompson, Manitoba, latitude 59°N. On the permafrost and lichen-encased earth, spongy and covered with Labrador tea plants and blueberries, Doug and Helen Webber have built their dream lodge. It took forty loads on a DC-3 to haul in the construction materials. Helen's commercial range was flown in and landed on the ice in the winter — four miles north of the lodge! She climbed onto her snowmobile, zipped up the lake and towed the range home, where it still graces her kitchen.

The lakes truly are so full of fish that, unless you're into tallying how many you catch, there's not much reason to be anything else but laid-back. We leisurely enjoyed the strong coffee and cinnamon buns that Helen and her friend Marie Woolsey served. We fished with tackle in the morning, sussing out the way these big fish behaved. By the afternoon, after a picnic in the sunshine of Mike's Beer-Battered Fish (p. 69). I was standing on the bow of the boat with a snow-white "zonker" on a 6/7 weight rod casting...once, twice, then the pike hit. All afternoon we caught and released.

Every evening the menu changed. Snow goose breasts were barbecued and served with wild rice and a delicious sweet onion salad. Over the few days we were there, we tasted all the lodge specialties, from Doug's smoked lake trout and roasted caribou to maple-marinated pickerel nuggets and dozens of squares and pastries.

71

Stuffed Beef Tenderloin with Rosehip and Roasted Red Pepper Sauce

Roses grow wild across the prairies, and in the autumn the hips, the fruit of the plant, become large and orange. You can easily oven-dry rosehips by spreading them on a tray and baking them at a very low temperature or until crisp. When brewed into a tea, using about 12 dried hips per cup (250 mL) of boiling water, they provide an important source of vitamin C.

This dish comes from Wanuskewin.

Rosehip and Roasted Red Pepper Sauce

This tangy, bright orange sauce can be sweetened to your personal taste with liquid honey.

2	sweet red peppers
2 cups (500 mL)	dried rosehips
3 cups (750 mL)	water
	Honey to taste
	Salt and freshly ground pepper to taste

✦ Place red peppers under the broiler and turn until charred and blistered on all sides. Place the peppers in a heavy paper bag or a pot with a tight-fitting lid; let stand for 10 minutes, then peel off skin and scoop out core, seeds and membrane. Purée pepper in a food processor until smooth. Set aside.

✦ In a saucepan, bring rosehips and water to a boil. Reduce heat and simmer for 20 to 30 minutes or until hips are soft. Strain the liquid and discard rosehips. Stir together rosehip liquid (it will be quite thick) and red pepper purée. Sweeten and season to taste.

Stuffed Beef Tenderloin

2 tbsp. (25 mL)	canola oil
3	shallots, finely chopped
2 cups (500 mL)	wild or cultivated mushrooms, stems removed, sliced
6 cups (1.5 L)	spinach leaves
4	slices fresh bread, cubed
1 cup (250 mL)	crumbled feta cheese
1 tbsp. (15 mL)	chopped fresh rosemary
1 tsp. (5 mL)	chopped fresh thyme
1 tsp. (5 mL)	chopped fresh sage
	Salt and freshly ground pepper to taste
2 lb. (1 kg)	beef tenderloin, butterflied
1	egg, beaten
1/4 cup (50 mL)	cracked black peppercorns
1 tbsp. (15 mL)	salt

✦ Heat 1 tbsp. (15 mL) oil in a heavy skillet over medium-high heat; add shallots and cook until tender. Add mushrooms and spinach; cook about 8 minutes or until spinach is wilted and mushrooms are soft. Set aside to cool.

✦ In a bowl, mix together bread, cheese, rosemary, thyme and sage. Add spinach mixture and toss to combine thoroughly. Season with salt and pepper.

✦ Open butterflied tenderloin and lay flat on a work surface. Place stuffing evenly over the surface and roll up jelly-roll style. Tie meat at even intervals. Heat remaining 1 tbsp. (15 mL) of oil in a skillet over high heat and brown tenderloin evenly on all sides. Let cool.

✦ Brush beaten egg over tenderloin and roll in cracked black pepper to coat entire surface. Sprinkle with salt. Bake in a pre-heated 375°F (190°C) oven for 1 hour or until thermometer inserted in roast registers 145°F (60°C).

✦ Warm sauce and serve over sliced beef tenderloin.

Makes 4 servings.

Wanuskewin, Saskatchewan

Wanuskewin means "seeking peace of mind." It is, indeed, a peaceful place. It is located west of Saskatoon on one of the great trade routes, and it was here on the cliffs that for thousands of years Native bands gathered without animosity to hunt buffalo. Today it is a national historic site where you can hike, enjoy some of the traditional foods and begin to understand the culture of the peoples of the plains. Stone tools, some 2,300 years old, and other 4,000-year-old artifacts are displayed in the museum.

Alberta Beef, Mushroom and Pepper Pasta Sauce

Alberta beef is renowned all over the world. This recipe pays homage to it and to the Ukrainian population scattered across the Prairies who might call this dish goulash.

A wine such as Baco Noir or Maréchal Foch would be perfect both with and in this dish.

4	slices bacon, diced
2	onions, peeled and diced
2 tbsp. (25 mL)	Hungarian paprika
1 tsp. (5 mL)	caraway seeds (optional)
2 lb. (1 kg)	round steak, cut in 1-inch (2.5 cm) cubes
1/2 tsp. (2 mL)	salt
1/2 tsp. (2 mL)	freshly ground pepper
1 cup (250 mL)	beef stock (p. 67)
1/2 cup (125 mL)	hearty red wine
1 cup (250 mL)	sour cream
2 tbsp. (25 mL)	all-purpose flour
3 tbsp. (45 mL)	canola oil
1 lb. (500 g)	Portobello mushroom caps, sliced
1	sweet red pepper, cut in 3/4-inch (2 cm) cubes
1	sweet green pepper, cut in 3/4-inch (2 cm) cubes
	Salt and freshly ground pepper to taste
12 oz. (375 g)	cooked Fresh Prairie Pasta (see right)

+ In a large saucepan, fry bacon over medium-high heat until crisp. Remove and set aside. Add onions to pan; cook 3 minutes. Add paprika and caraway seeds; cook, stirring constantly, 15 to 30 seconds or until paprika begins to darken. Add meat, tossing to coat thoroughly with paprika. Season with salt and pepper. Add beef stock and wine. Bring to a boil. Reduce heat; cover and simmer 1 1/2 hours, stirring occasionally. Uncover and simmer 30 minutes longer.

+ Whisk sour cream and flour together until smooth. Add to meat mixture. Cook, stirring constantly, until thickened.

+ In a large skillet, heat oil over medium heat. Add mushrooms and cook 2 to 3 minutes. Add peppers and cook, stirring constantly, until tender-crisp. Season with salt and pepper.

+ Place hot, well-drained pasta on 6 plates. Top with a generous portion of beef, then the mushroom and pepper sauce. Sprinkle with reserved crisp bacon. **Makes 6 servings.**

Fresh Prairie Pasta

The durum wheat grown in Canada is without question the finest on earth. Making pasta from scratch takes a bit of time, but the taste is well worth it, and with a pasta machine it's easy to do.

2 – 3 cups (500–750 mL)	all-purpose flour
3	eggs
2 tsp. (10 mL)	canola oil
1/4 tsp. (1 mL)	salt

+ Mound 2 cups (500 mL) of the flour on a work surface; make a well in centre. Put eggs, oil and salt in well. Beat eggs with a fork, gradually working flour into egg mixture until a soft dough is formed. Gather dough into a ball, leaving any bits of dough or excess flour behind. Knead dough on a lightly floured surface 10 minutes or until smooth and elastic. Add more flour as needed to prevent sticking. Cover with plastic wrap; let rest at least 30 minutes and up to 3 hours.

+ Divide dough into 4. Keep dough you aren't working with covered. On a lightly floured surface, roll out dough portion into a 5-inch (12 cm) strip. Dust lightly with flour. Feed through widest setting on pasta machine rollers 4 times. Set machine to next narrowest setting. Pass dough through once. Repeat, running dough through machine using a smaller setting each time to finest setting. Hang pasta over a pole 15 minutes to dry slightly (no longer). Repeat rolling with remaining dough.

+ Set machine to cut desired shape of pasta. Feed each sheet of dough through cutter. Lay pasta on tea towel. Cover with plastic wrap up to 1 hour, or refrigerate up to 2 days.

+ To cook, bring a large pot of salted water to a boil. Add pasta and cook over medium-low heat 5 to 7 minutes or until tender but still slightly firm. **Makes 12 oz. (375 g) pasta.**

Perfect Perogies

Once you've tasted homemade perogies, store-bought will never do. Make lots; freeze them and they're ready when you are.

Dough

1	egg
3/4 cup (175 mL)	warm water
2 tbsp. (25 mL)	canola oil
2 1/2 cups (625 mL)	all-purpose flour
1 tsp. (5 mL)	salt

Potato and Onion Filling

1 2/3 cups (400 mL)	mashed cooked potatoes (3 large potatoes)
2/3 cup (150 mL)	shredded sharp cheddar cheese
1/4 cup (50 mL)	dry cottage cheese (optional)
1	green onion, finely chopped
2 tsp. (10 mL)	finely chopped fresh dill or mint
	Salt and pepper to taste

Toppings

	Melted butter, sour cream, crisp diced bacon, cooked diced onions

✦ In a large bowl, beat egg, water and oil. Add flour and salt. Mix well. Knead on a lightly floured surface about 3 minutes or until smooth and elastic. Cover with a damp tea towel and let rest 1 to 2 hours.

✦ Combine mashed potatoes, cheddar cheese, cottage cheese, green onion, dill, salt and pepper. Mix well.

✦ Divide dough in half. Work with one portion at a time, keeping other one covered. Shape each portion into a roll 1 inch (2.5 cm) in diameter. Cut into 1/4-inch (5 mm) slices. Roll each slice into a 2 1/2-inch (6 cm) circle. Place about 1 tbsp. (15 mL) filling in centre of each circle, away from edge. Moisten edge with water; fold dough in half over filling. Seal edges with tines of a fork. (Freeze at this stage, if desired, by spreading perogies in a single layer on a baking sheet and, when frozen, packaging in tightly sealed plastic bags.)

✦ Cook perogies in a large pot of boiling salted water 5 to 8 minutes or until they rise to the top and look plump. Don't over-crowd; cook in several batches for even cooking. Transfer to a colander, drain well, then place in a buttered dish, turning to coat with butter. Keep warm while cooking remaining perogies, or reheat in a skillet.

✦ Serve with sour cream and butter or a mixture of crisp bacon and onions. **Makes about 45 perogies.**

Agribition

For one week in late November, Regina's Agribition showcases the best in big-time western farming. It is estimated that one-third of all Prairie farmers attend the marketplace, where nearly $4 million worth of livestock alone is auctioned. It's the place to come to see what's new and biggest and best.

Baked Autumn Vegetables, Barley and Wild Rice

This is one of the finest oven-baked "risottos." Use any combination of root vegetables so long as it equals about 8 cups (2 L) of 1-inch (2.5 cm) chunks.

1 cup (250 mL)	wild rice
1/4 cup (50 mL)	unsalted butter
2 cups (500 mL)	thinly sliced onions
1 cup (250 mL)	barley
2 cups (500 mL)	cubed, peeled sweet potatoes
2 cups (500 mL)	cubed, peeled parsnips
2 cups (500 mL)	cubed, peeled celeriac
2 cups (500 mL)	cubed, peeled squash
1 lb. (500 g)	mushrooms, cleaned and halved (optional)
1 1/2 tsp. (7 mL)	salt
1/4 tsp. (1 mL)	freshly ground pepper
2 cups (500 mL)	apple cider
2 cups (500 mL)	chicken stock (p. 66)

✦ Cover wild rice with cold water; let soak 4 hours. Drain and set aside.

✦ Melt butter in a large skillet over high heat. Reduce heat to medium. Add onions; sauté until golden. In a large casserole dish or small roaster, mix wild rice, onions and barley. Layer root vegetables and mushrooms on top. Sprinkle with salt and pepper. Pour cider and stock over mixture. Cover and bake in a preheated 375°F (190°C) oven for 1 1/2 hours or until the barley and rice are tender. **Makes 8 servings.**

Left: *Aerial view near Saskatoon, Saskatchewan*

Prairie Pulses

The term "pulse" refers to a plethora of beans, feed and food peas, lentils and chickpeas (a.k.a. garbanzo beans). And in western Canada, it's a huge business. The varieties of beans number into the dozens, and Canadian feed peas are exported all over the globe. Two crops in particular hold a lot of promise. Chickpea production, based in southern Alberta and Saskatchewan has been dubbed as "the next Cinderella crop." Chickpeas are a major food source in much of the world, particularly in India, Pakistan and Spain. Lentils are cultivated in the same areas and southern Manitoba. Like chickpeas, lentils form the protein base in regions with primarily vegetarian populations and where meat and fish are at a premium. With the highest average protein levels of all pulses (19 g/250 mL), they vary from the fat, light green Laird variety to the traditional French green, Spanish brown and red.

Sautéed Wild Amaranth and Dill

1 tbsp. (15 mL)	unsalted butter
1	large clove garlic, slivered
4 cups (1 L)	wild amaranth, washed
2 tbsp. (25 mL)	chopped fresh dill
1/4 cup (50 mL)	whipping cream (35%)
	Salt and freshly ground
	black pepper to taste

In Yorkton, Saskatchewan, you'll find living proof that much of Canada's best food is still cooked in our homes. Anne Musey's little bed and breakfast on Darlington Street is a haven of traditional Ukrainian foods. Wild mushrooms fill crepes, and rhubarb is a huge favourite, especially in a light chiffon dessert with fresh strawberries. Dill grows wild in the garden. Beans — the seeds were from the housekeeper of an old priest — are saved from year to year to mash with garlic for the Christmas feast. Peter Kobylka, the manager of the parish cultural centre, grows potatoes beside the Musey home and from time to time pops in to play his fiddle.

Amaranth, commonly known as pigweed, is a delicious green vegetable. Pick the young tender stalks and smaller, less-coarse leaves. Larger leaves are best parboiled 2 to 3 minutes before sautéing.

✦ *Melt butter in a skillet over medium heat. Add garlic; cook 30 seconds. Add amaranth with water still clinging to leaves. Sauté about 4 minutes, until leaves begin to wilt. Stir in dill, cream, salt and pepper. Cook about 3 minutes or until cream is slightly thickened.* **Makes 4 servings.**

76

Painted Eggs, Wedding Bread and Kasha

The Ukrainian presence in the Prairies, particularly in Manitoba and Saskatchewan, is a tribute to a people and their culture. The trek during the early years between 1891 and 1914 saw 170,000 Ukrainians immigrating to Canada. A first winter must have been horrific for these brave families, huddled in tiny sod huts on the vast Prairie grassland. The tenacity and the faith in the future that brought these people to Canada also sustained them. Their churches were important and still play a powerful role in community life. St. Mary's Church in Yorkton, Saskatchewan, is a magnificent example not only of art and architecture but also of the way a church binds a spiritual community into a physical one. There are perogy-making bees, which fill the big kitchen with tradition and fun. Hundreds of dozens of the stuffed dough dumplings are made for parties and weddings. The old food ways have been preserved and flourish better here in Canada than in Ukraine itself, and the belief is that as long as pysanky are made there will be peace in the land. These delicate, perfectly painted eggs are the pride of Ukrainian communities across Canada and are one of the most treasured gifts. The other gifts are the Ukrainian decorative breads, each wearing its tiny dough icons.

The day-to-day foods of a Ukrainian family are sprinkled with old dishes: kasha (porridge), holubtsi (cabbage rolls), nachynka (baked corn meal), fresh yogurt and huslianka (clabbered milk), studenets (jellied pork) and of course borscht, the national soup that has as many variations as it does cooks. Ceremony is important, too. Easter brings on paska and babka, both traditional holiday breads, and syrnyk, an old-country cheesecake. On Christmas Eve, the Holy Supper features twelve meatless dishes, symbolizing the twelve disciples, surrounding another fabulous bread, kolach braided with a candle, the star of Bethlehem, at the centre.

Above: *Anne Lukowich with Ukranian wedding bread, Saskatoon*

The first record of wheat being harvested in Alberta was on October 11, 1811, and on October 12, 1819, the first recorded agricultural export left Saskatchewan from Cumberland House to the Red River Settlement. Listed were "36 Kegs @10.Gall. of Potatoes, 8 Bushels of Barley, and 1 Bushel of Wheat."

Sourdough Rye Bread

Using sourdough as its base, a form of leavening well known across pioneer Canada, this recipe is a showcase for many of the finest Prairie ingredients.

2 cups (500 mL)	Easy Sourdough Starter (p. 52)
2 cups (500 mL)	warm water
3 tbsp. (45 mL)	canola oil
4 – 5 cups (1 – 1.25 L)	all-purpose flour
1/4 cup (50 mL)	golden or regular flax
1 tbsp. (15 mL)	salt
2 tsp. (10 mL)	instant yeast
2 cups (500 mL)	dark or light rye flour

✦ *In a large bowl, whisk together the starter, water, oil and 1 cup (250 mL) of the all-purpose flour until smooth. Beat in flax, salt and yeast. Stir in rye flour and enough all-purpose flour to make a soft dough. Turn dough out onto a floured work surface and knead 10 to 15 minutes or until smooth and elastic, adding all-purpose flour as necessary. Dough should feel slightly sticky.*

✦ *Place dough in well-oiled bowl, turning to coat with oil, and cover with a tea towel. Let rise until doubled, 60 to 70 minutes. Punch down dough and let rise again until doubled.*

✦ *Punch down dough and divide in half. Shape each half into a round or long loaf and place on a parchment-lined baking sheet. Cover with a tea towel and let rise until almost doubled, about 45 minutes. With the tip of a small sharp knife, slash the top of each loaf diagonally in three places.*

✦ *Place a pan containing 1/2 inch (1 cm) hot water on the bottom of a preheated 400°F (200°C) oven. Bake bread 50 to 60 minutes or until deep brown and loaves sound hollow when tapped on bottom.* **Makes 2 loaves.**

Whole-Wheat Bread with Borage Honey

One of the newest medicinal crops on the Prairies is borage. It's harvested for its oil but the honey is, without doubt, one of the most delicious produced anywhere in Canada. It is usually found creamed in tubs, ready to spread on toast. Here, it's used as a main ingredient in an old-fashioned whole-wheat bread.

2 3/4 cups (675 mL)	lukewarm water
1/3 cup (75 mL)	borage honey
1 tbsp. (15 mL)	active dry yeast
3/4 cup (175 mL)	canola oil
1 tbsp. (15 mL)	salt
1 cup (250 mL)	all-purpose or white bread flour
6 – 6 1/2 cups (1.5 – 1.6 L)	whole-wheat flour

✦ *Combine water and honey in a large warmed bowl, stirring to dissolve the honey. Sprinkle with yeast. Let sit 10 minutes or until foamy. Whisk in oil, salt and all-purpose flour. Beat well. Let rise until puffy, 30 to 60 minutes. Stir in enough of the whole-wheat flour to make a soft dough. Turn out onto a well-floured surface and knead in remaining flour. Continue to knead 2 to 3 minutes or until dough is smooth and elastic. Cover with a tea towel and let rise at room temperature until doubled, about 1 1/2 hours. Punch down and let rise again for 15 minutes. Punch down and cut in half, shaping each half into a loaf. Place in well-greased 9" x 5" (2 L) loaf pans. Cover and let rise till doubled, about 1 1/2 hours. Bake in a preheated 350°F (180°C) oven 30 to 35 minutes or until richly golden brown. Remove bread from pans while hot and cool on a wire rack 15 to 20 minutes before slicing.* **Makes 2 large loaves.**

77

Above: *Grain elevator, Rosthern, Saskatchewan*

Wild Rice and Birch Syrup Pudding

This recipe, from Calgary's River Café, uses birch syrup, the Prairie answer to maple syrup. Substitute the darkest maple syrup you can find or add molasses to the maple syrup that is boiled in early spring. At the restaurant they garnish the pudding with fruit and fresh mint leaves.

3 1/2 cups (875 mL)	water
1 cup (250 mL)	wild rice
3 cups (750 mL)	milk
1/4 cup (50 mL)	sugar
2	egg yolks
1/2 cup (125 mL)	whipping cream (35%)
1/4 cup (50 mL)	birch syrup
	(or 1/4 cup/50 mL maple syrup and
	1 tbsp./15 mL molasses)

✦ Bring 3 cups (750 mL) of the water to a boil in a heavy-bottomed saucepan; add wild rice and cook 20 minutes. Drain and rinse the rice with cool water. Return rice to saucepan and add milk, remaining 1/2 cup (125 mL) water and sugar. Simmer 20 to 30 minutes longer or until rice is tender.

✦ Whisk together egg yolks and cream. Stir into the rice mixture and cook, stirring constantly, over low heat 5 minutes or until thickened slightly. Remove from heat and stir in birch syrup. Cool to room temperature. **Makes six 1-cup (250 mL) servings.**

The Calgary Scene

Calgary is a happening food city. Earth to Table is one of the reasons. It's a farmer/chef organization that has brought dozens of the great local ingredients into the restaurant kitchens. As a result, local chefs are busy creating the new Albertan cuisine with such downright great ingredients as Prairie Sun Grains, Shepherd's Dairy sheep's milk yogurt and Hamilton's Barley Flour. Then there's the Cookbook Store, Gail Norton's fabulous culinary bookstore that not only sells books but invites top instructors from all over Canada and the United States to give lessons. The 11th Avenue location is also home to the Calgary Wine Academy, a division of J. Webb Wine Merchants. The entire cuisine scene is covered by City Palate, an excellent tabloid of food and commentary and gossip. Even the ads are great reading.

79

Above: *Peppers, Blackfoot Farmers' Market, Calgary, Alberta*

80

Saskatoon Berry and Rhubarb Pie

Saskatoon berries, also known as serviceberries, have sparked a debate over which wild fruit is the ultimate — these sweet purple berries or blueberries. Rich and full of summer's best flavour, the crops of saskatoon berries are sporadic, causing Prairie folks to protect their patches with the ferocity of mushroom hunters in morel season. This pie is wonderful warm with a big scoop of vanilla or Crème Fraîche Ice Cream (p. 46).

1	pastry for single crust (p. 81)

Topping

2/3 cup (150 mL)	packed brown sugar
1/2 cup (125 mL)	all-purpose flour
1/2 cup (125 mL)	old-fashioned rolled oats
1/3 cup (75 mL)	unsalted butter

Filling

4 cups (1 L)	saskatoon berries
2 cups (500 mL)	chopped rhubarb
3/4 cup (175 mL)	sugar
3 tbsp. (45 mL)	quick-cooking tapioca
1 tbsp. (15 mL)	lemon juice

✦ *Line a 9-inch (23 cm) pie plate with pastry.*

✦ *Combine brown sugar, flour and oats. Cut in butter with pastry blender or two knives until crumbly. Set aside.*

✦ *In another bowl, combine saskatoon berries, rhubarb, sugar, tapioca and lemon juice, mixing well. Spoon into pastry shell. Sprinkle oat topping evenly over filling. Bake on lower rack of a preheated 425°F (220°C) oven 15 minutes. Reduce heat to 350°F (180°C) and bake 30 to 40 minutes or until topping is brown and filling bubbly and tender. Cool on wire rack.*
Makes 6 to 8 servings.

Canola Oil Pastry

This easy-to-make pastry is very tender and tasty, great in any pie recipe.

Single Crust

1 cup + 2 tbsp. (275 mL)	all-purpose flour
1/2 tsp. (2 mL)	salt
6 tbsp. (90 mL)	canola oil
2 tbsp. (25 mL)	cold water

Double Crust

2 1/4 cups (550 mL)	all-purpose flour
1 tsp. (5 mL)	salt
3/4 cup (175 mL)	canola oil
1/4 cup (50 mL)	cold water

✦ *Stir together flour and salt in a mixing bowl. In another bowl, combine oil and water. Add to flour all at once. Stir lightly with a fork until dough comes together. Gather pastry into a ball. Divide into 2 portions for double-crust pie. Flatten balls slightly. Place 1 ball of dough between 2 large squares of waxed paper. Place on moistened surface to keep paper from moving. Roll out dough between waxed paper to desired size for recipe. Peel off top paper. Flip dough over with remaining paper onto pie plate. Gently peel off top paper. Ease dough into pan. For a top crust, roll remaining ball from double-crust recipe the same way and flip over filling. Cut slits for steam to escape. Bake as directed in recipe.*

To Bake Blind (without filling)

✦ *Cut out a 12-inch (30 cm) circle of aluminum foil or parchment paper. Fit into pastry shell. Fill with pie weights or dried beans (lima, kidney, etc.). Bake on lower rack of a preheated 425°F (220°C) oven 10 minutes. Cool 5 minutes, then remove beans. Lower heat to 350°F (180°C) and bake 15 to 20 minutes longer or until golden.*

Canola Oil

Canola oil is the lowest in dietary saturated fat. There is no cholesterol. When stored in the refrigerator it remains free running. But aside from the nutrition, canola oil's mild flavour never masks the tastes of other foods. When you substitute canola oil for solid fat in baking, you not only reduce calories because you use less but reduce your intake of saturated fatty acids. As well, the texture of your baked goods will be softer and moister.

Canola oil conversion chart

Solid fat	Canola oil
1 cup (250 mL)	3/4 cup (175 mL)
3/4 cup (175 mL)	2/3 cup (150 mL)
2 cup (125 mL)	1/3 cup (75 mL)
1/4 cup (50 mL)	3 tbsp. (45 mL)

Above: *Canola field, Saskatchewan*

Blackberry Custard Tart with Alberta Springs Rye Whisky–Laced Cream

Alberta Springs distills great rye whisky from the real thing, locally grown rye. It's used to give a special western flavour to this deliciously sweet summer tart.

Crust

1 1/2 cups (375 mL)	all-purpose flour
2 tbsp. (25 mL)	sugar
1/2 tsp. (2 mL)	salt
2/3 cup (150 mL)	cold unsalted butter, cut in cubes
1	egg yolk
2 tbsp. (25 mL)	water

Filling

1/2 cup (125 mL)	apple butter
3 cups (750 mL)	fresh blackberries

Custard

2/3 cup (150 mL)	sugar
4 tsp. (20 mL)	all-purpose flour
3	eggs
3/4 cup (175 mL)	half & half cream (10%)
1 tsp. (5 mL)	vanilla

Cream

1 cup (250 mL)	whipping cream (35%)
2 tbsp. (25 mL)	icing sugar
2 tbsp. (25 mL)	Alberta Springs Rye Whisky

83

✦ Put flour, sugar and salt in the bowl of a food processor; pulse to combine. Add butter cubes; pulse until mixture resembles coarse crumbs. Lightly beat together egg yolk and water; add to flour mixture and pulse to combine. Mixture will not form a dough but will be crumbly. Pat into bottom and sides of a 12-inch (30 cm) tart pan with removable bottom. Bake in a preheated 350°F (180°C) oven 15 minutes. Cool.

✦ Spread crust with thin, even layer of apple butter. Place blackberries in single layer, covering entire bottom of tart. Place tart on a baking sheet.

✦ For custard, stir together sugar and flour in a bowl. Beat in eggs, cream and vanilla. Pour over blackberries. Bake in a preheated 350°F (180°C) oven until custard is set, about 40 minutes. Cool. Before serving, beat cream to soft peaks. Add icing sugar and whisky; beat to stiff peaks. Serve a large dollop with each portion of tart. **Makes 12 servings.**

The Best Butter Tarts

What would a Canadian cookbook be without a butter tart recipe? These, developed by super-baker Jill Snider of Robin Hood Flour, a company that incidentally uses 100 percent Canadian wheat, are slightly runny and totally addictive!

	Pastry (p. 81) for a double-crust pie will be enough, if rolled 1/8 inch (3 mm) thick, to yield 24 tart shells.
1 cup (250 mL)	raisins
24	3-inch (8 cm) unbaked tart shells
2	eggs
1 cup (250 mL)	packed brown sugar
1 cup (250 mL)	corn syrup
1/2 cup (125 mL)	unsalted butter, softened
1 1/2 tsp. (7 mL)	vanilla
1/4 tsp. (1 mL)	salt

✦ Line muffin tins with tart shells; divide raisins evenly among shells. In a bowl, lightly beat together eggs, brown sugar, corn syrup, butter, vanilla and salt. Pour over raisins, filling shells about 3/4 full. Bake in a preheated 425°F (220°C) oven just until set, about 15 minutes. Cool on wire rack, then carefully remove from pan. **Makes 24 tarts.**

New Grains

The Grain Research Laboratory was founded in Winnipeg in 1913 with a mandate to conduct quality research. Since that time, the GRL has been instrumental in many agricultural innovations, including the development of Harrington, a malting barley that is considered the best in the world. New varieties of Canada Prairie Spring wheat are being bred specifically for the Asian noodle market. These grains must be white-hulled so that no flecks show in the perfect pasta. In the same facility are several "pilot plant" operations. Here, small test batches of bread are baked using various flours, and barley is malted. Although no beer is brewed on-site, the word is that one of the research scientists does hold the best Christmas party going.

85

Chocolate

Barr's Sweet Revenge Confection Company is a business specializing in candies made from Prairie products. Wheat is toasted and either made into brittle or coated with chocolate for "bark." Saskatoon and sea buckthorn berries, chokecherries and high-bush cranberries are all used to flavour the centres of chocolates.

Bernard Callebaut, a member of the family of famous chocolatiers, settled in Calgary and from there has opened a series of excellent boutique-style shops in western Canada. Callebaut chocolate is found in many of the nation's best pastry kitchens.

Utterly Decadent Chocolate Brownies

The secret of this recipe is to bake the brownies until they are barely set. They are so rich you'll never need to ice them. Nuts may be added, but they're hardly necessary. And try, if possible, to use the Prairies own Callebaut chocolate.

1/2 cup (125 mL)	unsalted butter
4 oz. (125 g)	bittersweet chocolate
1 3/4 cups (425 mL)	sugar
3	eggs
1 tbsp. (15 mL)	vanilla
1/4 tsp. (1 mL)	salt
1 cup (250 mL)	all-purpose flour
1 cup (250 mL)	semi-sweet chocolate chips

✦ *In a heavy saucepan over low heat, melt butter and chocolate, stirring constantly. Remove from heat; whisk in sugar till mixture turns creamy. Beat in eggs, one at a time. Whisk in vanilla, salt and flour to create a smooth batter. Stir in chocolate chips and spread evenly in a well-greased 8-inch (20 cm) square glass pan. Bake in a preheated 350°F (180°C) oven for 30 to 35 minutes or until barely set in the middle. Allow to cool in the pan before cutting.* **Makes 16 to 20 brownies.**

Matrimonial Cake

No one that I have talked to knows where and when wonderful old date squares changed their name, but in western Canada the title Matrimonial Cake applies everywhere from Victorian fast-food restaurants to truck stops in the middle of Saskatchewan. Here is a particularly delicious whole-wheat version.

2 1/2 cups (625 mL)	chopped dates
1 cup (250 mL)	water
1 1/2 cups (375 mL)	whole-wheat flour
1 tsp. (5 mL)	baking powder
1/2 tsp. (2 mL)	baking soda
1 cup (250 mL)	salted butter, softened
1 1/2 cups (375 mL)	quick rolled oats
1 cup (250 mL)	brown sugar

✦ In a small, heavy saucepan, combine dates and water. Cook, covered, over medium heat, stirring occasionally, until soft and smooth. Set aside to cool while making crust.

✦ In a large mixing bowl, blend flour, baking powder and baking soda. With a fork, blend in the butter. Add oats and sugar, stirring to combine thoroughly. Press half crust mixture into a lightly greased 8-inch (20 cm) square cake pan. Spread evenly with date filling. Top with remaining crust, pressing lightly to smooth. Bake in a preheated 350°F (180°C) oven 25 to 30 minutes. Allow to cool before cutting into squares. **Makes 20 to 24 small squares.**

87

On Grain

In 1884, Capt. William Clark was appointed Canada's first grain inspector in Winnipeg. He soon published his standards for the various grades of grain then being cultivated and laid the foundation of our present grading system. From the arrival of the railway to western Canada in the 1880s until the end of the homesteading era in the 1930s, agriculture flourished and the area farmed doubled and then doubled again. The export of wheat grew from a trickle of 1.5 million bushels in 1884 to more than 344 million bushels in 1928/29.

Above: *Grain sculpture at Rosthern, Saskatchewan*

Spicy Dill Pickles

The secret of dill pickles is lots of dill and cucumbers that are as fresh as possible. Pickling spice should be purchased fresh every year.

15	heads fresh dill
4 tsp. (20 mL)	pickling spice
1 gallon (4 L)	small cucumbers
5	small hot peppers
	or 1/2 tsp. (2 mL)
	crushed dried chilis
10 cups (2.5 L)	water
6 cups (1.5 L)	cider vinegar
1 cup (250 mL)	pickling salt

✦ Into each of five 1-quart (1 L) sterilized jars, stuff 2 heads of dill. Divide the pickling spice among the jars and fill with well-scrubbed whole cucumbers. Top with the remaining dill and hot peppers. Bring water, vinegar and salt to a boil, stirring to dissolve salt. Pour boiling brine over cucumbers and seal jars immediately. Store in a cool, dark place for at least 1 month. *Makes 5 quarts (5 L).*

Flavoured Canola Oil

Home economists Margaret Howard and Ellie Topp spent months perfecting the safest, most delicious way of making flavoured oils for the Saskatchewan Canola Development Commission. This is what they came up with.

1 cup (250 mL)	canola oil
3 tbsp. (45 mL)	chopped herbs

✦ Place oil and herbs in a glass measuring cup. Set on a pie plate and bake in a preheated 300°F (150°C) oven 1 hour or until the herbs begin to turn brown. Cool on a rack for 30 minutes. Strain through a coffee filter or several layers of cheesecloth. Store in an airtight glass container and refrigerate up to 1 month. *Makes 1 cup (250 mL).*

Flavour variations for 1 cup (250 mL) canola oil:

✦1 tbsp. (15 mL) fresh rosemary, 1 small hot chili pepper, sliced, and 2 large garlic cloves, halved lengthwise

✦ 2 strips lemon rind and 4 sprigs fresh sage or thyme

Left: *Near Saskatoon, Saskatchewan*
Above: *Organic chives*

Husband Farm

A good example of the Prairie entrepreneurial spirit is found at the Husband farm in southern Saskatchewan, 13 kilometres (8 miles) west of Wawota. Of their 650 hectares (1600 acres), Carol and John Husband have set aside 25 hectares (60 acres) for fifty specialty herbs, ranging from small areas of anise hyssop and black cumin to field-sized plots of coriander and caraway. They grow and dry amaranth, chickpeas, red and French lentils, black chickpeas and peas. They also market their own specialty soup mixes, manufacture basil and cilantro pestos, teach classes on the use of culinary herbs, hold workshops on herbal teas and operate a summertime "market barn," where they sell fresh vegetables and a neighbour's elk and lamb. They grow, and thus preserve, some of the original grains that the first settlers brought with them to the New World. A nearby miller grinds them into flour that Carol uses to maintain her Swedish tradition of home baking.

89

Chapter 3
Ontario

Ontario spreads a delicious buffet — of historic dishes brought by the earliest settlers to the culinary traditions that honour the province's most recent immigrants to the new foods developed by a dynamic research and manufacturing community. It's a region of great food festivals and vital farmers' markets. Its many culinary regions produce fabulous food, from the east with its cheeses and apples to the west with tomatoes and peaches and the north with its huge wild harvest.

The fertile soil of the province has been farmed for centuries. In the area which is now known as southwestern Ontario, the Iroquois planted corn about AD 500. Then tobacco was added, and by AD 1200 beans, sunflowers and squash also flourished. Among the first European settlers were the Scots, who farmed along the river valleys from the Grand to the Ottawa and built sturdy towns like Guelph and Fergus. The Scots brought with them the food traditions and substantial dishes of their homeland, and it is still possible to find cooks who regularly make girdle scones (biscuits that are cooked on a special rimless cast-iron skillet), oat breads and Scottish meat pies.

The Irish cleared forests all over the province, planting orchards and providing a backbone of solid agricultural practice. My own Irish ancestors handed down their respect for the harvest and their love springing directly from necessity of seasonal food. As did most settlers, they ate and preserved the harvest from the time the earliest rhubarb was cut for pies and jam until the last parsnip was dug and added to stew or stored in the root cellar.

In the early 1800s the first wave of Mennonites immigrated to Upper Canada and settled near the Niagara River and in Berlin (now Kitchener) and Markham, just north of Toronto. These German Mennonites introduced all sorts of delicacies, many of which you can still find at farmers' markets in Waterloo County: pungent kochkase, or cooked cheese; salty dry summer sausage; and sweet shoofly pie, a sticky, molasses-laden pastry. With the help of those Mennonites already successfully settled in Ontario, Russian Mennonites arrived in the later 1800s. They brought another array of traditional dishes, from fruit platz, which I've heard called "pie by the yard," and pluma moos, simply stewed dried fruits. At the New Hamburg Relief Sale, both culinary cultures are combined, and those bidding on the handmade quilts donated by virtually every congregation in Ontario can savour pancakes drenched with this season's maple syrup as well as the best apple fritters and long john doughnuts I've ever eaten.

Left: *Harvesting grapes for ice wine, Niagara*
Above: *Cookstown greens*

Finnish lumbermen immigrated to Thunder Bay (then Fort William and Port Arthur) in the early 1900s. Like all settlers they clung to old food traditions, like piirakka, a buttery, baked sourdough filled with savoury pudding and topped with egg salad, that can still be found in restaurants such as the venerable Hoito or the Scand, within blocks of one another in downtown Thunder Bay.

Toronto has seen some dramatic changes. The old town of York, as Toronto was once known, was the centre of agricultural trade. In its early days it really was called "hogtown" because of the porkers that were allowed to run at large until a proclamation in 1800 banned them from the streets.

Since World War II, Toronto has grown in culinary variety. There are more Italians in the city than in any city outside Italy. The Italians who came to Toronto and into most other urban areas in Ontario helped to change our tastes from a preference for overdone roast beef to a taste for ripe tomatoes and spicy sausage. Italians often owned produce stores, and across the city, backyards bloomed with basil and grapes. In late summer, tons of tomatoes, generally the variety called Roma, are still processed in the old-fashioned way. Bushels of the fleshy fruit are harvested and pressed into a purée. The purée is then funnelled into glass jars of every description, including old, well-washed pop bottles. When the jars are sealed or the last crown caps are attached to the pop bottles, they are carefully layered in an old oil drum, water is added with a garden hose, a fire is built underneath, and the tomato sauce is cooked for hours.

In recent years Toronto has become one of the most ethnically diverse cities on earth, with colourful markets and restaurants in which you can taste the world. Among its neighbourhoods, it boasts many Chinatowns, which more accurately should be called Asiatowns, and a vibrant Caribbean community.

The foundation of Ontario's food culture is its diverse populations and their culinary heritage. In the past two decades, however, the range of crops flourishing in the province has changed. A new generation of rural entrepreneurs has expanded the burgeoning wine industry, and innovative research in plant breeding, much of it under the auspices of the University of Guelph, has selected, trialed and introduced new strains from Gus Tehrani's great black cherries and Tony Hunt's wheat to Al Sullivan's giant raspberries and Adam Dale's fabulous strawberries, many of which have taken decades to perfect.

Above: *A Taste of the Danforth festival, Toronto*
Right: *St Lawrence market, Toronto*

The University of Guelph, and more specifically, the Ontario Agricultural College, is at the heart of agricultural research for the province. The provincial ministry of agriculture, based in Guelph, has turned over all its research programs and facilities to OAC. From ice cream and cheese-making to plant breeding and farm management, the university can claim dozens of success stories. In 1910, OAC 21 barley became the foundation for the modern malting industry in Canada, and in 1999 the college was the first in Canada to brew its own beers from the progeny of that famous grain.

Ontario's growing areas are exceedingly rich. In the most gentle of these climatic regions, the area that stretches languorously from the Niagara along the north shore of Lake Erie to Windsor, there are white and ruby-dappled peaches; apricots and cherries; plums of all description; melons; grapes, both table and wine; and even an experimental plot or two of kiwifruit. The figs that grow in the microclimate of the Niagara region proper are soft and luscious. Southwestern Ontario tomatoes are among the best in Canada, and major processors like Aylmer and Primo have their factories and research facilities there. Hundreds of hectares that used to grow tobacco have been turned over, with the help of the Simcoe Research Station team of crop scientists, to more healthful crops, like peanuts and ginseng. Sweet potatoes — a variety known as *Beauregard* — are now commercially available, and tree nuts, such as sweet chestnuts and heart-nuts, may soon be grown in commercial quantities. Lake Erie yields golden whitefish caviar, and the lake is famous for its tiny yellow perch, best savoured at the Erie Beach Hotel in Port Stanley, south of Simcoe.

This is wine country, with three defined wine-growing regions — Niagara, Lake Erie North Shore and Pelee Island — while near Guelph, Kitchener-Waterloo and Cambridge there are more breweries than anywhere else in Canada. Beer is big!

In the large triangular area that begins roughly north of Highway 401 and continues northward along the eastern shore of Lake Huron, corn and soybeans are the two most prevalent crops. There are hundreds of hectares of white and coloured beans, all heralded at the Zurich Bean Festival every year in late August. Swinging north toward the counties of Grey and Bruce, the Bluewater Highway (#21) leads to beef cattle territory. In lakeside towns like Southampton, Port Elgin and Kincardine and up as far as Tobermory at the very tip of the Bruce Peninsula, there are small but determined freshwater fishing fleets. In the summer season you can buy lake trout, splake, pickerel and freshwater herring, sometimes right off the boats. Craigie's, a tiny dockside café in Tobermory, serves fabulous dinners of whitefish and chips. Great smoked fish is sold in many small peninsula businesses.

Right: *Frost on kale, Langdon Hall, near Cambridge*

Moving eastward on our map but still in the central region, the rocky terrain is criss-crossed by dozens of spring-fed streams, many of which are now used to supply water for trout and arctic char aquaculture. A wide crescent around Georgian Bay at the base of the Niagara Escarpment is famous for its apple orchards and cider mills. Toward Haliburton and Huntsville are myriad small lakes. This is the southern end of the Canadian Shield and it's wild blueberry country. Cranberries flourish, and once a year the village of Bala celebrates this tart, red fruit. There are dozens of hardwood maple forests.

Eastern Ontario may be characterized by apples and cheese but it's also known for maple syrup and some of the best soy products, including an excellent tempeh, a type of fermented beans formed into ready-to-use blocks. It was in Kingston that Canada's first cookbook was printed in 1831. *The Cook Not Mad; Or Rational Cookery: Being a Collection of Original and Selected Receipts* was fully plagiarized from a volume printed in the United States. The Central Experimental Farm in Ottawa, now more a museum than a working research facility, can claim many milestones in Canadian agriculture. One of the most significant was the development of Marquis wheat, a strain of hard red spring wheat that was more cold tolerant and helped to open western Canada to agriculture.

Grand and glorious, northern Ontario covers most of the geographic area of the province. Here, game graces many dinner tables. The wild harvest is huge, from serviceberries (a.k.a. saskatoons) and chokecherries to wild rice and hazelnuts. There's some of the best angling in the country, and fishers come from all over for the superb pickerel. Small farm markets have sprung up across the north in which you can buy local honeys and great breads along with all the other cold-hardy or short-season produce.

Driving across the north you can find hidden culinary treasures like the sausages made in Timmins by the Dabrowski family and the curious pink-frosted confections called Persians in Thunder Bay. There's a Garlic Festival in Sudbury and a Haweaters Festival on Manitoulin Island in praise of the hawthorne trees that fill the hedgerows. On that island is also one of the most authentic pow wows, at Wikwemikong, with great wild game burgers. One of Canada's pre-eminent potato growers, Murray Becker, has his farm near Nipissing. On property nestled between two river valleys, he harvests seed potatoes that reflect both the history of the tubers — with a selection of old varieties including the richly hued blues — and the future of the crop — with many of the newest varieties, including Ruby Gold and Temagami.

If there's one word that characterizes Ontario in culinary terms, it's "abundance." Discover the province's great tastes...region by region. Savour them. Take a detour off the beaten pathways and drive the back roads. Pause a while to talk to growers, and buy from them. Pick up a bushel of this or that and preserve the harvest, all the while sharing it along with the stories you're sure to have collected.

95

Above: *Scott Thompson harvesting cranberries at Johnston's cranberry marsh near Bala*

Ice Wine

No harvest in the world could be colder than that of ice wine. Winemakers wait until the winter temperatures dip to well below freezing. Then, in the middle of the night, dressed in thermal layers and carrying clippers, they head to the vineyards where grapes hang in hard, frozen clusters. All night long, pickers clip Vidal and Riesling grapes that have been dried and sweetened by months on the vine. Pressing occurs immediately and the precious golden drops are collected and vinified.

Canada is the world's largest producer of this magical beverage, which tastes of apricots and honey and late-autumn sunshine. It is appropriate that it was an ice wine, Inniskillin's 1989 Vidal, that brought Canada its first truly prestigious medal in world wine competition, the Grand Prix d'Honneur at Vinexpo in Bordeaux.

Pam's North Gower Cheese and Asparagus Strudels

Deep in the country, in a beautifully restored log home, Pam Collacott operates the Trillium Cooking School. The nearby village of North Gower, southwest of Ottawa, has a long history of cheese-making. The North Gower Cheese Manufacturing Company, founded circa 1867, was the first in Carleton County and operated as a farmers' co-operative. In 1952 it closed and was revived again in the mid-nineties. Today, North Gower is home to a superb little cheese factory where cheese-maker Ulrich Bollinger milks Brown Swiss cows and creates wonderful cheddar, gouda and yogurt. The stars of the show are the white, mild cheese curds, lightly salted and sometimes seasoned with green onion.

2 cups (500 mL)	asparagus
1/2 cup (125 mL)	chopped leeks, white part only
1 tbsp. (15 mL)	unsalted butter
2 – 3 tsp.	minced fresh tarragon
(10 – 15 mL)	(or 3/4 tsp./4 mL dried tarragon)
	Salt and freshly ground pepper to taste
6	sheets phyllo pastry
1/3 cup (75 mL)	unsalted butter, melted
6 oz. (175 g)	mild North Gower cheddar,
	cut in 6 portions

✦ *In a medium skillet, sauté asparagus and leeks in butter until tender-crisp, 2 to 3 minutes. Season with tarragon, salt and pepper. Set aside.*

✦ *Brush 1 sheet of phyllo with melted butter. Fold in half cross-wise and brush with a little more butter. Place 1/6 of asparagus mixture on one end of phyllo. Top with one portion of the cheese. Fold in end and sides of phyllo and roll up like a jelly roll. Place on a lightly oiled or parchment-lined baking sheet. Repeat with remaining ingredients. Bake in a preheated 400°F (200°C) oven 15 minutes or until pastry is browned and crisp. Serve warm.*
Makes 6 servings.

Warm Wild Mushroom Terrine

Hidden away in cottage country is one of the finest inns in North America. The Inn and Tennis Club is a magnificent resort in Ontario's "near north" on Lake Manitouwabing. Ben and Sheila Wise have worked for decades creating an ambience of utter elegance with a dining room to match. In some ways the inn still reflects its humble beginnings as a summer camp, but today, as a member of the prestigious international association of Relais & Chateaux, the five-star luxury retreat provides such "camping" needs as world-class golf and tennis instruction, culinary retreats and full spa facilities.

On one special weekend each year, inn guests are guided into northern forests to hunt for mushrooms. This is a recipe that was developed by the chef to use the harvest.

1 lb. (500 g)	chanterelle mushrooms
1/2 lb. (250 g)	morel mushrooms
1/2 lb. (250 g)	oyster mushrooms
3 tbsp. (45 mL)	unsalted butter
	Salt and freshly ground pepper to taste
	Water or chicken stock
	(p. 66) as needed
1/4 cup (50 mL)	white wine
3 tbsp. (45 mL)	whipping cream (35%)
2 oz. (50 g)	ground veal
1	egg
	Chopped chives

◆ Clean mushrooms with a dry cloth, discard stems and chop coarsely. Melt 2 tbsp. (25 mL) of the butter in a large skillet over medium heat. Add mushrooms and cook in batches, adding more butter as needed, stirring often, 8 to 10 minutes or until tender. Drain and reserve pan juices (if any). Place mushrooms in a bowl and season generously with salt and pepper. Cool to room temperature.

◆ Add enough water or chicken stock to reserved pan juices to measure 1/2 cup (125 mL). Add to skillet with wine and 2 tbsp. (25 mL) of the cream. Return to heat, stirring to scrape up any brown bits from the bottom of the skillet. Bring to a boil, reduce heat and cook 4 to 5 minutes or until reduced by half; stir in remaining butter and set aside.

◆ Place veal, egg, remaining 1 tbsp. (15 mL) cream and a pinch of salt and pepper in a blender and purée until smooth. Add veal mixture to mushrooms, stirring to combine. Butter an 8" x 4" (1.5 L) loaf pan and line the bottom with parchment. Spoon mushroom mixture into pan, packing well, and set pan in a small roasting pan. Fill roasting pan with water to halfway up the sides of the loaf pan. Bake in a preheated 350°F (180°C) oven 30 to 35 minutes or until set and heated through. Cover the terrine with foil and let rest 30 minutes.

◆ Cut the terrine into 1-inch (2.5 cm) slices and arrange on 4 to 6 plates. Rewarm the sauce and drizzle over each serving. Garnish with chopped chives. **Makes 4 to 6 servings.**

97

Château des Charmes

The twentieth anniversary of Château des Charmes Estate Winery allowed the Bosc family a moment of reflection. "Twenty years ago, we were ahead of our time — that really means there wasn't a market for what we were making," says Paul André Bosc, son of founder Paul Michel Bosc. However, it is clear that the next two decades will be as radical as the past two, also thanks to the Bosc family and recent research. In March 1993, the Niagara wine industry was devastated by a late-winter freeze. Half the crop was lost, costing tens of millions of dollars. In the region three of every ten winters can be so severe as to do significant damage. Now, the Bosc family, in partnership with the National Research Council and Dr. John Paroshy of the University of Guelph, have identified a gene that protects grapes from stress and implanted that gene into Chardonnay and Cabernet Franc vines. It is expected that these vines will be able to withstand 5°C cooler growing conditions than their parents. The world's first such vines were planted in 1997 at Château des Charmes St. David's Bench vineyard. "We're the only growers in Canada who are hoping for a severe winter. We need to see whether these vines will make it," Paul André says. Although the vines are not yet bearing fruit, the potential for Niagara is astounding. It may now be feasible to more than double the current 8,000 hectares (20,000 acres) of vineyard. Next market? The world!

Left: *Donald Ziraldo, one of Niagara's wine pioneers and co-founder of Inniskillin Wines*

Shiitake

The Norfolk/Haldimand region has a profusion of shiitake mushroom growers. The quiet forests and barns are filled with spore-inoculated oak logs, each growing the woodsy, delicious mushrooms. Most of the production is exported either fresh or dried. Shiitake mushroom powder is as delicious a seasoning as I've ever encountered. One of my chef friends rolled a slice of foie gras (my favourite food) in it before popping it into a searing-hot pan. Even writing about it, my mouth waters. The photo above was taken at Andy's Capps mushrooms, near Walshingham.

Shallot and Shiitake Mushroom Tart

This tart recipe is from one of Ontario's finest chefs, Mark Bussieres. In the 1980s while so many other restaurants were glorifying foods from the rest of the world, Mark was identifying and cooking the regional foods of Huron County in the kitchens of the Benmiller Inn, near Goderich. He then took his crusade to Toronto and opened Metropolis, the first restaurant in Ontario to truly celebrate the province's bounty. He has now returned to his roots in Gananoque, near Kingston, where at The Cook Not Mad restaurant he is, once again, searching out the most interesting ingredients in the area and encouraging his diners to experience many delicious "new" tastes.

Mark notes that this tart makes "a great appetizer and works well with a squirt of curried mayonnaise and/or the earthiness of a fresh beet coulis."

1/4 cup (50 mL)	canola oil
1 lb. (500 g)	shallots, sliced
1 tbsp. (15 mL)	minced garlic
1/4 tsp. (1 mL)	crushed dried rosemary
4 – 6 oz. (125 – 175 g)	shiitake mushrooms, sliced
1/2 tsp. (2 mL)	salt
1/4 tsp. (1 mL)	freshly ground black pepper
1	411 g package frozen puff pastry, thawed
4 oz. (125 g)	soft goat's milk cheese

✦ In a heavy saucepan, heat 3 tbsp. (45 mL) of the oil over very low heat. Gently cook shallots and garlic, covered, stirring frequently, until tender and beginning to turn golden brown, 20 to 30 minutes. Stir in rosemary and allow to cool.

✦ Heat remaining oil in a non-stick skillet over medium-low heat; sauté shiitake mushrooms until tender, 5 to 6 minutes. Season with salt and pepper; set aside to cool slightly.

✦ Roll 2 puff pastry pieces into 10" x 4 1/2" (25 x 11 cm) long rectangles. Cut each piece into 3. Place on baking sheet. Top with sautéed shallots and mushrooms. Slice goat's milk cheese into 6 equal portions and place on top of tarts. Bake in a pre-heated 425°F (220°C) oven 5 to 7 minutes or until browned and golden. Serve warm. **Makes 6 servings.**

To make a curried mayonnaise, replace oven-dried tomatoes with 1 tsp. (5 mL) curry powder in recipe on p. 119 or stir the same amount of spice mixture into 1 cup (250 mL) high-quality mayonnaise.

To make beet coulis. A small amount may be made by cooking 1 medium beet, peeled and diced, in 1/2 cup (125 mL) stock or lightly salted water until tender. Purée the mixture, adding additional liquid if necessary, until it is saucelike.

99

Woolwich Dairy Ravioli with Smoked Tomato and Basil Sauce

This sauce is light yet filled with overtones of wood smoke and fresh basil. It is perfect with the delicate ravioli stuffed with prize-winning chèvre from Woolwich Dairy.

To prepare wood chips, measure the amount required and cover with boiling water. Let stand 8 to 10 hours or overnight. Drain before using.

Prepared wonton wrappers streamline the entire recipe. Wrap leftover wrappers and either freeze or refrigerate them.

Smoked Tomato and Basil Sauce

2 cups (500 mL)	smoking wood chips, soaked in boiling water
12 – 15	plum tomatoes, halved
1	head garlic
3 tbsp. (45 mL)	canola oil
2	shallots, minced
1/4 tsp. (1 mL)	salt
1/4 tsp. (1 mL)	cayenne
1 cup (250 mL)	finely sliced fresh basil

Raviol Filling

1	200 g package plain or flavoured chèvre, softened
1 tbsp. (15 mL)	minced chives and chive blossoms
1 tbsp. (15 mL)	minced Italian parsley
2	cloves garlic, minced
1	shallot, finely chopped
1/2	I-lb. (454 g) package wonton wrappers Additional fresh herbs, edible flowers and freshly grated hard goat's milk cheese

+ Place wood chips in a shallow foil pan. Heat barbecue to high. Set pan on coals until chips begin to smoke, about 5 minutes. Place halved tomatoes directly on warming rack above the chips; reduce heat to low, close lid and smoke 15 minutes. Let tomatoes cool. Peel and seed tomatoes, reserving juices. Coarsely chop tomatoes; set aside.

+ Separate garlic cloves and peel. In a heavy saucepan combine oil and garlic. Cover and cook over low heat, stirring frequently, 20 to 30 minutes or until browned and soft. Add shallots; cook till transparent, stirring and mashing the garlic during the cooking. Add reserved tomatoes and their juices, salt, cayenne and basil. Stir until basil is barely wilted. Remove from heat.

+ In a small bowl, thoroughly combine chèvre, chives and chive blossoms, parsley, garlic and shallot. Set aside.

+ Brush wonton wrappers lightly with cold water. Top each with 1 tsp. (5 mL) filling and fold over, pinching edges tightly, to make small triangles. If not using immediately, cover with a tea towel. Drop ravioli into a large pot of boiling salted water. Simmer until they pop to the surface and are puffy and soft, 3 to 4 minutes. Drain and transfer to a large serving bowl. Toss with Smoked Tomato and Basil Sauce; top with fresh herbs, edible flowers and goat's milk cheese.

Makes 36 to 40 ravioli or 6 to 8 servings.

101

Woolwich Dairy

Woolwich Dairy is one of Canada's busiest and oldest goat cheese producers. For years the dairy's founders, Pat and Ramelle Harkins, took their products from their farm north of Guelph to Toronto's St. Lawrence Market, where chefs and the public could taste-test and buy. It was at the St. Lawrence that Woolwich began to build its reputation. When Olga and Tony Dutra purchased Woolwich, they brought with them an established cheese-making tradition. Business boomed and they quickly became Canada's largest producer of goat cheese. In 1997 they moved the plant into new facilities in Orangeville. The milk, which comes from all over the province, is made into award-winning chèvre, gaisli (a firmer mozzarella-style product) and cheddar. And — although Olga and Tony rarely attend — Woolwich Dairy is still at the St. Lawrence Market.

The Royal Agricultural Winter Fair is the world's largest indoor agricultural exhibition, bringing rural Canada to the glass-walled, recently renovated coliseum at Toronto's CNE grounds. It's a fabulous experience! Visitors come from around the globe to check out Canada's agricultural expertise. Down Dairy Lane you'll see some of our finest cheeses. The Gay Lea Co-operative donates hundreds of kilograms of salted butter for students from the Ontario College of Art to carve. It's cold work, standing in a see-through, well-chilled display refrigerator from 8:30 A.M. till evening.

People go to the Royal for the horses and Holstein cattle but also for the food. More than 200 entries arrive the week before the show. Cases of chili sauce and dills, mustard pickles and jewel-like jellies are tasted and savoured all day long by twelve judges selected from the best of Toronto's home economists and food writers. Cooking demonstrations occur daily, featuring almost without exception the best of Ontario and Canadian ingredients.

Above: *A pile of piglets at Royal Agricultural Winter Fair*

Ontario Bean Soup with Basil

Southwestern Ontario is known for its great beans, from black turtle and adzuki to cranberry and Dutch brown. They are such an important crop that the Hensall District Cooperative built a $1.5-million bean-drying facility in 1995.

Although this recipe calls for romano and kidney beans, you can add almost any other kind of cooked bean.

1/4 cup (50 mL)	unsalted butter or canola oil
1	large onion, chopped
1	clove garlic, minced
4	medium potatoes, peeled and diced
4	carrots, diced
2	stalks celery, chopped
6 cups (1.5 L)	vegetable (p. 103) or chicken stock (p. 66)
2 cups (500 mL)	diced peeled plum tomatoes
1 tsp. (5 mL)	salt
1/2 tsp. (2 mL)	freshly ground black pepper
1	large sprig fresh basil (or 1 tsp./5 mL dried basil)
1 cup (250 mL)	sliced green beans
1 cup (250 mL)	peas
1	19 oz. (540 mL) can romano beans, rinsed
1	19 oz. (540 mL) can white or red kidney beans, rinsed
1 cup (250 mL)	pasta shells
2 tbsp. (25 mL)	chopped fresh parsley
	Freshly grated Ontario Parmesan or Asiago cheese

✦ Melt butter in a large saucepan or Dutch oven over medium heat. Add onion and cook, stirring occasionally, 4 minutes or until softened. Stir in garlic, potatoes, carrots and celery. Toss to coat with butter and cook 3 to 4 minutes. Add stock, tomatoes, salt, pepper and basil. Bring to a boil, reduce heat and simmer 10 minutes or until vegetables are almost tender. Add green beans, peas, romano beans, kidney beans and pasta; simmer 10 minutes more or until pasta is tender. Remove basil sprig. Stir in parsley. Serve in wide soup bowls and pass cheese to sprinkle on each serving. **Makes 8 to 10 servings.**

Nettie's Vegetable Stock

Nettie Cronish is as passionate about vegetarian cooking as she is good-natured — although she may never forgive me for introducing her children to a Wellington County pig roast. (They adored the crisp cracklings.) For her, vegetarian cookery is a matter of commitment and of taste. A truly good vegetarian stock is a must. Most are insipid, but this one, from her own files, is one of the best I've tasted.

2 tbsp. (25 mL)	canola oil
2	cloves garlic, minced
2	onions, sliced
2	leeks, white part only, sliced
4	carrots, chopped
4	stalks celery, sliced
1	potato, peeled and diced
6	tomatoes, quartered or
	1 28-oz. (796 mL) can crushed
	tomatoes
1/2 lb. (250 g)	mushrooms, sliced
2/3 cup (150 mL)	dried lentils
6	sprigs Italian parsley
4	sprigs fresh basil
4	bay leaves
2 tsp. (10 mL)	salt
1/2 tsp. (2 mL)	black peppercorns
10 cups (2.5 L)	water

✦ Heat oil in a 3-quart (3 L) saucepan over medium heat. Add garlic, onions and leeks; cook, stirring, 5 minutes or until onions begin to soften. Stir in carrots, celery and potato; cook, stirring, 10 minutes, adding a few spoonfuls of water from time to time to prevent sticking.

✦ Add tomatoes, mushrooms, lentils, parsley, basil, bay leaves, salt, pepper and water. Bring to a boil, reduce heat to medium-low, cover and simmer 30 minutes. Strain through a fine sieve and discard solids. Cool before refrigerating. *Makes 10 cups (2.5 L).*

103

Above: *Tomato planting*

Simcoe Region

The sandy soil of the Simcoe region, specifically Norfolk and Haldimand counties, is one of the most underappreciated culinary regions in Canada. As Dr. Arthur Loughten, the past director of the Simcoe Research Station, says, "We can grow anything." This is the home of Music garlic, with its purplish tinge and large, potent cloves. More hectares of asparagus are planted here than in any other region of Canada. Here you'll find the hottest horseradish and Witloof endive, the fine bleached product so often associated with Belgium. Shiitake growers abound. It was here that Ontario's first legal hemp was planted. Near Vittoria, the Racz family operates Kernal Peanuts, and roast and sell them at their farm. The Norfolk Fruit Growers, a co-operative cold-storage and marketing association with a great little retail operation called the Apple Place, is based in Simcoe. Fields of Asian vegetables (bok choy, gai lohn, mustard greens and Chinese cabbage) flourish.

Elora Road Butternut Squash and Buttermilk Soup

Every year John and Katy Piskoric harvest a wagonload of squashes, which they sell at their small stand near Highway 6 on the Elora Road north of Guelph. Their crops include ropes of strong-flavoured garlic, the sweetest corn, huge onions with the leaves often still attached and wonderful peppers. Butternut squash is chosen for this recipe because it has a high yield of deep orange flesh, though buttercup or Hubbard may also be used. This soup is so intensely flavoured that I garnish it with plain yogurt, preferably Saugeen Country brand, manufactured near Durham, Ontario.

2 tbsp. (25 mL)	canola oil
1	large onion, coarsely chopped
2	cloves garlic, minced
1 tbsp. (15 mL)	minced fresh ginger
1 tsp. (5 mL)	cumin seeds*
1/2 tsp. (2 mL)	black mustard seeds*
1 tbsp. (15 mL)	garam masala*
4 cups (1 L)	diced butternut squash
4 cups (1 L)	chicken stock (p. 66)
	Salt and freshly ground pepper to taste
1 cup (250 mL)	fresh or frozen corn kernels (about 2 cobs)
1	sweet red pepper, minced
1 cup (250 mL)	buttermilk or half & half cream (10%)
	Plain yogurt and red pepper flakes for garnish

✦ Heat oil in a large soup pot over medium heat. Add onion, garlic and ginger; cook, stirring, 3 to 5 minutes or until ingredients begin to turn golden. Add cumin seeds and mustard seeds. Stir and cook 30 to 60 seconds or until the mustard seeds begin to pop. Add garam masala, stir and cook another 30 seconds. Stir in squash, tossing to coat with spice mixture. Add stock, cover and bring to a boil. Reduce heat and simmer until squash is tender. Season with salt and pepper. Let cool 10 minutes before puréeing with a hand blender or in a food processor. Return to medium heat. Add corn and red pepper. Cook, covered, 3 to 4 minutes. Stir in buttermilk and heat until steaming. Serve in heated soup bowls, topped with a spoonful or squirt of yogurt and red pepper flakes. **Makes 6 to 8 generous servings.**

* Available at East Indian or Asian grocery stores.

Hank Saito

In Japan only a few farmers still grow chujuro, an old variety of Asian pear. But in the Niagara region, Hank Saito tended his orchard of 100 chujoro trees until 1999. The trees' story is the stuff of legends. Before the Second World War, a friend of Hank's immigrated to Canada with a few of the trees. When he was interned in British Columbia, his entire orchard was destroyed except for a single tree. Upon his release, he took cuttings from that lone chujoro, grafted them onto Bartlett pear rootstock and gave them to friends who, Hank believes, may still have them in their B.C. backyards. Hank himself was given two tiny trees. One became the mother of the orchard he planted in the 1980s. Hank admits that, during Ontario winters, his pears are labour intensive. "They grow better in B.C," he says. With an infectious smile, he adds, "With global warming, maybe there's hope."

Grilled Lake Huron Splake with Fava Beans and Arugula

In the summer the Old Prune restaurant is particularly popular with patrons of the Stratford Festival in Stratford, Ontario. In the winter it is the home of the renowned Stratford Chefs School, holding classes and dining evenings that allow students, many of whom have come from other careers, to learn to cook for the love of it.

Chef and instructor Bryan Steele created this recipe with some of the region's best ingredients. Splake, a cross between speckled and lake trout, has a lightly pink flesh.

1/2 lb. (250 mg)	baby new potatoes
5 tbsp. (75 mL)	canola oil
2	cloves garlic
1	sprig fresh thyme
1/2 lb. (250 g)	baby Barletta onions (or pearl onions), peeled
2	slices smoked bacon, chopped
1/2 lb. (250 g)	shucked and peeled fava beans
4	splake fillets (about 4 oz./125 g each), boned and skin left on
	Salt and pepper to taste
1	bunch arugula

✦ Place potatoes on a sheet of foil. Drizzle with 1 tbsp. (15 mL) of the canola oil. Crush one of the garlic cloves and add to potatoes along with thyme. Fold the foil and crimp edges to seal. Bake in a preheated 375°F (190°C) oven 45 to 50 minutes or until tender. Set aside.

✦ In a large skillet, heat 2 tbsp. (25 mL) of the canola oil over medium-low heat. Add onions and bacon; cook, stirring occasionally, 10 minutes or until onions are just tender. Mince the remaining garlic clove and add to pan along with fava beans. Cook 3 minutes, taking care not to burn the garlic. Remove from heat.

✦ Brush splake fillets on both sides with remaining 2 tbsp. (25 mL) canola oil and season with salt and pepper. Heat barbecue to medium-high and brush rack with oil. Grill splake fillets 2 to 3 minutes on each side or until skin is crisp and is slightly pink in the centre. Remove from the grill and keep warm.

✦ Return fava beans to medium heat and add arugula, tossing until arugula is just wilted. Season with salt and pepper.

To Serve

2 tbsp. (25 mL)	lemon juice
	Canola oil

✦ Divide fava beans among 4 dinner plates and place a piece of grilled splake on top. Arrange potatoes around each plate and drizzle with lemon juice and canola oil. Serve immediately. Makes 4 servings.

107

Herbs

Richters Herbs in Goodwood, Ontario, northeast of Toronto, is a serious herb-growing company. Their catalogue lists hundreds, both culinary and medicinal. When I first began ordering from them, the variety was huge but most of their plants were familiar. Today, there are dozens of unusual scents and flavours from around the world that are new to me — from annatto, the natural food dye, and kombucha, the medicinal mushroom, to samphire, a shore-loving sea plant, and yerba buena, an ancient tea plant. Nor are their "gourmet vegetables" run of the mill. Richters sells everything from burdock to tomatillos.

Left: *Harvesting white asparagus, Jensen Farm, south of Simcoe*

Potato-Crusted Rainbow Trout with Braised Fruited Savoy Cabbage

Hillebrand Estates Chef Antonio de Luca writes, "This recipe symbolizes the nature of our cuisine. It was literally developed at the back door of our kitchen during the summer of 1997 when John Laidman, our forager, arrived with the day's produce. The day was a special one. It was the first time in the year when all the primary ingredients of the dish — the peaches, the corn, the cabbage — were at their peak of ripeness." He modestly continues, "All we had to do was combine them." The trout is covered with a layer of thinly sliced potatoes that, when cooked quickly then flash baked, form a golden brown rust. When cooking the trout make sure you use a high-quality oven-proof non-stick skillet. It must be cooked quickly just before serving. This recipe is for two servings, and I would not recommend increasing that.

4 tbsp. (50 mL)	unsalted butter
1	shallot, finely chopped
2 tbsp. (25 mL)	minced dried peaches or apricots
1 tsp. (5 mL)	minced fresh ginger
3 cups (750 mL)	coarsely shredded Savoy cabbage
1 cup (250 mL)	fish stock (p. 189) or water
1/3 cup (75 mL)	Hillebrand Estates Harvest Chardonnay
2	peaches, peeled and cut in 6 wedges each
2/3 cup (150 mL)	fresh corn kernels (about 3 cobs)
	Salt and freshly ground pepper to taste
2	rainbow trout fillets (about 7 oz./200 g each), skin on and scaled
1	small baking potato
2 tbsp. (25 mL)	canola oil

✦ Melt 2 tbsp. (25 mL) of the butter in a large skillet over medium heat. Add shallot, dried peaches and ginger; cook, stirring, 1 to 2 minutes or until fragrant. Stir in cabbage, stock and wine. Bring to a boil, reduce heat to medium and cook, covered, 20 minutes or until most of the liquid is absorbed. Add peaches, corn, salt and pepper; continue cooking until peaches are warmed through. Remove skillet from heat and cover to keep warm.

✦ Sprinkle trout on both sides with salt and pepper; set aside, skin side down. Melt 1 tbsp. (15 mL) of the butter. Peel potato and using a vegetable peeler, thinly slice crosswise. Place potato slices in a large bowl and toss with melted butter and a pinch of salt and pepper. Arrange potato slices on each fillet, slightly overlapping them to completely cover the fish.

✦ In a large non-stick skillet, melt remaining 1 tbsp. (15 mL) butter with canola oil over medium-high heat. Carefully place fillets, potato side down, in skillet. Cook, undisturbed, 2 to 3 minutes or until potatoes are golden brown. Carefully transfer fillets to a baking sheet, skin side down. Bake in a preheated 450°F (220°C) oven 5 to 7 minutes or until edges are opaque.

To Serve

A variety of sprouts
Chopped fresh chives

✦ Remove peach wedges from braised cabbage and arrange wedges around the edge of 2 dinner plates. Mound some of the cabbage on each plate and top with sprouts and a piece of trout. Drizzle any liquid from the cabbage around each plate, garnish with chives and serve immediately. **Makes 2 servings.**

109

International Plowing Match

The International Plowing Match (IPM) is big-time farming and terrific fun. No matter where in the province it travels, the display of farming expertise is worth a drive. The planning begins more than five years in advance and takes up huge chunks of volunteer time. Farm families are a proud lot, and when it comes to be their turn to host this fabulous event, they pull out all the stops. What will you see at the IPM? Well, first there'll be machinery — gigantic combines and perfectly polished tractors. There are animals and cooking demonstrations and all sorts of country-fair concessions. But the highlight, as the name suggests, is plowing. Men and women compete on new and antique tractors and with horses to determine just who can cut a perfect furrow. And when you tire of tractors, there is horseshoe pitching, log sawing and bag tying before it's time to go back to the food booths for a buffalo burger or a sausage on a bun and glasses of fresh local cider. For people who don't live on farms, and that's most of us, it's a wonderful opportunity to see a cross-section of agricultural Canada.

Hickory Roast Pheasant with Jerusalem Artichoke, Sourdough and McIntosh Stuffing

This recipe from Auberge du Pommier in Toronto is truly Ontario.

1	head garlic
3 tbsp. (45 mL)	canola oil
	Salt and pepper
1 tbsp. (15 mL)	unsalted butter
1/2 cup (125 mL)	diced peeled Jerusalem artichokes
1	McIntosh apple, diced (about 1 cup/250 mL)
1 tbsp. (15 mL)	dry mustard
2 tsp. (10 mL)	liquid honey
1 tsp. (5 mL)	cider vinegar
4 cups (1 L)	cubed day-old sourdough bread
1 tbsp. (15 mL)	chopped fresh thyme
3 cups (750 mL)	hickory shavings, soaked in warm water
1	pheasant (about 3 lb./1.5 kg)

✦ Cut a slice from top of garlic head and place head on a square of foil. Drizzle with 2 tsp. (10 mL) of the oil and sprinkle with a pinch of salt and pepper. Wrap garlic in foil and bake in a preheated 400°F (200°C) oven 35 to 45 minutes or until tender. When cool enough to handle, squeeze softened garlic from each clove.

✦ Melt butter in a skillet over medium heat. Cook artichokes and apple 10 minutes or until golden brown and tender. Remove pan from heat and stir in softened garlic.

✦ In a small bowl, stir together mustard, all but 1 tbsp. (15 mL) of the oil, honey and vinegar. Add mustard mixture, bread cubes and thyme to apple mixture, stirring to combine.

✦ Heat one side of barbecue to medium-high. Drain hickory chips and place in foil container; place on heated side of barbecue and close lid.

✦ Rinse pheasant under cold running water and dry thoroughly. Fill the cavity with stuffing and truss bird. Place any remaining stuffing on a piece of greased foil and close tightly. Rub pheasant with remaining 1 tbsp. (15 mL) oil and sprinkle with salt and pepper; place over indirect heat on barbecue. Cook 1 hour and 20 minutes, turning often, or until meat thermometer inserted in thickest part of thigh registers 180°F (85°C) and juices run clear. Thirty minutes before pheasant is done, place foil packet containing any remaining dressing on barbecue and cook until heated through. Remove pheasant to heated platter and tent with a piece of foil. Let stand 15 minutes before carving. **Makes 6 servings.**

Above: *Ted Mascka with garlic*

Garlic

The Garlic King (a.k.a. The Garlic Man of Fishlake), Ted Mascka, is a soft-spoken gentle man with a mission — to make Canada self-sufficient in garlic production. His goal is laudable, especially given the poor quality of the imported bulbs (irradiated, they are literally dead and will not germinate when planted). On his farm in Demorestville, Ontario, near Belleville, he raises and hybridizes up to thirty varieties of garlic, some of which have been judged as among the best in the garlic world. His Fishlake #3 (a.k.a. F3) topped the University of Saskatchewan cultivar trials, with his F1 and F2 coming in sixth and seventh, respectively. To help Canada grow better garlic, Ted has established a mail-order business, sending seeds and garlic bulbs from coast to coast.

Apple Trees

The McIntosh apple was discovered in 1811 among a number of other apple trees by John McIntosh when he was clearing his land at Dundela, near Morrisburg in eastern Ontario, then known as Upper Canada. His son, Allan, learned how to graft apples and by 1835 they were in the apple business. The original tree lived for more than 90 years and can be credited for producing the line of apples, McIntosh Red, that is still Canada's most popular. Ontario grows more than half of the Canadian production.

Venison Medallions, Wild Blueberry Sauce and Corn and Chive Fritters with Fresh Pea, Wild Leek and Mint Timbale

Langdon Hall is unique. Hidden on its own 80 hectares (200 acres) of private Carolinian forest near Cambridge, Ontario, the American Revival mansion, built by Langdon Wilks, a direct descendant of John Jacob Astor, has been perfectly restored by owners Bill Bennett and Mary Beaton. The inn has a large kitchen garden, which the kitchen brigade harvests all summer long. This recipe was developed by former chef Louise Duhamel.

Wild Blueberry Sauce

1 tbsp. (15 mL)	unsalted butter
1	onion, finely chopped
2 tsp. (10 mL)	minced fresh ginger
1	clove garlic, minced
1 cup (250 mL)	port
1/4 cup (50 mL)	red wine vinegar
	Zest and juice of 1 lemon
1 tbsp. (15 mL)	red currant jelly
1 cup (250 mL)	wild blueberries

✦ Melt butter in a saucepan over medium heat. Add onion, ginger and garlic; cook 5 minutes or until softened. Stir in port, vinegar and lemon zest and juice; simmer until reduced by half, about 15 minutes. Stir in jelly and half the blueberries; purée in a blender until smooth. Return to saucepan and stir in remaining blueberries; heat through. Keep warm until needed. *Makes 2 cups (500 mL).*

Fresh Pea, Wild Leek and Mint Timbale

2 tbsp. (25 mL)	unsalted butter
1	leek, white and pale green part, chopped
1/2 lb. (250 g)	fresh or frozen green peas
1 cup (250 mL)	whipping cream (35%)
1/4 cup (50 mL)	chopped fresh mint
4	egg yolks
2	eggs
1/4 tsp. (1 mL)	salt
1/4 tsp. (1 mL)	freshly ground pepper

✦ Melt butter in a skillet over medium heat. Add leek and cook 2 to 3 minutes or until softened. Stir in peas and cream; cook 5 minutes or until slightly reduced. Place pea mixture in blender along with mint and purée until smooth. Add egg yolks, eggs, salt and pepper. Blend again until smooth. Butter four 1-cup (250 mL) ramekins and place in a roasting pan. Pour pea mixture into ramekins. Pour very hot water into roasting pan to come halfway up the sides of the ramekins. Bake in a preheated 350°F (180°C) oven 30 minutes or until set. Keep warm. *Makes 4 timbales.*

Corn and Chive Fritters

1 cup (250 mL)	fresh corn
1 tbsp. (15 mL)	chopped fresh chives
1	egg, separated
2 tbsp. (25 mL)	all-purpose flour
1/4 tsp. (1 mL)	salt
1/4 tsp. (1 mL)	freshly ground pepper
	Canola oil for deep-frying

✦ In a bowl, stir together corn, chives and egg yolk. In a separate bowl, whisk egg white until frothy. Gently fold egg white into corn mixture along with flour, salt and pepper. Heat oil in a deep-fryer to 365°F (185°C). Drop corn batter by heaping tablespoonfuls into hot oil and fry 2 to 3 minutes or until puffy and golden. Drain on paper towels. *Makes 8 fritters.*

Venison Medallions

4	venison loin filets (2 oz./50 g each)
	Salt and pepper to taste
1 tbsp. (15 mL)	canola oil

✦ Season venison filets lightly with salt and pepper. Heat oil in a skillet over medium-high heat. Sauté venison 2 to 3 minutes on each side or until medium-rare.

To Serve

✦ Place 1 medallion on each of 4 dinner plates and top with some Wild Blueberry Sauce. Arrange 1 timbale and 2 fritters on each plate. Garnish with fresh herbs. Serve immediately. *Makes 4 servings.*

113

Wild Marjoram–Roasted Eigennsen Farm Duck Breast and Duck Confit with Garden Vegetables

Michael and Nobuyo Stadtländer serve this duck with their own garden vegetables. You can order duck fat from some butchers. Wild marjoram, with its tiny blue flowers that bees love, grows across the province and is somewhat like a mild oregano. Start with 2 whole 4-lb. (2 kg) ducks, cut in pieces.

Duck Confit

4	cloves garlic, minced
2 tsp. (10 mL)	salt
1 tsp. (5 mL)	crushed black peppercorns
2	bay leaves, crumbled
1/2 tsp. (2 mL)	dried thyme
4	legs from two 4-lb. (2 kg) ducks
4 cups (1 L)	rendered duck fat

✦ Combine garlic, salt, peppercorns, bay leaves and thyme. Rub into duck legs. Place in bowl, cover and refrigerate overnight.

✦ In a large oven-proof saucepan, melt duck fat over medium heat. Brush coating from duck legs and place legs in hot fat. Cover with lid or foil; bake in a preheated 325°F (160°C) oven 1 1/2 hours or until duck is very tender. Let cool in fat until ready to serve.

To make juniper honey, crush 1 tbsp. (15 mL) whole juniper berries and combine with 1/2 cup (125 mL) red wine and 2 tbsp. (25 mL) wildflower honey in a small saucepan. Bring to a boil, reduce heat and simmer 5 minutes. Strain, pressing the berries to release all their flavour. Return liquid to clean saucepan and cook another 3 to 5 minutes or until dark and syrupy. Refrigerate till needed. Makes 1/4 cup (50 mL).

Duck Stock

2	duck carcasses (legs and breasts removed)
2	carrots, quartered
2	stalks celery, quartered
1	onion, quartered
1	bay leaf
2	sprigs fresh thyme
1/2 tsp. (2 mL)	juniper berries
1/2 tsp. (2 mL)	black peppercorns
6 cups (1.5 L)	chicken stock (p. 64)

✦ Break carcasses into pieces and remove duck meat from bones. Place bones in a lightly oiled roasting pan. Roast in a preheated 400°F (200°C) oven 30 minutes or until golden. Stir in carrots, celery, onion, bay leaf, thyme, juniper berries and peppercorns; roast about 45 minutes, stirring occasionally, or until fragrant and deeply browned. Place bones and vegetables in a large saucepan, scraping brown bits from roasting pan. Pour in stock. Bring to a boil, reduce heat and simmer 2 hours. Strain, discarding solids. Return stock to saucepan and boil until reduced by half. **Makes about 2 cups (500 mL) stock.**

Duck Breast and Sauce

4	duck breasts
1	bunch fresh wild marjoram
2	shallots, sliced
1/4 cup (50 mL)	red wine
2 cups (500 mL)	Duck Stock (recipe above)
2 tsp. (10 mL)	raspberry vinegar
1 tsp. (5 mL)	juniper honey
	Salt and black pepper to taste

✦ Heat an oven-proof skillet over medium-high heat. Sear duck breasts, skin side down, about 3 minutes; turn and sear 2 minutes. Set breasts aside. Place marjoram stems in skillet; top with duck breasts, skin side down. Bake in a preheated 400°F (200°C) oven about 10 minutes or until just rare. Remove duck breasts to a platter; keep warm. Discard marjoram stems. Drain all but 1 tbsp. (15 mL) fat from skillet. Add shallots and cook about 2 minutes or until golden. Add red wine; cook until almost evaporated. Stir in Duck Stock; boil 5 minutes. Stir in raspberry vinegar and juniper honey. Season with salt and pepper.

To Serve

✦ Thinly slice duck breasts and fan onto 4 serving plates. Place a confit leg of duck on each plate and surround with sauce. **Makes 4 servings.**

Michael Stadtländer

It was at Sooke Harbour House on Vancouver Island that I first met Michael Stadtländer. I arrived in midafternoon and he was in the then-tiny kitchen of the inn, beginning to prepare dinner. "Would you like to see how to skin a wolf eel?" was his first question. And that was the beginning of a rich and long culinary relationship. The dinner, for which I still have the handwritten menu, centred on the snowy white flesh of the eel bathed with wild blackberry butter sauce. It was the first of many magical Stadtländer encounters. We have followed each other — me to his various cooking gigs: the Feast of Fields, which he helped found with chef Jamie Kennedy; Nekah, a restaurant that was so leading-edge it was too far ahead of its time and probably still would be today. And he, with his wife, Nobuyo, trekked to Quadra Island in B.C., where I had rented a tiny home surrounded by fruit trees to finish a manuscript. That was a summer of touching the earth and the ocean. He stole my plums and brought them back as preserves. I caught salmon and Nobuyo topped it with her own miso, then Michael barbecued it under the cherry trees on my terrace overlooking the sea. Now, north of Toronto on the edge of the Niagara Escarpment near Singhampton, he's cooking again at Eigennsen Farm, a rustic property that doubles as their home and business.

Few chefs I've met understand the essence of food like Michael. He grows it, he harvests it and he loves to share it. Menus evolve over the day in the forest or fields or markets of Huron County.

On a blistering hot day in late June, Roger Dufau, one of the early pioneers of regional cookery in Canada, and I travelled north along the dusty back roads to Eigennsen. We began the evening with a walk along a rutted lane into the hot summer farm fields. The massive heaps of lichen-smeared rocks spoke of another era when immigrant families tried to scrape out a living from this gravelly, unforgiving soil. Little cooking havens — small outdoor kitchens — lined the way. Soon the lane became a path and plunged into the resin-scented forest — cooling and silent — where, in a woodsy clearing, slate dining tables balanced firmly atop logs.

In the farmhouse dining room, guests toasted each other while the twisted driftwood chandelier reminded me of the summer we had spent on Quadra Island. Candles were lit, the light flickering on the gilt-rimmed ceiling and walls the colour of aged Pomerol. Small Japanese plates arrived with grilled bits of suckling pig and a warmish German-style salad. Baby radishes, sliced paper thin, were strewn on the plate.

Next we each received a few spoonfuls of light lobster bisque in deep bowls and then backyard-smoked whitefish from Georgian Bay dolloped with its own caviar, the burnished skin pulled back to reveal the cream-coloured flesh. Two sauces — the first a garden pea, the second a fresh yogurt, both dotted with grains of wild rice — ringed the small fillet. Perfect, once again. It glowed. An intense black currant sorbet broke the meal.

The squab we had seen Michael carrying earlier was served atop a few leaves of young lettuce and blessed with foie gras. The lovage leaves rolled into the thinnest pasta and draped like tissue around roasted veal with only a rich jus for sauce.

Dessert? Nobuyo brought out a composition plate that made the tastebuds dance, even for the most satiated. Lemon foam was set on a wild blueberry compote. There was maple caramel ice cream in a tiny maple hazelnut tuile, apricots infused with Jack Daniels and chunks of Georgian Bay apples in caramelized puff pastry. Finally, a pair of truffles, bits of velvet chocolate ganache rolled in coconut.

This was more than just a meal — it was the heart and soul of great Canadian cuisine.

Above: *Michael and Nobuyo Statländer at Feast of Fields*

Four Seasons Film Festival Chicken Pot Pie

The restaurants in The Four Seasons Hotel in Yorkville in downtown Toronto are among the best dining experiences in Canada — upscale, inventive and delicious. This, however, is a homespun dish, hearty and full of seasonal vegetables and a full-blown annual tradition at the hotel at the George Christy luncheon during the Toronto International Film Festival. Once a year a collection of stars and glitterati get together and enjoy this quintessential comfort food.

1 tbsp. (15 mL)	vegetable oil
	onion, diced or
	12 pearl onions
4	carrots, peeled and chopped
4	stalks celery, chopped
1/2 cup (125 mL)	chopped mushrooms
2 cups (500 mL)	chicken stock (p. 66)
1/3 cup (75 mL)	unsalted butter
1/3 cup (75 mL)	all-purpose flour
1 cup (250 mL)	whipping cream (35%)
4 cups (1 L)	cubed cooked chicken
3/4 cup (175 mL)	green peas, fresh or frozen
1 tbsp. (15 mL)	chopped fresh thyme or
	1 tsp. (5 mL) dried thyme
1 tsp. (5 mL)	salt
1/4 tsp. (1 mL)	pepper
8 oz. (250 g)	frozen puff pastry, thawed
1	egg, beaten

✦ Heat oil in a large skillet over medium heat. Add onion, carrots, celery and mushrooms; cook, stirring, 5 minutes. Add 1/2 cup (125 mL) of the chicken stock; cover and simmer about 5 minutes or until tender. Set aside.

✦ Melt butter in a large saucepan over medium heat. Add flour; cook, stirring constantly about 2 minutes or until bubbling but not browned. Whisk in remaining chicken stock and cream until sauce is thickened and smooth. Stir in vegetable mixture, chicken, peas, thyme, salt and pepper; simmer 2 to 3 minutes. Pour into six 10 – 12 oz. (300 – 375 mL) ramekins or oven-proof soup bowls.

✦ On lightly floured surface, roll out puff pastry as thinly as possible. Cut rounds slightly larger than tops of ramekins. Place pastry over filling, pinching to seal the edges. Brush lightly with egg and, with a sharp knife, slash the tops to allow steam to escape. Bake in a preheated 375°F (190°C) oven 30 minutes or until pastry is puffed and golden and filling is bubbling. Serve immediately. **Makes 6 servings.**

117

Cookstown Greens

David Cohlmeyer of Cookstown Greens in the rolling hills north of Toronto has been on the leading edge for as long as I've known him. Not content to simply grow three or four specialty crops, David routinely grows hundreds of unusual and delicious fruit and vegetable varieties in his greenhouses and in the fields surrounding his home. He is renowned for his salad mix in which there are often thirty-five varieties of greens. Chefs buy everything from candy-stripe beets to salsify from him, and on Saturdays, at Toronto's public organic market on Markham Street, he sells a wide selection of his produce. Look for purple carrots, red-fleshed radishes and sprouts of every description from chickpea to coriander. If you dine at Scaramouche, Truffles (in the Four Seasons Hotel) or tiny Giancarlo on Clinton Street, the chances are the vegetables are from David's farm.

Right: *David Cohlmeyer of Cookstown Greens*

Portobello Mushroom Burgers on Onion Buns with Aylmer Dried Tomato Mayonnaise and Yukon Gold Fries

Portobello Mushroom Burgers

1/4 cup (50 mL)	canola oil
2 tbsp. (25 mL)	red wine vinegar
1 tbsp. (15 mL)	chopped fresh thyme
	large Portobello mushrooms, stemmed
	Salt and pepper to taste

✦ In a small bowl, whisk together oil, vinegar and thyme. Brush bottom and top of each mushroom with mixture and sprinkle with salt and pepper. Arrange mushrooms cap-side up, in a baking pan and broil 5 minutes or until softened. Serve on Onion Buns spread with Aylmer Dried Tomato Mayonnaise and Yukon Gold Fries on the side. **Serves 6.**

Yukon Gold Fries

6	Yukon Gold potatoes
2 tbsp. (25 mL)	canola oil
	Salt and pepper to taste

✦ Cut each potato lengthwise into 8 wedges. Toss in a bowl with oil and spread in a single layer on a baking sheet. Bake in a pre-heated 375°F (190°C) oven 15 minutes. Turn and bake another 15 minutes or until fries are golden brown and tender. Sprinkle with salt and pepper. **Serves 6.**

Aylmer Dried Tomato Mayonnaise

1	egg
1 tbsp. (15 mL)	lemon juice
1 tsp. (5 mL)	Dijon mustard
1/2 tsp. (2 mL)	salt
1/4 tsp. (1 mL)	cayenne
1 cup (250 mL)	canola oil
1/4 cup (50 mL)	chopped oven-dried tomatoes (see below)

✦ In a food processor, combine egg, lemon juice, mustard, salt and cayenne. Process for 1 minute. With processor still running, slowly drizzle in oil until all the oil is used and mixture is thick. Add oven-dried tomatoes and process until smooth. Taste and adjust seasoning. **Makes 1 1/4 cups (300 mL).**

Oven-dried Tomatoes

Plum tomatoes

✦ Slice plum tomatoes in half lengthwise and scoop out seeds and pulp. Place, single layer, cut side up, on an oiled baking sheet. Bake in a 300°F (150°C) oven 45 minutes.

Onion Buns

✦ Use half the Soft Bread Roll recipe (p. 194). Before shaping rolls, knead 1 cup (250 mL) cooked chopped onion into dough. Divide dough into 12 portions and shape into rolls. Let rise. Brush with eggwash (p. 23). Sprinkle with a few spoonfuls chopped onion and bake as directed. **Makes 1 dozen.**

119

Yukon Gold

Gary Johnston is a modern agricultural hero! He is the breeder of the famous Yukon Gold, a potato that is found, named, on menus and in grocery stores around the world. Now retired, he is still breeding potatoes and it takes years. As he says, "Potato breeders have to be a patient lot." Let's hope that we'll soon taste his new cultivars.

Cipaille/Sea Pie

Just a little south of North Bay, Ontario, there's a region of pink granite and small silvery lakes connected by marshy stretches and filled with Indian arrowhead and purple loose-strife. Here you'll discover a seventy-two-year-old tradition: every second Sunday in August, the parish that cradles the tiny village of Astorville holds a fund-raising picnic that preserves its special Canadian culinary heritage, served up in ancient lumber-camp iron kettles. It's a celebration in two languages — French and English.

This is country food at its best, featuring the wonderful layered meat pies known as cipaille, or sea pie in English, which are hauled, golden brown and sizzling, from a series of big outdoor wood-fired ovens and taken to the arena to be eaten. As Jeanne McKenney says as she walks around the hall on the day of the picnic, carrying platters and visiting with diners, "This is one of the better things you can do in your lifetime. What would Astorville be without the picnic?" The answer is summed up in a comment made by Bea Besstte, an octogenarian who has been helping at the picnic for more than seventy years. "The picnic has paid our debts. It has built our parish." Bea, who began selling tickets when she was twelve years old, became, as years rolled by, the organizational linchpin. Her record books attest to her skill at detail. In a carefully written logbook, she's kept meticulous lists of donations, costs and volunteer rosters. But best of all it's in this book that she's kept the recipe for sea pie.

The menu at the Astorville picnic is honest and homespun. Half a tonne of sea pie is accompanied by baked beans (fèves au lard) liberally dosed with salt pork, onion and molasses; cabbage salad (salade au choux); and dozens of desserts. Auditorium tables sag under the weight of the fixin's.

The planning begins in March, and by July the volunteers all have jobs: there are potato peelers, onion choppers, sea pie assemblers, baked bean cookers, pie bakers, transportation specialists (the guys who have the sturdiest half-ton trucks), and probably best of all, all-night fire stokers, those hardy individuals who tend the ovens, sitting in the semi-darkness telling stories and quaffing their favourite frothy beverages. It's a massive oper-ation turned into serious fun by the dedication of a whole parish full of good-hearted people.

Astorville Cipaille/Sea Pie

The pastry for this pie is adapted from a recipe in one of Bea Bessette's many notebooks containing decades of handwritten lists of contributors and donations. Although any lard may be used, these parish bakers insist on Tenderflake.

Pastry

5 cups (1.25 L)	all-purpose flour
2 tsp. (10 mL)	salt
1 tsp. (5 mL)	baking powder
1/2 tsp. (2 mL)	baking soda
1 1/4 cups (300 mL)	chilled lard
1	egg
1 cup (250 mL)	ice water

Filling

3 lb. (1.5 kg)	lean boneless beef, cut in 1-inch (2.5 cm) cubes
2	onions, minced
1 1/2 tsp. (7 mL)	salt
3/4 tsp. (4 mL)	freshly ground pepper
2 lb. (1 kg)	lean boneless pork, cut in 1-inch (2.5 cm) cubes
1 1/2 lb. (750 g)	boneless chicken breast, cut in 1-inch (2.5 cm) cubes
2 cups (500 mL)	water

✦ In a large bowl, stir together flour, salt, baking powder and baking soda. Cut in lard until crumbly. In another bowl, whisk together egg and ice water. Using a fork, combine liquid and dry ingredients till moistened. Gather dough into ball. Cut into 3 equal pieces; cover with damp towel and set aside.

✦ Spread beef over bottom of a large, lightly oiled roasting pan. Sprinkle with one-third of the onions, 1/2 tsp. (2 mL) of the salt and 1/4 tsp. (1 mL) of the pepper. Roll 1 piece of dough on a lightly floured surface till large enough to cover meat. Tuck in edges of pastry if necessary. Spread pastry with pork cubes, sprinkling with another third of the onions, 1/2 tsp. (2 mL) salt and 1/4 tsp. (1 mL) pepper. Roll out second piece of dough and cover pork. Spread with chicken and remaining onion, salt and pepper. Roll out last piece of pastry, trimming any uneven edges, and place on top, tucking in if necessary to cover meat.

✦ With the handle of a wooden spoon, punch a 1-inch (2.5 cm) hole in the centre of the pie all the way to the bottom of the pan. Pour water into the hole; cover roasting pan with lid or a double layer of foil. Bake in a preheated 325°F (160°C) oven 4 hours or until crust is deep golden brown. **Makes 12 generous servings.**

Waterloo County Roasted Pig Tails

The inspiration for this dish came from the Myers family. Evelyn Myers worked for years at the Heidelberg Tavern, one of the best places in Waterloo County for pig tails.

These pig tails are tender and glistening with an almost caramelized crust. Although they are traditionally roasted whole, we've cut them into chunks to make them easier to serve. They're great with jugs of local beer, sauerkraut and whipped mashed potatoes.

3 lb. (1.5 kg)	meaty pig tails (5 or 6)
3/4 cup (175 mL)	corn syrup
1/2 cup (125 mL)	ketchup
1/4 cup (50 mL)	Worcestershire sauce
1 tbsp. (15 mL)	dry mustard
2 tsp. (10 mL)	ground ginger
1 tsp. (5 mL)	cayenne

✦ Wash pig tails thoroughly. Place in large saucepan or Dutch oven; cover with cold water. Bring to a boil, skimming foam from surface periodically. Simmer, covered, for 1 hour. Drain, let stand till cool enough to handle and slice each tail into 3 or 4 pieces. Transfer to a large shallow baking dish or roasting pan.

✦ In a bowl, stir together corn syrup, ketchup, Worcestershire sauce, mustard, ginger and cayenne. Pour over meat, stirring to coat evenly. Bake in a preheated 350°F (180°C) oven, turning several times to glaze, 1 to 1 1/2 hours or until shiny and crisp. **Makes 4 servings.**

121

The Vintners Quality Alliance

The Vintners Quality Alliance (VQA), a national organization dedicated to the development and promotion of fine Canadian wines, has established an appellation-of-origin system for wine labelling. According to this system, each bottle of wine produced in Canada must indicate its provincial or geographic origin.

Provincially designated wines are identified by appellation of "Ontario" or "British Columbia" and must be made entirely of the finest French hybrid and European vinifera grape varieties. In the case of "varietal" wines (wines named after the grape from which they are produced, like Chardonnay or Cabernet Sauvignon), the bottles must contain at least 75 percent of that named variety.

122

Falling under even more stringent rules are those wines produced in specific viticultural areas such as Niagara Peninsula or Lake Erie North Shore in Ontario or Okanagan Valley or Vancouver Island in British Columbia, to name a few. Grape origin is strictly controlled, and only the classic grape varieties such as Reisling, Chardonnay, Pinot Noir and Cabernet Sauvignon may be used. At the highest level, the wine should carry the name of the individual vineyard, or the words "Estate Bottled," in which case the grapes are entirely from that property.

Yearly the winemakers who take part in the VQA program submit their new vintages to an expert tasting panel for blind tastings, and only after that are the VQA medallions awarded.

The appellation-of-origin system was established in Ontario in 1989. A year later the British Columbia Wine Institute adopted the general philosophy and recently it has been adopted Canada-wide. Although it has become a marketing success, the real benefit to Canadian consumers is that they can be absolutely guaranteed that the label information is correct.

Crisp Almond Meringues and White Peaches with Late-Harvest Vidal Sabayon

Vineland Estates Winery has a restaurant with the most panoramic view in the Niagara region. It looks down the rolling vineyards right to Jordan Harbour on Lake Ontario. White peaches are among the rarest and sweetest produced in Niagara. Typically found in Japan and Europe, they are not often grown in Canada. Their perfumed flesh is a cream colour and around the pit are whorls of brilliant red. For this recipe other large, fully ripe, mid- to late-season peaches may be substituted. Try Red Haven, Loring or Jubilee, but taste them first. They must be sweet and fragrant.

Meringue Disks

4	egg whites
3 tbsp. (45 mL)	granulated sugar
3 tbsp. (45 mL)	icing sugar
2 tbsp. (25 mL)	ground almonds (optional)

✦ In a large bowl, using electric mixer, beat egg whites until frothy. Gradually beat in granulated sugar, then icing sugar. Beat about 5 minutes in total or until egg whites become very shiny and stiff. Fold in almonds. Place mixture in piping bag; pipe into 24 3-inch (8 cm) circles on parchment-lined baking sheet. Bake in a preheated 200°F (95°C) oven about 2 hours or until completely dry but not coloured. Let cool on parchment.

Peaches

1/2 cup (125 mL)	white grape juice
2 tbsp. (25 mL)	demerara sugar
1 tbsp. (15 mL)	unsalted butter
12	white peaches, halved and pitted

✦ In a large saucepan, combine juice, sugar and butter; bring to a boil. In batches, place peaches, cut side down, in a single layer in saucepan. Simmer, covered, 6 minutes; turn, simmer 2 minutes. With slotted spoon, carefully transfer to a plate and slip off skins.

Raspberry Sauce

| 2 cups (500 mL) | fresh raspberries |
| 2 tbsp. (25 mL) | icing sugar |

✦ Purée raspberries with sugar in a food processor or blender. Pass through a sieve to remove seeds.

Late-Harvest Vidal Sabayon

1/2 cup (125 mL)	late-harvest Vidal or ice wine
1/4 cup (50 mL)	sugar
4	egg yolks

✦ Just before serving, make the sabayon. In top of a double boiler over simmering water, whisk together wine, sugar and egg yolks 6 minutes or until very thick and pale yellow. Place top of double boiler in a bowl of ice water and continue whisking 4 minutes or until sabayon is cooled.

To Serve

✦ Place 1 peach half on top of each meringue and decorate with raspberry sauce and sabayon. **Makes 12 servings.**

123

Above: *Nuts from Grimmo's Nut Farm, Niagara.*
Clockwise, from upper left, *black walnut, sweet chestnut, Persian walnut, Korean pine nut, native hazelnut, heart-nut.*

The Benko family at Norfolk County Estate Winery makes wine from their own apples (Golden Delicious, Mutsu, Empire, Idared and, of course, McIntosh). The juices are vinified as varietals or blended with local plums, strawberries, elderberries and pears.

Roasted Pears with Caramel Sauce and Whipped Cream

This recipe comes from a team of chefs, Laura Buckley and Gillian Talacko, who graduated from the Stratford Chefs School together before setting up their catering business in Toronto. It's an endlessly versatile recipe. Instead of caramel sauce you can use a fruit purée. Or you can ignore the pears and spoon the sauce over the best ice cream you can find. Or combine them both and you'll have one of the most delicious seasonal desserts going.

Caramel Sauce

1 1/2 cups (375 mL)	sugar
1/2 cup (125 mL)	water
1 cup (250 mL)	whipping cream (35%)

✦ Combine sugar and water in a heavy-bottomed saucepan. Heat over medium-low heat, without stirring, until sugar is dissolved completely. Increase heat to high; cook, swirling pan occasionally to prevent burning, until sugar-water turns golden. Remove from heat and slowly whisk in cream. Be careful: the caramel will sputter and bubble as you add the cream.

✦ Refrigerate any leftover sauce for up to 1 month. Reheat in microwave or by placing sealed container in hot water.

Roasted Pears

4	ripe pears (Bosc or Bartlett)
2 tbsp. (25 mL)	unsalted butter
2 tbsp. (25 mL)	sugar

✦ Peel, quarter and core pears. Heat an oven-proof pan, preferably cast iron, over medium heat. Add butter; allow to melt. Add pears, sprinkle with sugar and toss to coat. Place pan in a preheated 450°F (220°C) oven and bake 5 to 10 minutes, turning pears occasionally, or until pears are golden brown and tender when pierced with a knife.

To Serve

1 cup (250 mL)	whipping cream (35%)
	Fresh mint for garnish (optional)

✦ Whip cream. Place 1 pear on each of 4 plates. Add a large dollop of whipped cream. Drizzle with caramel sauce. Garnish with fresh mint. **Makes 4 servings.**

Above: *George Benko at Norfolk Estate Winery*

Compote of Niagara Plums and Blueberries in Brandy

Lovely over ice cream in the middle of winter! Piercing the plum skins helps prevent them from splitting during processing.

4 lb. (2 kg)	firm ripe Santa Rosa or Italian prune plums, washed
3 cups (750 mL)	water
1 1/2 cups (375 mL)	sugar
1 cup (250 mL)	liquid honey
6	slices peeled fresh ginger
3 cups (750 mL)	blueberries, washed
1/3 cup (75 mL)	Niagara brandy

✦ *Pierce each plum twice with a sterilized skewer or needle. In a large saucepan or Dutch oven, combine water, sugar and honey. Bring to a boil; add plums. Simmer, covered, 2 minutes. Remove from heat.*

✦ *Divide ginger slices between two 1-quart (1 L) Mason jars. Place one-quarter of the blueberries in each jar. Gently spoon plums into jars. Top with remaining blueberries. Divide brandy among jars; pour in syrup. Fit with new two-piece lids. Process in boiling-water bath 20 minutes.* **Makes about 8 cups (2 L) plums, enough for 12 servings.**

The Best Bran Muffins

Years ago, my aunt, Sadie Ovens, then the cook at a summer camp in Muskoka, shared this recipe. Although there have been a number of modifications over the ensuing decades, these moist muffins have made my kitchen a morning destination for many friends.

They are incredibly forgiving. You can omit the apples and raisins and add all sorts of other fruits and nuts — even a handful or two of granola. I scraped the remains of a post-Christmas bowl of cranberry sauce into the batter one time, and added chopped late-harvest pears and candied ginger another. My favourite is still a healthy addition of chopped dates with a few walnuts. I guess what I'm saying is that this recipe is foolproof...the sort that endears itself to me forever.

1 cup (250 mL)	brown sugar
1/2 cup (125 mL)	canola oil
1	egg
1 cup (250 mL)	natural bran
1 cup (250 mL)	sour milk or buttermilk
1/4 cup (50 mL)	fancy molasses (optional)
1 tsp. (5 mL)	vanilla
1 cup (250 mL)	whole-wheat flour
1 tsp. (5 mL)	baking soda
1/2 tsp. (2 mL)	baking powder
1/2 – 3/4 cup (125 – 175 mL)	chopped nuts
1/2 cup (125 mL)	golden raisins
1 cup (250 mL)	chopped unpeeled apple

✦ *In a large mixing bowl, whisk sugar, oil and egg about 2 minutes or until light in colour. Stir in bran, sour milk, molasses and vanilla. In a separate bowl, sift or stir together flour, baking soda and baking powder. Stir into the bran mixture, combining well. Fold in nuts, raisins and apple or whatever other addition you've chosen.*

✦ *Spoon into 12 paper-lined or well-greased muffin tins. Bake in a preheated 400°F (200°C) oven 20 to 22 minutes or until dark brown. Let cool 5 minutes before removing from pan.* **Makes 12 muffins.**

125

Ontario Wine Regions

Within the Niagara wine region are other areas quite definable in themselves. "The Bench," for instance, sweeps along the Niagara Escarpment's craggy outcroppings with its eastern terminus being St. Catharines. It plateaus into a narrow fertile band of well-drained clay loam over limestone bedrock and the climate is the coolest of the Niagara Peninsula. Riesling flourishes there. Throughout the lower Niagara region, from the Lakeshore through Queenston to St. Davids, the soil varies from sandy loam to coarse and gravelly deposits. It's these potential subappellations that are challenging the expertise of winemakers like Jean-Laurent Groux of Hillebrand Estates Winery. "In France," he says, "the job of finding out what grows best where took 2000 years; here we are trying to do it in ten to twenty."

The Lake Erie North Shore region spans the flat, former seabed between Windsor and Blenheim. Dominated by heavy clay soil, this region has the most heat units in all of Canada. But the lake is so shallow, it has little to no moderating effect. At LeBlanc Estate Winery near Harrow, winemaker Lyse LeBlanc creates lush, rounded vintages with very limited production of Pinot Gris, Riesling, Gewürztraminer, Vidal, Pinot Noir and Cabernet Sauvignon.

Pelee Island is a few kilometres offshore in Lake Erie. It was here, in the 1860s, that the first grapevines in Ontario were planted. A winery was established in 1873 on a latitude the same as northern California's. The 80 hectares (200 acres) of Pelee Island Winery vineyards have a climate so unusual that the harvest must be completed within 24 to 48 hours.

Above: *Grape vine in late fall*

Canadian Cheeses with Glazed Onion and Raisin Compote and Rosemary-Infused Local Honey

Chef Michael Olson of On the Twenty in Jordan is one of Niagara's culinary pioneers. His menus change frequently — sometimes from hour to hour, depending on the availability of local, seasonal ingredients. He selects cheeses from across Ontario and Quebec. With them he serves these easy-to-create condiments and crisp oat cakes similar to those on p. 196.

The wine used is from the Cave Spring Cellars winery, operated by Len Pennachetti and Helen Young, adjacent to the restaurant. Travellers can enjoy a full-fledged wine tasting, dine and then stay overnight at the couple's upscale Vintner's Inn.

Glazed Onion and Raisin Compote

1 tbsp. (15 mL)	unsalted butter
3	onions, cut in long strips
1 cup (250 mL)	Cave Spring Cellars Late-Harvest Riesling
3/4 cup (75 mL)	golden raisins

✦ In a large non-stick skillet, melt butter over very low heat. Add onions and cook, stirring occasionally, about 20 to 25 minutes or until soft and caramelized. Add wine and raisins, stirring with a wooden spoon and scraping any browned caramelized onion bits from the bottom of the pan. Cook slowly to allow the raisins to absorb the wine. Once the wine is fully absorbed — it will take 7 to 10 minutes — remove from heat. Refrigerate until needed. Serve compote warm or at room temperature. *Makes about 2 cups (500 mL).*

Rosemary-Infused Local Honey

Chef Olson suggests that other pungent herbs, such as lavender, thyme and sage, may be used. He also varies the kind of honey, from light to dark buckwheat.

1 cup (250 mL)	local honey
3 – 4	stems fresh rosemary, washed if necessary and patted dry

✦ Place honey in a small non-stick saucepan with a heavy bottom. Warm over low heat. Chop rosemary coarsely and add to honey. Steep rosemary in honey over the lowest heat for 1 hour, stirring occasionally. Strain into a jar, seal and refrigerate until needed.

To Serve
Fresh rosemary

✦ Warm honey slightly and swirl onto serving plates. Top with cheese. Spoon compote onto side of plate and garnish with fresh rosemary. *Makes 1 cup (250 mL).*

Big Cheese

In eastern Ontario there's an unofficial "cheese route" that leads north from Belleville. Sop first at Plainfield. Maple Dale Cheese (founded c.1888) and cheddar are synonymous. Try their extra-old. Up highway 37 in Madoc you'll find Eldorado, so named because Ontario's first gold was discovered nearby. As it is for Maple Dale, cheddar is Eldorado's forte. Back down highway 62, stop at Ivanhoe Cheese. Founded around 1870, it is Canada's oldest cheese company. Try their cheddar, but pay particular attenetion to their Swiss-style cheese. In the 1830s Hiram Ranney, a farmer from Vermont, moved to Oxford County and started making cheese with the milk from his five cows. By 1853, he owned more than a hundred cows and shipped a 1,200-lb. (545 kg) cheese to the London Exhibition in Great Britain. By Confederation, in 1867, Ontario had at least 200 cheese factories and that year the Canadian Dairyman's Association was founded in Ingersoll, Ontario. Cheese-making was big business. In 1893, the railway sheds in Perth were the nursery for the Canadian Mite, a cheese that weighed in at 22,000 lb. (10,000 kg). It was shipped to Chicago for the World's Fair, where it crashed through the floor of the exhibit hall.

Chapter 4
Quebec

Quebec is a magnificent province of wild rivers and dense maple forests, of flowery
meadows and rich farmland, of apple orchards and fishing fleets. For all that, when the bloom of summer fades
and the first snowflakes flutter earthward, it is winter that still, as it has for centuries, shapes the province and
its people. Soft snowbanks drape sensuously over the hard Canadian Shield. Blue ice ribbons weave together
the rocky Laurentian outcroppings that outline the highways on which Quebecers speed into the country to ski
and to dine. The people of Quebec are in tune with the season, its isolation, its harshness.

Old Quebec foods reflect this season. As winter stormed down the St. Lawrence River valley centuries
ago, home cooks set fires in their hearths and created the ancient belly-warming dishes that helped build the
region. Bubbling, steaming soupe aux pois; richly spiced, meat-filled tourtière with all its regional variations;
cipaille or cipate, layers of pastry filled with everything from game to seafood; dumplings cooked in the first
maple syrup of the season and called grand-pères; and galettes de sarrasin, or buckwheat pancakes, made with
the only grain that would grow in the thin, inhospitable soil of the Canadian Shield.

Although these historic dishes bring back nostalgic moments, they are rarely found in modern Quebec.
But in the springtime, many cosmopolitan Quebecers still make a pilgrimage into the countryside for the almost
sacred rite of *les cabanes au sucre,* or sugar shacks. While the maple sap flows from the trees into tanks, the
sugar bush owners set up rustic restaurants. All around the province, families gather to eat and drink the foods
of old Quebec. Rough wooden tables in makeshift dining halls are loaded with platters of omelettes, pancakes,
bacon and sausages. Huge bowls of delicious fèves au lard (pork and beans), boiled potatoes, *ragout de pattes
de cochon avec boulettes* (a meatball and pigs' feet stew), jambon à l'érable (maple-glazed ham), *ketchup
maison,* warm breads and pickled beets fill all the space. Jugs of fresh maple syrup are on every table, and

diners are expected to pour this first taste of spring over absolutely everything. Beer
is served but so is "cariboo," a potent, knee-bending drink that is basically white
alcohol and red wine. When the main course is over, everyone is urged to eat more
pancakes and then perhaps a piece of tarte au sucre, or sugar pie. Outside, still-
boiling syrup is poured onto the snow to make *la tire,* or taffy, which is twirled and
pulled on a wooden stick.

Left: *A baker at James McGuire's Le Passe Partout*
Above: *Saint-Benoit du Lac*
Right: *Maple syrup pie*

130   Originally Quebec's economy was based on primary industry — logging, mining, fishing and agriculture. Today, many things have changed, including the tastes of Quebecers, who have encountered the world at their doorstop with a true French appreciation of gastronomy. Young culinarians abound — men and women who have travelled and brought home an understanding of fresh ingredients and their possibilities. Now we can dine on duck foie gras and sturgeon caviar, artisanal breads and fine local cheeses.

     The ethnic influences that have affected the food of Quebec date back for centuries. Early French settlers were welcomed by the First Nations with corn, bean, squash and, of course, maple syrup. The Irish who poured into Canada down the St. Lawrence were quickly assimilated into the cities and rural communities. Their foods were typically of the land, medieval in nature, with lots of potatoes and cabbages. The Scots who became the early business elite of Montreal brought with them oatmeal and good scones and the hearty fare of Great Britain. The Jews provided Montrealers with the best smoked meat and bagels in the country. The Loyalists who came north from the United States and settled thickly in the area we know as L'Estrie, or the Eastern Townships, brought Boston baked beans and chowders.

     La cuisine régionale au Québec is based on many ingredients that are specific to certain areas. Gourganes, oversized red-streaked beans that are similar to the French fèves de marais, are a staple in the Charlevoix on the north shore of the St. Lawrence River. Year after year, the seeds have been saved by the families of the original settlers. There you will find superb lamb flavoured by the seaside pastures and slightly salty. Éperlans, or smelts, the tiny river fish, can be had battered and deep-fried at roadside stands. Venison and caribou and a prolific harvest of wild mushrooms are on many restaurant menus in the autumn.

     On the rural south shore of the St. Lawrence is the region known as Kamouraska. Villagers dwell in whimsical houses with wide porches and swooping rooflines. Their long skinny farms are remnants of the eighteenth-century seigneuries, and because the farms all face onto the river, the local diet often includes sturgeon, eel and smelt. Just downriver is another definable culinary region, La Gaspésie, or the Gaspé, with its succulent

Above: *Auberge Georgeville*
Right: *In Quebec city – scaling the heights*

fresh seafood. The people of the Gaspé are often called *mangeurs de morue* (cod eaters). Lobster, shrimp, salmon, scallops have all been harvested for many centuries. It is here that you find *herbes salée,* fresh herbs preserved in salt, an ingredient not frequently used in modern cookery but an important component in historic dishes of both Quebec and Acadian Atlantic Canada.

Upstream, around and in Quebec City, are still more delicacies — quail and apples and grapes from l'Île d'Orléans and virtually any vegetable that will grow in the rich island soil.

The rolling hills south of Montreal support the province's largest English-speaking population. L'Estrie produces some of the best maple syrup in Canada and superb lamb, apples and cheese. The monks at one lakeside monastery, L'Abbaye de Saint-Benoît-du-Lac, make feta and Ermite blue cheese, sparkling hard cider and chocolate.

Quebec's northland is the domain of the Cree. Life on the winter trapline is hard and cold. Base camps are pitched in the wilderness by the trappers. The floors of the large canvas tents are deeply covered with spruce boughs and the foods are very traditional. In the centre of each tent is a portable wood-fired stove around which wild geese are impaled on wooden spits to roast. Blueberries bubble in a large pot and dried fish are hung from the crossbeams. Trappers arrive back at the camp to the aroma of roasting beaver. The tail is the most prized morsel. An elder seated on a thick bear skin prepares a moose head for cooking. Bannock is fried and shared while outside the wind lashes the forest and drifts the lake with snow.

Above: *Cheeses and cider at L'Abbaye de Saint-Benoît-du-Lac*

The cheese-makers of Quebec are national treasures. No other region of Canada can claim as many fine
cheese-makers. When Brother Alphonse Juin made the first Trappist cheese in Oka in 1893 he set the stage for
their proliferation. Oka is still being made, albeit in rather larger amounts since it is now owned by Agropur,
the largest dairy cooperative in Canada. The original curing rooms are still in use and the monks have opened
a small store next door.

Sprinkled across all regions are culinary entrepreneurs. One makes lavender flower jellies and herb
pestos while another haunts the hedgerows and meadows to gather wild herbs and fruits, from sumac and
hawthorn to highbush cranberry and chokecherry, for exotic preserves. One farmer raises wild boar to make
superb sausage and mills his own grain for heavy Germanic breads baked on-site. A fourth-generation
orchardist presses apples and ferments the juice to vinegar in oak barrels. There are innovators who produce
fine Sève, a maple syrup eau-de-vie, and Chicotai, a cloudberry liqueur made in the Côte Nord. Artisanal cider-
makers are slowly making inroads into a marketplace until now dominated by large, mediocre producers. There
are mushroom foragers and wild game farmers by the dozen. Maple production has evolved to the point where
one inventive fellow is making a sparkling, low-alcohol maple beverage called Sevillant that is sold in a cham-
pagne-style bottle.

There's a culinary synergy in this province. Diners push chefs to explore new frontiers. Chefs challenge
producers to grow new ingredients and producers are responding faster than ever. Positive rivalry between
regions abounds. It would seem, at least from my vantage point, that this is an exciting, pride-filled time in the
food life of Quebec.

Left: *Cheeses at la ferme Piluma, Saint-Basile de Portneuf, west of Quebec City,*
Clockwise from top, *Lechevalier Mailloux, Angelus, Sarah-Brizou, Saint-Basile de Portneuf*
Above: *Ice sculpture, Winter Carnival, Quebec City*

Caramelized Warm Purse
of Ermite Cheese with Georgeville Maple Syrup and Brambleberries

This recipe comes from Auberge Georgeville, the longest-operating hotel in Quebec. Built in 1889 for steamboat passengers travelling on Lac Memphrémagog, the inn is once again becoming famous for food and wine. Special attention is given to Eastern Townships ingredients — from Ayers Cliff goat's milk cheese and lamb to local trout and honey.

Wild garlic is a special springtime treat and is available in the forests of the region. If you can't pick your own a good substitute would be regular garlic or the roots and stems of well-cleaned and minced garlic chives. The Ermite cheese is from the abbey at Saint-Benoît-du-Lac.

Sauce

1 tsp. (5 mL)	unsalted butter
1 tsp. (5 mL)	minced wild garlic
1 tsp. (5 mL)	minced shallot
1/2 tsp. (2 mL)	cracked black peppercorns
Pinch	salt
1 tbsp. (15 mL)	dry white wine
3/4 cup (175 mL)	Canadian balsamic vinegar or high-quality organic cider vinegar
1/3 cup (75 mL)	Georgeville maple syrup
1 tbsp. (15 mL)	brambleberries or cranberries

Filling

1 1/4 cups (300 mL)	hazelnuts
5 oz. (150 g)	Ermite blue cheese
2 oz. (50 g)	cream cheese
1 tsp. (5 mL)	maple syrup
1 tsp. (5 mL)	balsamic vinegar

8	sheets phyllo pastry
1/2 cup (125 mL)	butter, melted
3 tbsp. (45 mL)	brown sugar

✦ Heat butter in a small saucepan over medium heat. Add garlic and shallot; cook about 1 minute, stirring, or until softened but not browned. Add peppercorns and salt; cook 20 seconds. Stir in wine. Allow wine to evaporate almost completely before adding vinegar, maple syrup and berries. Bring to a boil, reduce heat and simmer until liquid is reduced by one-third. Strain and reserve. This sauce will keep, refrigerated, up to 1 month.

✦ Toast hazelnuts on a baking sheet in a preheated 350°F (180°C) oven about 7 minutes or until fragrant. Place on a clean tea towel and fold towel over nuts. Gently roll nuts inside towel to loosen skins. Don't worry about getting all the skins off. Cool hazelnuts completely, then coarsely chop in a food processor.

✦ In a food processor, process blue and cream cheese until smooth. Add maple syrup, vinegar and 1 cup (250 mL) of the nuts. Pulse just to combine. Transfer to a small bowl; freeze 30 minutes. Between your palms, quickly roll cheese mixture into 12 walnut-sized balls. Roll balls in remaining hazelnuts.

✦ On a clean work surface, lay 1 sheet of phyllo with long end facing you; lightly brush with butter and sprinkle with some brown sugar. Repeat layering, buttering and sugaring for 4 layers in total with the top layer only buttered. Cut into 6 squares. Place a ball of cheese mixture onto each section. Gather phyllo up in a clockwise manner, pleating the pastry until it resembles a "beggar's purse." Pinch top together securely. Repeat with remaining ingredients. Brush lightly with butter and sprinkle with sugar. Place purses on a parchment-lined baking sheet and bake in a preheated 350°F (180°C) oven 10 minutes or just until golden and cheese is softening.

To Serve

Assortment of nuts and berries (optional)

✦ Spoon warm sauce onto 12 plates. Place 1 "purse" in centre of each. Garnish with berries and nuts, if desired. *Makes 12 servings.*

Blue Trout

Truite au bleu is a legendary dish in gastronomic circles. The fish is so fresh — it must be alive till mere seconds before it is plunged into boiling court bouillon — that it's curled and dusky blue on the plate. Until late one autumn I thought that I would never dine on this fabled dish. But Bill Nowell, the naturalist/biologist who oversees the 26 000-hectare (65,000-acre) private preserve of Chateau Montebello, and Marcel Mundel, the hotel's Alsatian-born executive chef, fulfilled my fantasy.

The smell of marsh dampness and cedar mingled as Chef Mundel fired up the stoves. First came steaming bowls of venison consommé, followed by fluffy quenelles encasing tart cranberries, and then the blue trout, curled and sensual on our plates. No fish could be finer!

Fresh Havre Saint-Pierre Scallop Tartare with Île d'Orléans Strawberry Vinaigrette

Daniel Vézina is one of Canada's great chefs! Laurie Raphaël, the restaurant he named after his two children, also happens to be one of the finest in Canada. Vézina works 18-hour days cooking and coaching young chefs in his Quebec City kitchen. As avid a user of the region's produce as any chef in the province, he has received kudos and recognition not only from his peers (he was voted Quebec's Chef of the Year in 1998) but also from his guests, who crowd his dining room virtually every night.

The scallops for this recipe are from Havre Saint-Pierre on the most easterly part of the St. Lawrence River's north shore, near Anticosti Island. The strawberries are from the lush gardens of Île d'Orléans. Substitutions can be made but remember that only the most flavourful would satisfy a chef like Daniel.

1/2 cup (125 mL)	canola oil
1/4	bunch fresh basil
1/2 lb. (250 g)	fresh sea scallops
1/3 cup (75 mL)	diced and hulled local strawberries
2 tbsp. (25 mL)	minced fresh chives
2 tbsp. (25 mL)	lemon juice
1/2 tsp. (2 mL)	salt
	Freshly ground pepper to taste

✦ *In a blender, purée oil and basil. Strain oil through cheesecloth. Set aside.*

✦ *Remove and discard the muscle from the side of each scallop. Finely dice scallops and toss with 1/3 cup (75 mL) basil oil, strawberries, chives and lemon juice. Season with salt and a grinding or two of pepper. Divide mixture evenly among 4 metal rings that have been set on salad plates. Refrigerate while preparing vinaigrette.*

Strawberry Vinaigrette

2	egg yolks
2 tbsp. (25 mL)	raspberry vinegar
1 tbsp. (15 mL)	Dijon mustard
6 tbsp. (90 mL)	canola oil
3 1/2 oz. (100 g)	whole local strawberries (about 3/4 cup/175 mL)
2 tbsp. (25 mL)	water (optional)

✦ *In a food processor or blender, blend egg yolks, vinegar and mustard. Add oil in a slow steady stream while motor is running. Drop in strawberries, one at a time, and keep processing till mixture is creamy, adding water if mixture becomes too thick.*

To Serve

Mesclun greens and interesting lettuces such as mizuna and tatsoi.

✦ *Gather greens into 4 bundles by holding them at the base. Insert into top of each of the four scallop tartares. Remove metal rings. Spoon vinaigrette around each tartare and drizzle with remaining basil oil. **Makes 4 servings.***

135

Coarse Country Pâté Jean Claude

James MacGuire, chef at Le Passe Partout in Montreal, serves a variety of house-made pâtés that complement his incredible breads. Four simple factors ensure the success of this spread. First, the ingredients must be absolutely fresh. Second, the fat must be chosen properly; pork jowls have a type of fat that does not melt completely and hence the pâté doesn't shrink. Third, all the ingredients must be very cold. Finally, the baking must be slow. A meat thermometer is a must!

According to James, Jean Claude Frentz, who lives just outside Paris, is one of the world's greatest charcuteriers. His recipe has been liberally adapted by MacGuire.

12 oz. (375 g)	pork jowls
10 oz. (325 g)	boned pork shoulder, trimmed of all fat
10 oz. (325 g)	very fresh pork liver
2 tsp. (10 mL)	unsalted butter
1	small onion, chopped
1	clove garlic minced
3 tbsp. (45 mL)	drained green peppercorns
2 tbsp. (25 mL)	cognac
1 tsp. (5 mL)	salt
1/4 tsp. (1 mL)	coarse black pepper
1/4 tsp. (1 mL)	sugar
1	egg
	Pork caul fat or
	very thinly sliced back fat

+ Cut pork jowls, shoulder and liver into 1-inch (2.5 cm) cubes. Transfer to a mixing bowl, cover and chill thoroughly in the freezer, without freezing, about 1 hour.

+ In a heavy saucepan, melt butter over low heat. Add onion; cover and cook 4 to 5 minutes or until transparent. Add garlic and continue to cook, covered, 30 seconds. Remove from heat, transfer to a small bowl and chill thoroughly.

+ Grind meats coarsely and return to freezer to chill again for 1 hour. Add onion mixture, green peppercorns, cognac, salt, pepper, sugar and egg. Mix thoroughly. Pour into buttered 8" x 4" (1.5 L) loaf pan.

+ Soak caul fat in cold water 5 minutes. Drape over pâté like a tablecloth. Trim off excess, leaving only 1 inch (2.5 cm) overlapping the edge of the pan. Tuck this overlap down along the sides of the meat. (Alternatively, place a layer of back fat over pâté.) In either case, cover with parchment and three layers of foil. Place pan on a double-thickness baking sheet or 2 stacked cookie sheets. Insert a meat thermometer into the centre and bake in a preheated 300°F (150°C) oven about 2 hours or until temperature registers 180°F (80°C). Remove from oven and place a heavy weight — a second loaf pan with full cans in it works well — on the centre of the covered pâté. This prevents air pockets and discoloration. Chill 12 to 24 hours before slicing. Serve with fresh crusty bread and some good homemade pickles or mustard. **Makes 12 servings.**

137

Pan-Seared Foie Gras

To understand how to handle this most delicate product, I commandeered Jean Soulard, the executive chef of the magnificent Château Frontenac in Quebec City. Foie gras must be cooked carefully. Too much heat makes it dissolve into a puddle.

In the midst of the busy Château kitchen, Jean cooked and I took notes while my mouth watered in anticipation.

This recipe is based upon a mere three ingredients: foie gras (this time from Saint-Apollinaire south of the city), cassis from Île d'Orléans and a little unsalted butter. As Soulard insists, "The nuances of the ingredients must show!" The garnish of sautéed apples or pears completes that mandate: peel 1 or 2 apples or Bosc pears and cook them slowly, covered, over medium-low heat in a little oil or butter until tender.

5 oz. (150 g)	foie gras
2 tbsp. (25 mL)	all-purpose flour
2/3 cup (150 mL)	crème de cassis
1 tbsp. (15 mL)	unsalted butter
	Salt and freshly ground pepper to taste
	Sautéed apples or
	pears as garnish (see above)

138

1. Slice foie gras into 4 3/4-inch (2 cm) pieces.

2. Place a non-stick skillet over high heat. Lightly dust the foie gras with flour.

3. When the pan is very hot, lay foie gras into it in a single layer. Sauté 30 seconds. In that time it will brown. Flip and sauté about 15 to 20 seconds longer.

4. Remove and keep warm on a heated plate. Drain off any accumulated fat. Add cassis to the pan and let it boil rapidly 15 to 20 seconds or until reduced by half.

5. Remove from heat; whisk in butter and season with salt and pepper. Place foie gras on 4 heated plates.

6. Garnish with apples or pears and spoon on sauce or squirt sauce from squeeze bottle. **Makes 4 servings.**

Foie Gras

The best foie gras is creamy in colour and nearly blood-free. The best livers weigh about 500 to 600 grams (a little over one pound) and should always be cooked over high heat. If the pan is not hot enough, the foie gras will simply melt into a golden pool. For best results, the foie gras should be sliced about 3/4 inch (2 cm) thick. Finally, a non-stick skillet is best.

Super Chef

The stamina required to be a fabulous chef is massive. But Executive Chef Jean Soulard of Le Château Frontenac has taken it to new heights. He's officially an "iron man," having competed in the Montréal Triathlon, where he swam 4 kilometres in the Olympic pool, biked 150 kilometres on the Gilles Villeneuve track, and finished with a 14 kilometre run. Training is easy for him. He simply hops on his mountain bike and visits the producers he's nurturing in Saint-Basile.

139

Baked Buckwheat Crepes with Sauteed Vegetables and Oka Cheese Sauce

At La Seigneurie des Aulnaies (founded c. 1656) in Saint-Roch-des-Aulnaies on Highway 132 west of Rivière-du-Loup, visitors to the historic site can watch grain being milled using a nineteenth-century water wheel, have a picnic and even buy some flour, including an excellent stone-ground buckwheat called *sarrasin*.

Buckwheat Crepes

2/3 cup (150 mL)	all-purpose flour
1/3 cup (75 mL)	buckwheat flour
1 3/4 cups (425 mL)	buttermilk
2	eggs
2 tbsp. (25 mL)	vegetable oil

✦ In a mixing bowl, stir together all-purpose and buckwheat flours. In a separate bowl, whisk together buttermilk, eggs and oil; whisk into flour mixture until thoroughly blended and very smooth. Cover; let stand at room temperature at least 20 minutes and up to 2 hours.

✦ Heat a lightly oiled crepe pan or small skillet over medium heat. Pour in about 1/4 cup (50 mL) batter, swirling pan to evenly coat bottom. Cook 1 to 2 minutes or until top surface appears dry. Turn and cook about 15 seconds. (Crepes will get easier to handle as you go. Adjust heat and batter thickness to produce a thin, well-browned crepe.) Stack crepes and keep warm.

To Serve

✦ Place about 1/4 cup (50 mL) filling on each of 12 crepes and roll or fold to enclose filling. Arrange in 9" x 13" (4 L) buttered baking dish. Spoon sauce evenly over crepes and bake in a preheated 350°F (180°C) oven 20 minutes or until sauce is bubbling. Serve on 6 heated plates. **Makes 6 servings.**

Filling

3 tbsp. (45 mL)	unsalted butter
1 cup (250 mL)	each cauliflower pieces, broccoli florets, corn kernels, diced celery, and sweet green and red pepper strips
1	onion, diced
1 cup (250 mL)	sour cream
1/2 tsp. (2 mL)	salt

✦ Heat butter in a large skillet or wok over medium-high heat. Add vegetables and stir-fry about 5 minutes, adding a little water to partly steam them if desired. Remove from heat; stir in sour cream and salt.

Oka Cheese Sauce

2 1/4 cups (550 mL)	milk
2 tbsp. (25 mL)	butter
2 tbsp. (25 mL)	cornstarch
1/4 tsp. (1 mL)	dry mustard
8 oz. (250 g)	Oka cheese, shredded

✦ Heat 2 cups (500 mL) of the milk and butter in a saucepan over medium heat until bubbles just begin to form around the edges. In a bowl, stir cornstarch together with remaining milk; add to hot milk. Cook, stirring, about 2 minutes or until thickened. Whisk in mustard and cheese until smooth. Keep warm.

Découvrez les Économusées

Quebec's great little museums show visitors the province's true economic heritage. Buckwheat and wheat are ground into flour at a watermill (c.1825) and a windmill (c.1836) on Île-aux-Coudres. Nearby, at La Laiterie Charlevoix at Baie Saint-Paul, artisanal cheddar cheese is made. From apple growers and beer brewers to honey makers, these small ventures preserve an important part of old Quebec.

Warm Eastern Townships Duck Salad

This salad is laced with maple syrup and topped with the duck that has made the eastern Townships' Brome Lake area so famous. Choose duck breasts that are lean but still have the skin on. Dried cranberries or fresh wild blackberries make a wonderful addition to this delicious salad.

	Mesclun, Belgian endive and Boston lettuce
2	duck breasts (3 – 4 oz./75 – 125 g each)
	Salt and freshly ground black pepper to taste
1 cup (250 mL)	canola oil
3	shallots, minced
4	Portobello mushrooms, stems removed, sliced
1/3 cup (75 mL)	Quebec cider vinegar
3 tbsp. (45 mL)	maple syrup

◆ Arrange salad greens on 8 plates. Refrigerate until needed.

◆ Score fat side of duck breasts and sprinkle with salt and pepper. Heat an oven-proof sauté pan over medium-high heat. Sear breasts, fat side down, until deep golden. Turn breasts; sear another 15 to 30 seconds and place in a preheated 450°F (220°C) oven 10 minutes.

◆ Meanwhile, heat 1/4 cup (50 mL) of the oil in a separate sauté pan over medium heat. Add shallots; cook, stirring, until transparent but not browned. Stir in mushrooms and cook 3 to 4 minutes or until beginning to soften. Stir in remaining oil, vinegar and maple syrup. Season with salt and pepper.

◆ Thinly slice duck and add to sauté pan, stirring carefully to coat slices evenly.

To Serve

◆ Arrange mushrooms and duck on salad greens. Drizzle with warm dressing. Garnish with a few more grindings of black pepper. **Makes 8 servings.**

Summer Arugula Salad with Goat's Milk Cheese, Tomato Confit and Basil Vinaigrette

Early in my career, I wrote extensively on Canada's country inns. The finest ones always mirrored the personalities of the innkeepers themselves. Auberge Hatley is one of the most gracious simply because of innkeepers Robert and Liliane Gagnon. Like the Gagnons, the inn is elegant and sophisticated yet welcoming.

Chef Alain Labrie uses Quebec's great goat's milk cheese (he recommends Tournevent) for this delicious summer salad. The basil comes from the inn's garden and the apple cider vinegar is made nearby.

In Quebec extra-virgin sunflower oil is now available. A perfect substitute in other parts of the nation would be cold-pressed canola oil from Alberta or hazelnut oil from British Columbia. Flax oil works well, too.

2	ripe tomatoes, peeled, quartered and seeded
1/4 cup (50 mL)	local honey
1	large clove garlic, minced
Pinch	cayenne
10 oz. (300 g)	plain goat's milk cheese
8	basil leaves
2 tbsp. (25 mL)	high-quality apple cider vinegar
1 cup (250 mL)	packed fresh basil leaves
1/3 cup (75 mL)	sunflower oil
	Salt and freshly ground pepper to taste

✦ Place tomatoes in a small, heavy skillet or saucepan with honey, garlic and cayenne. Cook over low heat 5 minutes. Let cool. With slotted spoon, remove any tomato pieces. Set aside. Reserve remaining liquid.

✦ Line four 2-inch (5 cm) high moulds (small soufflé dishes are perfect) with plastic wrap, leaving a 4-inch (10 cm) overlap around each dish. Divide cheese into 8. Into each mould, press 1 cheese section. Top with one-eighth of the cooked tomato pieces, 1 basil leaf, then remaining cheese, basil and tomato. Gather up plastic wrap, twist tightly and refrigerate 2 hours.

✦ Meanwhile, purée cider vinegar and 1 cup (250 mL) basil in a food processor or blender till smooth. With motor running, add oil slowly. Season with salt and pepper. Just before serving, return reserved tomato-garlic-honey to medium-low heat. Cook, uncovered, 2 to 3 minutes or until syrupy.

To Serve
Fresh young arugula leaves
Edible flowers
Slivers of red pepper

✦ Drizzle warm tomato-garlic-honey onto 4 salad plates. Arrange arugula leaves on top. Unmould goat's milk cheese terrine on top. Slice each terrine in half with a very sharp knife and spoon on basil vinaigrette and garnish with flowers and pepper. *Makes 4 servings.*

143

Cider Vinegar

One of the best-known producers of cider vinegar in Quebec is Pierre Gingras. His vinaigrerie (vinegar production house) is in Rougemont, centre for much of the apple industry. Unfiltered and cloudy, his well-balanced vinegar is aged in oak barrels, and he is one of the few producers in Canada to be able to make that claim.

Right: *Cider vinegar aging in oak barrels, Michel Jodoin's cidrerie*

Onion Soup à la Blanche de Chambly

In Chambly, the beer brewery Unibroue has set up Fourquet Forchette, an interpretation centre featuring not only the beer of Unibroue but also the early foods of Quebec. The menu is written in French, English and Amerindian. It's worth a visit just to taste the impressive selection of excellent local cheeses — at last count seventeen.

Salt onion soup lightly because cheddar cheese, in this case full-flavoured l'Ancêtre, usually contains ample salt on its own.

2 tbsp. (25 mL)	unsalted butter
4 cups (1 L)	chopped or thinly sliced cooking onions
2	large sprigs fresh thyme
2	bay leaves
4 cups (1 L)	beef stock (p. 67)
1	12-oz. (341 mL) bottle Blanche de Chambly beer
	Salt and freshly ground pepper to taste
12	thin slices crusty baguette, toasted
1 1/2 cups (375 mL)	shredded l'Ancêtre cheddar or other very high-quality old cheddar

✦ Melt butter over medium heat in a large, heavy soup pot. Add onions; cook, stirring frequently, 10 to 12 minutes or until beginning to brown. Add thyme, bay leaves, stock and Blanche de Chambly. Season lightly with salt; grind in pepper. Bring to a boil, cover and reduce heat to low. Simmer 20 to 25 minutes or until onions are very tender. Remove thyme and bay leaves.

✦ Ladle into 4 oven-proof onion soup bowls. Place 3 baguette slices on each and sprinkle generously with cheese. Broil till bubbling and melted. Carefully transfer to napkin-lined serving plates. Serve immediately. **Makes 4 servings.**

Unibroue Beers

Unibroue is a made-in-Quebec success story. It all began in 1992 with Blanche de Chambly, a white, bottle-fermented beer that features unmalted Quebec wheat and a very pale barley malt. In 1996, this beer was named "the best white in the world" by the Chicago-based Beverage Tasting Institute.

The company's multi-award-winning beers have a craft-brewed taste, and each has had a special drinking glass designed to show off the carbonation and the density of the beer. The stronger the beer, the bigger the glass. All of the beers have a Québécois story attached to their names. After Blanche de Chambly came Maudite, a mahogany brew that is rich and smooth. The name means "damned" in homage to the lumbermen of local myth who, at Christmastime, sold their souls to Satan to paddle an airborne canoe home to their families from the wilds of northern Quebec. La Fin du Monde refers to the explorers who sailed to North America, the ends of the earth. Raftman honours the courage of the lumberjacks and log drivers of Quebec's river systems. La Gaillarde's recipe dates back to the sixteenth century when women did the brewing.

145

Matane Shrimp Chowder

Tiny, sweet, Matane shrimp harvested in the icy Gulf of St. Lawrence stud this steaming, winter-rich chowder.

1/4 cup (50 mL)	unsalted butter
1 cup (250 mL)	chopped onions
1 cup (250 mL)	minced celery
1/2 tsp. (2 mL)	winter savory
4 cups (1 L)	cubed peeled potatoes
2 cups (500 mL)	fish (p. 189) or
	chicken stock (p. 66)
1 lb. (500 g)	Matane shrimp
2 cups (500 mL)	half & half cream (10%)
	Salt and freshly ground pepper or
	cayenne to taste
	Crisp bacon bits for garnish

✦ *In a large, heavy saucepan, melt butter over medium heat. Add onions, celery and savory; cover and cook 5 to 7 minutes or until soft but not browned. Stir in potatoes and stock. Bring to a boil, reduce heat and simmer until vegetables are tender. Mash the mixture coarsely. Return to heat; stir in shrimp. Bring to a boil; stir in cream. Season with salt and pepper and heat till steaming. Stir and simmer 5 minutes. Ladle into heated soup bowls and top with bacon. **Makes 8 servings.***

146

Montreal Bagels

A heap of hardwood is piled beside the bagel oven at St. Viateur Bagel Shop in Montreal. As the coals dim, a log is added. Dough is hand-twisted, boiled in sugar-water, then spread on a long, slim paddle to be skillfully placed onto the hot brick beside the fire. A quick flip and a pull, and the finished bagels are back on the paddle then out quickly into a waiting wooden bin.

Above: *Marco Sblano of St. Viateur Bagel Shop, Montreal*

Pot en Pot "Tante Yvonne" aux Fruits de Mer

Where better to cook seafood and become a champion at it than on Les Îles de la Madeleine? Yvonne Bouffard developed her prize-winning recipe in a regional competition organized in 1983 by Mme. Suzanne Leclerc, recently retired from the provincial ministry of agriculture. Pot en pot is a traditional Acadian recipe that usually contains fatty beef, chicken, pork, duck or goose with onions and potatoes. It's baked in pastry and the seasoning is most often the old Atlantic Canadian herb, savory.

Here Mme. Bouffard has replaced the meat with the seafood for which Les Îles is famous and spiked the pastry with dry mustard and parsley. The treasured family recipe was shared by her niece, Ann Cantin of Quebec City.

Seafood Filling

1 cup (250 mL)	water
2 cups (500 mL)	diced peeled potatoes
1 cup (250 mL)	chopped celery
1	onion, chopped
1	carrot, coarsely grated
1/4 cup (50 mL)	shallots or green onion, chopped
1 tsp. (5 mL)	fish seasoning*
1 lb. (500 g)	small bay scallops
1 lb. (500 g)	medium-large raw shrimp,
	peeled (about 2 cups/500 mL)
1 lb. (500 g)	lobster meat, cut in chunks
	(about 2 cups/500 mL)
	Salt and freshly ground pepper to taste
1/2 cup (125 mL)	unsalted butter
1	12 oz. (385 mL) can evaporated milk or
	1 1/2 cups (375 mL) half & half cream
	(10%)
1/4 cup (50 mL)	cornstarch

Biscuit Dough

4 cups (1 L)	all-purpose flour
2 1/2 tbsp. (35 mL)	baking powder
2 tsp. (10 mL)	salt
2 tsp. (10 mL)	dry mustard
2 tsp. (10 mL)	chopped fresh parsley
2/3 cup (150 mL)	lard
1 3/4 cups (425 mL)	milk

✦ *In a large saucepan, combine water, potatoes, celery, onion, carrot, shallots and fish seasoning. Bring to a boil, cover and simmer 5 minutes. Add scallops, shrimp and lobster meat. Cover and continue to cook 5 minutes. Season with salt and pepper. Stir in butter and evaporated milk, stirring till butter melts.*

✦ *Mix cornstarch with a little cold water until smooth. Stir into seafood mixture and bring to a boil, stirring constantly. Cover and set aside while preparing crust.*

✦ *In a large mixing bowl, stir together flour, baking powder, salt, mustard and parsley. Cut in lard with a pastry blender till mixture resembles coarse meal. Add milk all at once, stirring gently with a fork until a soft dough is formed. Press dough together to form a ball. Divide dough into 2 portions, approximately 2/3 and 1/3 of the dough. Cover small portion and save for top crust.*

✦ *Roll out larger portion on a floured surface until it measures 17" x 13" (43 x 33 cm) about 1/4-inch (5 mm) thick. Fit dough into a 9" x 13" (4 L) casserole or lasagna dish. Press dough out to cover bottom and at least 2 1/2 inches (6 cm) up the sides of the pan. Pour in filling. Brush edge with water. Roll remaining dough to fit top of dish. Place over filling, sealing edges with a fork. If desired, decorate top with 3 small fish cut from the remaining dough. Prick top crust with a fork to simulate waves and to let steam escape. Bake in a preheated 350°F (180°C) oven 30 to 40 minutes or until pastry is golden brown. Let stand 10 minutes before serving. Makes 10 to 12 servings.*

* Fish seasoning may be replaced with 1 tsp. (5 mL) dried dill and 1/4 tsp. (1 mL) dried thyme.

Magdalen Islands

For a brief summer moment, Les Îles de la Madeleine, sandy slashes in the cold Gulf of St. Lawrence, shed their winter isolation and frolic in the sun. Every year there seems to be a new colour trend in house paint... raspberry red and blueberry blue are currently hot. For centuries Les Madelinots have lived with, spoken with and worshipped the sea. From Basque sailors and Jacques Cartier's earliest explorations to the ultra-fast car ferries and airline shuttles of today, the islands have been the destinations for generations of visitors, be they shipwrecked sailors, Acadians fleeing deportation or modern tourists in search of the best beaches and much of the most interesting food in Atlantic Canada. Originally an attempt at self-sufficiency (a.k.a. survival), la cuisine régionale is today nurtured by a handful of utterly devoted chefs. Local ingredients are the foundation. Here you'll find mackerel and snow crab; shark and seal; lobster and tiny cultured scallops with their roe, in the French fashion. In the autumn there are golden chanterelles by the bushel basket and tiny wild cranberries that locals make into pie and serve at island celebrations with custard sauce after a meal of cod cakes.

A cluster of restaurants on Les Îles de la Madeleine is worth noting. At Au Vieux Couvent, moules au poivre vert are creamy, messy and fabulous. At Le Table de Roy, Johanne Vigneault works miracles with seafood. For the adventurous, Auberge Chez Denis à François makes a ragout of seal with the islands' golden chanterelles. At La Marée Haute, the seasonal carte will contain the islands' salted lamb, lumpfish caviar, sea snails en brochette, mussels and island-harvested berries, including golden raspberries, which are made into marmalade.

147

Fillets of Trout with Ginger-Perfumed Carrot Sauce

Anne Desjardins of L'Eau à la Bouche in Sainte-Adèle apologized for the simplicity of this full-flavoured dish.

In the summer Anne's foragers bring her wild ginger, which she uses in this recipe. She suggests that if you have a supply you will need to use more than called for in this recipe because wild ginger is milder than commercial. She invented the seasoning and drying of the scaled trout skin. She cuts the skin into slices or rectangles and lays them on a parchment-lined baking sheet before sprinkling with salt and lightly dusting with cayenne. It is then baked, turned once with tongs, in a preheated 375°F (190°C) oven 7 to 10 minutes or until crisp and golden. The skins shrink to half their size during the drying. Store them in a tightly covered container.

When I arrived with a bottle of cold-pressed flax oil from Alberta, Anne tasted it and decided that it would be a perfect accompaniment for the delicate spring-raised trout.

Ginger-Perfumed Carrot Sauce

1/2 cup (125 mL)	carrot juice
1/2 cup (125 mL)	dry white wine
1	shallot, coarsely chopped
1	1-inch (2.5 cm) piece fresh ginger, peeled and sliced
1 tbsp. (15 mL)	whipping cream (35%)
	Salt to taste
	Lemon juice (optional)

✦ Combine carrot juice and wine in a small saucepan. Bring to a boil over high heat. Add shallot and ginger: reduce heat and cook, uncovered, until reduced by half. Strain into another small saucepan, pressing on solids. Whisk in cream and salt. Taste and add a few drops of lemon juice if needed. Keep sauce warm.

Leeks

4 cups (1 L)	julienned leeks
1 tbsp. (15 mL)	flax oil
1 tbsp. (15 mL)	water
1/2 tsp. (2 mL)	salt

✦ In a large saucepan or skillet, toss leeks with flax oil, water and salt. Cook, stirring often, over medium heat till wilted but still green. Keep warm.

Trout

4	rainbow trout fillets, skinned
1 tsp. (5 mL)	salt
1 tbsp. (15 mL)	grated fresh ginger
1 tbsp. (15 mL)	finely minced chives or green onions
1 tbsp. (15 mL)	lemon juice

✦ Lay the trout, skinned side up, on a work surface. Sprinkle with salt, ginger, chives and lemon juice. Roll up loosely from the widest end. Allow some of the tail end of the fillet to remain unrolled to make standing it up easier. Place in a steamer over boiling water. Cover and cook 4 minutes or until the fish is opaque.

To Serve
Flax oil

✦ Place a mound of leeks in the middle of 4 heated plates. Top with trout and drizzle with Ginger-Perfumed Carrot Sauce and additional flax oil. **Makes 4 servings.**

L'eau à la Bouche

At L'eau à la Bouche in Sainte-Adèle, Anne Desjardins and Pierre Audette were near enough to Montreal to survive financially, far enough away to follow their personal visions. Chef Desjardins is one of the best interpreters of the new provincial cuisine. She thoughtfully creates dishes with the traditional ingredients of old Quebec. Comfort food never tasted so good. A slim Gaspé salmon scallop on a little puddle of fennel-scented butter sauce, quail breasts from the lower Laurentians atop a wintry mixture of cabbage and bacon, a colourful confit of red and yellow peppers spooned over thin slices of spiced farm-raised goose, and, of course, the foie gras, fresh and fatty and perfect. Each meal culminates with a selection of well-aged French and Quebec cheeses to spread on Anne's savoury nut bread.

Rack of Pork Stuffed with Apples and Roasted Hazelnuts

Hovey Manor's Chef Roland Ménard creates entire menus around the ingredients of L'Estrie, or the Eastern Townships. He buys his apple cider from the abbey at Saint-Benoît-du-Lac. If you cannot purchase Fine Sève, the maple eau-de-vie, substitute Calvados in the sauce.

3 lb. (1.5 kg)	rack of pork (4 – 6 bones)

Maple Marinade

1	green onion, finely chopped
1/2	small carrot, diced
1	clove garlic, minced
1/3 cup (75 mL)	maple syrup
1/3 cup (75 mL)	Dijon mustard
1	sprig fresh thyme, chopped
1/2	sprig fresh rosemary, chopped
1/2 tsp. (2 mL)	freshly ground black pepper

Apple Stuffing

1	large apple, peeled and diced
1/2 tsp. (2 mL)	cinnamon
1/2 cup (125 mL)	toasted hazelnuts, chopped (p. 21)
1/4 cup (50 mL)	finely diced red onion
1/4 cup (50 mL)	maple syrup
3 tbsp. (45 mL)	apple cider
	Salt and freshly ground black pepper to taste

Cider Sauce

1 tsp. (5 mL)	vegetable oil
1/2	red onion, chopped
1	clove garlic, crushed
1/4 cup (50 mL)	Fine Sève
1/2 cup (125 mL)	apple cider
1 1/4 cups (300 mL)	chicken stock (p. 66)
1 tsp. (5 mL)	tomato paste
	Fresh thyme
	Salt and freshly ground black pepper to taste

✦ Place pork roast in a shallow dish. In a bowl, combine green onion, carrot, garlic, maple syrup, mustard, thyme, rosemary and pepper. Spread marinade over roast. Cover and refrigerate at least 4 hours, turning occasionally.

✦ To prepare stuffing, combine apple, cinnamon, hazelnuts, onion, syrup and cider. Season with salt and pepper.

✦ Drain meat. With a very sharp knife, make an incision through the meatiest part of the roast. With your fingers, enlarge the incision until it is 2 inches (5 cm) in diameter. Stuff with apple mixture.

✦ Place roast on a rack in a small roasting pan lined with foil (the marinade and filling may stick to the pan during cooking). Roast in a preheated 400°F (200°C) oven 60 minutes or until meat thermometer inserted in centre of meat reads 165°F (72°C).

✦ Meanwhile, prepare sauce. Heat oil in a small saucepan over medium heat. Add onion and garlic; cook about 2 minutes or until just softening. Stir in Fine Sève, cider, stock, tomato paste and thyme. Bring to a boil, reduce heat and simmer, uncovered, about 20 minutes or until slightly thickened. Strain. Season with salt and pepper. Serve thick slices of pork (1 bone per serving) with Cider Sauce. Garnish with fresh thyme.

Makes 4 to 6 servings.

151

Maple vinegar *is becoming a staple in many commercial kitchens. It is magnificent in salad dressings with a bit of dry or Dijon mustard, a few fresh herbs, some canola oil, freshly ground black pepper and a touch of salt. Make your own by stirring together 1 cup (250 mL) cider vinegar and 1/2 cup (125 mL) maple syrup. Refrigerate until needed.*

Blackcurrants

When he saw the wild grapes that prolifer-ated on what we now know as l'Île d'Orléans, Jacques Cartier called it Île de Bacchus. The garden of Quebec City, it's an agricultural island where the farmers were once called les poireaux, or leek-pickers. Acres of leeks still grow there, but it wasn't for them or the wild asparagus or the apples or the great roadside snack bars that I came. Just over the bridge is the tiny blackcurrant farm of Bernard Monna. The crème de cassis that Monna produces is filled with the intense berry flavour that only a purist can create. No added concentrates here. All Monna farms is blackcurrants. Although he's also a sculptor and a salmon fisher, this is his heritage. His great-great-grandfather was a liquorist in France, making, among others, crème de menthe. From his 2.5 hectares (6 acres) he has the capacity to pro-duce 10,000 bottles. Some is cassis madérisé, both filtered and unfiltered, perfect with a blue cheese like Saint-Benoît's Ermite. And, of course, there's his crème de cassis, thick and fruity and fabulous.

Roasted Duck Breast with Peppered Pears and Blackcurrant Sauce

When blackcurrants are in season they are widely available in Quebec's great farmers' markets. Store them by spreading a single layer on a baking sheet and freezing overnight. When frozen, bag them tightly and return to freezer. You'll be able to use them all winter long.

5 tbsp. (75 mL)	cold unsalted butter
1	shallot, minced
1 cup (250 mL)	dry red wine
1 1/2 cups (375 mL)	beef stock (p. 67)
	Salt and freshly ground black pepper to taste
1 cup (250 mL)	blackcurrants
2 tbsp. (25 mL)	brandy
3	ripe Bosc pears, peeled, halved and cored
1/4 tsp. (1 mL)	freshly ground black pepper
6	boneless duck breasts

✦ *Melt 2 tbsp. (25 mL) of the butter in a small saucepan over medium heat. Add shallot; cook, stirring, 3 minutes or until soft-ened. Pour in wine; bring to a boil and reduce by half. Add beef stock. Continue to boil until reduced by one-third. Season with salt and pepper. Gently stir in blackcurrants; simmer 7 minutes or until berries are tender. Pass sauce through a fine sieve to remove seeds. Return to saucepan over low heat. Cut remaining butter into chunks and whisk into sauce a little at a time. Whisk in brandy. Keep warm.*

✦ *Sprinkle pears with pepper and place in a steamer over boiling water; steam 7 minutes or until very tender.*

✦ *In a large oven-proof skillet over medium-high heat, brown duck breasts on both sides. Roast in a preheated 400°F (200°C) oven, skin side down, about 10 minutes or until just rare.*

To Serve
Blackcurrants

✦ *Slice duck breasts thinly and fan them out on 6 plates. Accompany each serving with 1 pear half and surround with Blackcurrant Sauce. Garnish with fresh blackcurrants.*
Makes 6 servings.

Pork Tenderloin in Charlevoix Blueberry Sauce

There are a few meals that will never fade in my memory. One such occurred when my second son, Brad (then a mere twelve years old), and I dined at La Pinsonnière, a fine inn in Charlevoix. We had a window seat that overlooked the St. Lawrence, quite wide at this point. The evening mist rolled in as the sunset illuminated the waters. Candles lit the room, which then, as now, was filled with fine Quebec art. It was a simple moment where all was right with the world. This recipe is one adapted from that menu, now well over a decade old but still absolutely delicious!

4	pork tenderloins (about 3/4 lb./375 g each)
1 tbsp. (15 mL)	canola oil
1	onion, finely chopped
3	cloves garlic, halved
1/2 cup (125 mL)	dry white wine
1 cup (250 mL)	chicken stock (p. 66)
1/4 cup (50 mL)	blueberry liqueur or cassis
	Bouquet garni (made of 1 thyme sprig, 1 bay leaf, celery leaves and 3 peppercorns)
1 1/2 cups (375 mL)	blueberries
1/2 cup (125 mL)	whipping cream (35%)
	Salt and freshly ground black pepper to taste

✦ In a large, heavy oven-proof skillet over medium-high heat, sear tenderloins on all sides. Roast in a preheated 400°F (200°C) oven about 30 minutes or until meat is barely pink inside. Place on a platter; cover with foil and keep warm.

✦ In a skillet, heat oil over medium heat. Add onion; cook about 4 minutes or until softened. Stir in garlic; cook 30 seconds. Deglaze pan with wine, stirring until wine is almost evaporated. Stir in stock, blueberry liqueur and bouquet garni. Bring to a boil, reduce heat and simmer 5 minutes or until slightly reduced. Stir in blueberries; simmer another 5 minutes.

✦ In a blender, purée sauce; return to saucepan. Stir in whipping cream, salt and pepper. Bring just to a boil before serving.

To Serve

Blueberries

✦ Slice tenderloins into rounds. Place a pool of sauce on 6 to 8 plates and fan pork tenderloins out on sauce. Garnish with fresh blueberries. **Makes 6 to 8 servings.**

153

Pâté à la Viande

There are as many versions of tourtière as there are cooks in Quebec. It's just one of those great old family traditions. In the urban areas of the province, tourtière means ground pork and spices such as cinnamon and cloves. The filling is cooked before being transferred into an unbaked pie shell. In the country, however, this dish is called pâté à la viande, and it is a deep-dish pastry-lined casserole filled with raw meats and potatoes, sometimes combined the night before in order to blend the flavours, and then slowly baked for 6 to 7 hours.

According to Micheline Mongrain-Dontigny, the province's expert on the old foods of Quebec, these huge tourtières are feast dishes... the basis of both the Christmas meals and large parties where they are truly the focal point. In her book *Traditional Québec Cooking: A Treasure of Heirloom Recipes*, (Les Editions La Bonne Recette, 1995), the first to be translated into English, she writes lovingly and definitively on the roots of the provincial cuisine.

An observation: This appears to be a pie that would serve many. It's not. When I originally thought that it would feed six or even eight, it served four! Nevertheless, it is one of the most delicious I've ever tasted.

1 lb. (500 g)	ground lean boneless pork shoulder
1	clove garlic, minced
1	medium potato, peeled
1 cup (250 mL)	boiling water
1/2 tsp. (2 mL)	salt
1/4 tsp. (1 mL)	freshly ground black pepper
1/4 tsp. (1 mL)	dry mustard
1/4 tsp. (1 mL)	ground cloves
1/4 tsp (1 mL)	cinnamon
	Dry bread crumbs or
	cold water, as needed
	Pastry for double-crust
	9-inch (23 cm) pie shell (p. 81)
	Eggwash (p. 23)

✦ In a medium saucepan, combine pork, garlic, whole potato, boiling water, salt, pepper, mustard, cloves and cinnamon. Cover and bring to a boil, reduce heat and simmer 1 hour or until potato is cooked. Remove potato with slotted spoon and mash thoroughly. Stir potato into meat mixture. Taste and adjust seasoning. If there is too much liquid stir in dry bread crumbs until mixture has the consistency of thick spaghetti sauce. If the mixture is too dry, add water. Remove from heat, cover and cool completely. The mixture can be refrigerated up to 2 days.

✦ Pour meat mixture into pie shell. Brush edge of shell with eggwash and cover with top crust, sealing well. Crimp edges and brush with eggwash. With a sharp knife, cut several slits in the top crust. Bake in a preheated 400°F (200°C) oven 15 minutes; reduce heat to 350°F (180°C) and bake an additional 25 to 30 minutes or until crust is golden and filling is bubbling through the slits. **Makes 4 servings.**

Award-Winning Beer

The name McAuslan is synonymous with great beer. Ellen Bounsall, one of North America's few female brewmasters, presides over the creation of her award winners. Some, like her pumpkin ale, spiced and tasting of autumn, are seasonal. In the summer she makes one of the nicest raspberry beers I've tasted. But it's her Oatmeal Stout that has won kudos and awards, including the platinum medal at the World Beer Championships.

Tourtière du Saguenay

According to Micheline Mongrain-Dontigny, this is the real tourtière. There is no better dish than this one after a day of snowmobiling or skiing. It must be baked slowly, and as it browns and bubbles it perfumes the entire house. The absolute best baking dish is an old cast-iron Dutch oven. But failing that just make sure that whatever casserole you use it is at least 4 inches (8 cm) deep and will hold about 12 – 14 cups (3 – 3.5 mL) of filling. Traditionally lard pastry is used. The amount of pastry used in this recipe is equivalent to that used to line three 9-inch (23 cm) pie shells. Roll two-thirds for the bottom crust and the remaining pastry and trimmings for the top.

Tourtière is always served with beet pickles and a variety of relishes. I serve it with Valerie's Version of Lady Ashburnham's Pickles (p. 205), a really wonderful old-fashioned cucumber relish.

1 lb. (500 g)	lean pork shoulder
1 lb. (500 g)	beef, venison or boned wild fowl meat
1 lb. (500 g)	veal shoulder or boneless chicken
6	medium onions, chopped
1 tsp. (15 mL)	salt
1 tsp. (1 mL)	freshly ground pepper
4	large potatoes, peeled
	Pastry for three 9-inch (23 cm) pie shells (p. 81).
	Eggwash (p. 23)

◆ Chop the meats into 1/2-inch (1 cm) cubes. Combine them in a large bowl with onions, salt and pepper. Mix thoroughly with your hands. Cover with plastic wrap and refrigerate overnight.

◆ Dice potatoes into 1/4-inch (5 mm) cubes and transfer to a medium bowl. Add 4 – 6 cups (1 – 1.5 L) of cold water. Cover with plastic wrap and refrigerate.

◆ The next morning, line the baking dish with pastry. Drain potatoes, reserving the water, and combine with meat mixture. Transfer to baking dish and add enough of the reserved potato water, about 3 cups (750 mL), to bring it up to the top of the meat, adding additional cold water if needed.

◆ Brush outer edge of pastry with eggwash and cover with top crust; seal. In the centre cut a 2-inch (5 cm) hole and insert a small "chimney" of foil; seal the base with eggwash and a bit of the pastry trimming. Brush entire surface with eggwash. Bake in a preheated 350°F (180°C) oven 1 hour; reduce heat to 250°F (120°C) and continue to bake for 6 to 8 hours or until richly golden brown. Check from time to time during baking to make sure that the meat is not too dry and that the juices can be seen in the foil chimney. If not, add a little hot water through the hole. **Makes 10 to 12 servings.**

155

Right: *Ducks at Le Canard Goulu, St.-Apollinaire, southwest of Quebec City*

Braised Quebec Lamb Shanks with White Beans

Quebec has four distinct lamb-raising regions — l'Estrie (Eastern Townships), the Charlevoix, Bas-Saint Laurent, including Kamouraska, and Mauricie-Bois-Francs, a huge area halfway between Montreal and Quebec City on the north shore of the St. Lawrence. Each region claims different tastes. Some, like Charlevoix, boasts a slightly salty flavour because the lambs graze in the tidal region of the lower St. Lawrence River.

Whichever lamb you use, this rustic, bistro-style dish is best served with garlic-infused mashed potatoes, baked root vegetables and roasted squash. Although it calls for beef stock, lamb bones may be substituted in the Beef Stock recipe on p. 67.

156

1 cup (250 mL)	dried white beans
6	Quebec lamb shanks
	Salt and freshly ground pepper to taste
2 tbsp. (25 mL)	canola oil
4	cloves garlic
1 cup (250 mL)	finely diced carrots
1/2 cup (125 mL)	diced onion
1/2 cup (125 mL)	diced celery
2 tbsp. (25 mL)	chopped fresh rosemary
1	bay leaf
1 tbsp. (15 mL)	minced fresh thyme
1/4 cup (50 mL)	tomato paste
1 cup (250 mL)	dry red wine
4 cups (1 L)	beef stock (p. 67)

✦ Soak beans in 8 cups (2 L) cold water 8 to 10 hours or overnight. Drain beans, place in a large saucepan, and cover with 8 cups (2 L) cold water. Bring to a boil, reduce heat to low, cover and simmer 30 minutes. Drain beans and set aside.

✦ Season the lamb lightly with salt and pepper. Heat oil in a large roasting pan over high heat. Brown lamb on all sides. Set lamb aside. Drain off all but 1 tbsp. (15 mL) fat. Stir in garlic, carrots, onion and celery. Cook, stirring constantly, 3 to 5 minutes or until slightly softened. Add beans, herbs, tomato paste and wine. Bring to a boil, whisking constantly. Add beef stock. Add lamb shanks in a single layer. Return to a boil.

✦ Roast, covered, in a preheated 350°F (180°C) oven 1 1/2 hours. Uncover and continue to roast an additional 1 1/2 hours or until meat is very tender and richly browned. Discard bay leaf. Serve in heated rimmed soup bowls, ladling sauce over shanks. *Makes 6 servings.*

Food Festivals

Across the entire region, throughout the year Quebecers celebrate food, wine and beer. The festivals begin in March with Le festival Beauceron de l'érable in Saint-Georges in the Beauce region and Le salon des vins, bières et spiritueux de Montréal, and continue with another Festival de l'érable in the region Mauricie-Bois-Francs in May. In June Le Mondial de la bière takes place in old Montreal, while in Matane on Le Gaspésie they celebrate les crevettes (shrimp). By July, blueberry season is in full swing, and in Saguenay-Lac-Saint-Jean the small berry comes into its own at the award-winning Festival du bleuet de Mistassini. In October, Le festival de la galette de sarrasin at Louiseville allows Quebecers to taste a part of their culinary history. Finally, in Bromont, and this may be my personal favourite, there is Le festival internationale du canard — or how many ways are there to cook a duck?

Roast Free-Range Capon with Lavender Flower and Thyme Dusting

Reminiscent of the famous French herb mixture from Provence, this seasoning mixture will perfume your kitchen as the chicken roasts to golden perfection.

1	capon (8 lb./3.5 kg)
4 – 5	sprigs fresh thyme
1 tsp. (5 mL)	salt
1 tbsp. (15 mL)	canola oil
1 tbsp. (15 mL)	dried lavender flowers
1 tsp. (5 mL)	dried thyme
1/2 tsp. (2 mL)	crushed black peppercorns

✦ Stuff the capon with the thyme sprigs and half the salt. Truss the bird loosely. Rub capon with canola oil and sprinkle with lavender, thyme, pepper and remaining salt. Place in a roasting pan, breast down. Roast in a preheated 425°F (220°C) oven 15 minutes. Turn breast up and continue to roast 10 minutes. Reduce heat to 350°F (180°C) and roast 2 1/4 hours. The skin will be golden brown. Cover pan with tea towel and let rest 15 to 20 minutes before carving. Serve with garlic mashed potatoes or Barley Risotto (p. 183). **Makes 6 to 8 servings.**

Lac St.-Jean Blueberry-Honeyed Carrots

I first bought Lac St.-Jean wild blueberry blossom honey at Le Marché les Halles du Vieux Port, the fabulous farmers' market in Quebec City. This honey is slightly darker in colour than clover honey but not as brown as buckwheat.

4 cups (1 L)	sliced carrots
2 tbsp. (25 mL)	unsalted butter
2 tbsp. (25 mL)	blueberry honey
1/2 tsp. (2 mL)	cinnamon
1/2 tsp. (2 mL)	vanilla

✦ Steam carrots about 6 to 8 minutes or until tender-crisp. Drain, reserving 2 tbsp. (25 mL) cooking liquid. Return carrots and reserved liquid to low heat; stir in butter, honey, cinnamon and vanilla. Cover and keep warm till serving. **Makes 8 servings.**

Great Bread

Quebec City's Eric Bouderon is one of the finest bread bakers in Canada. He studied artisanal bread baking in France at the same school as the other renowned Quebec bread guru, James MacGuire, and his tiny sandwich shop and bakery is a must for anyone who adores sourdough. Try the walnut bread or the loaves infused with herbes de Provence. His breads can be found throughout the region in specialty markets and on the tables of the finest restaurants.

Les Éboulements

When I first arrived at Les Éboulements, east of Quebec City, the sun had tipped westward, turning the fields copper. Jean LeBlond, a broadcaster-turned-newspaper-owner-turned-gardener, has connected with many of the region's top chefs. He now grows a list of crops that could be considered a who's who of the veggie world in Quebec. Tiny baby fennel (he gets four crops a year), blue potatoes, a field full of celeriac, perfect miniature sweet corn and a greenhouse of Thai, habanero and Bolivian rainbow peppers. His fields, protected by hedgerows of wild fruit trees and watered by a cress-filled stream, are flourishing.

Pain aux raisins.

Pain de seigle.

e blé ent

Pain rustique.

Buckwheat and Buttermilk Bread

Buckwheat flour, or *sarrasin* as it is known in Quebec, was one of the staples of early pioneer life. The grain, tough and hardy, was ground at local mills and then made into crepes and bread. This updated recipe makes absolutely delicious bread that goes well with some of the province's fabulous cheeses. It is particularly delicious toasted. Stone-ground whole-wheat flour makes a slightly coarser but even more flavourful bread. I always use Fermipan yeast in this recipe.

2 cups (500 mL)	all-purpose or white bread flour
1/4 cup (50 mL)	brown sugar
2 tbsp. (25 mL)	Fermipan yeast
1 tbsp. (15 mL)	salt
2	eggs, beaten
1 1/2 cups (375 mL)	very warm water
	(120 – 130°F/50 – 55°C)
1 cup (250 mL)	buttermilk, at room temperature
1/3 cup (75 mL)	canola oil
2 1/2 cups (625 mL)	coarsely chopped dried fruits
	(apricots, plums and apples)
1 1/2 cups (375 mL)	buckwheat flour
1 cup (250 mL)	whole walnuts
4 – 4 1/2 cups	whole-wheat flour
(1 – 1.125 L)	

✦ In a large mixing bowl, combine all-purpose flour, sugar, yeast and salt. In a separate bowl, whisk together eggs, water, buttermilk and oil. Add to dry ingredients and beat with an electric mixer or whisk 2 minutes. Stir in fruits, buckwheat flour and walnuts, combining thoroughly. Gradually beat in whole-wheat flour, a cupful at a time, to make a soft dough. Turn out onto a floured surface and knead, working in additional all-purpose flour if needed, till dough is smooth, elastic and no longer sticky, about 10 minutes. Place in oiled bowl, turning to coat all sides. Cover with lightly greased waxed paper and a tea towel. Let rise at room temperature until doubled, 1 1/2 to 2 hours.

✦ Punch down and cut in half. Cover and let rest 10 minutes. Shape into 2 round loaves and place on lightly oiled or parchment-lined baking sheets. Cover and allow to rise again until doubled, 1 to 1 1/2 hours. Bake in a preheated 350°F (180°C) oven 25 to 35 minutes. Baking time may vary with shape of loaves. Bake till loaves are deep golden brown and sound hollow when tapped. Cool on a rack. **Makes 2 loaves.**

Left: *Luc Mailloux and Sarah Tristan*

Lechevalier Mailloux Cheese

The region of Portneuf, west of Quebec City, is rural Quebec in the finest sense. The sun seemed barely over the horizon when we pulled into the driveway of La Ferme Piluma, home of Luc Mailloux and Sarah Tristan and the soon-to-be-famous Lechevalier Mailloux cheese (judged in 1998 to be the finest in the nation by the Dairy Farmers of Canada), and two other lait cru or unpasteurized cheeses, Saint-Basile de Portneuf and Sarah Brizou. (See photo p. 132) These are handmade cheeses in the truest sense. The milk is never chilled and it is gravity fed from milking parlour to the fromagerie. At one point in the production each cheese must be turned, day and night, every 30 minutes.

159

Mead

Hydromel and the more commonly heard vin de miel are French for "mead." Honey is mixed with spring water, acidified, then fermented before being aged in barrels. Finally it is filtered through diatomaceous earth and bottled. In the summertime, the Musée de l'abeille (honey museum) in Chateau-Richer (Route 138) offers a tasting of their full product line. They produce about 20,000 bottles of hydromel yearly. Their house-made ice creams are amazing: honey vanilla, wild honey with caramel and a delicious wild blueberry sorbet. When I visited, they were baking exquisite desserts and pastries. My favourite? Peach Danish with honey cream. And chocolates? Try the honey-roasted almond chocolate bark!

Rustic White Bread with Local Honey

Fred Lallemand left his native Alsace and immigrated to Montreal after the Franco-Prussian war of 1870–71. He set up business refining vegetable oils into shortening. For a brief time he moved to New York but came back to Montreal to found the company that still bears his name. He began to produce bakers' yeast in 1923 and today the company ships the Fermipan-brand yeast all over the world.

3 cups (750 mL)	very warm water (120 – 130°F/50 – 55°C)
2	eggs
1/3 cup (75 mL)	liquid honey
1 tbsp. (15 mL)	salt
6 – 7 cups (1.5 – 1.75 L)	all-purpose or white bread flour
2 tbsp. (25 mL)	Fermipan or bakers' yeast

✦ *In a large mixing bowl, whisk together water, eggs, honey and salt. Beat in 2 cups (500 mL) of the flour. Add yeast and continue to beat 1 to 2 minutes. Stir in the remaining flour, a cupful at a time, until a soft dough forms. Turn dough out onto a floured surface; knead 5 minutes or until smooth and elastic. Cover with a tea towel and let rise at room temperature until doubled, about 1 1/2 hours. Punch down and let rest 15 minutes. Punch down again, cut into thirds and shape into loaves. Place in greased loaf pans; cover and let rise until doubled, about 1 1/4 hours. Bake in a preheated 375°F (190°C) oven 25 to 30 minutes or until richly golden brown. Cool on racks. **Makes 3 loaves.***

Top Wines

Being on the Wine Spectator's Grand Award list for a decade is a feat in itself. But being the only restaurant that has garnered such a long-standing honour in all of Canada and being located, not in a major urban area but rather in a tiny village in the Laurentian mountains of Quebec an hour north of Montreal, is indeed impressive. "I used to know the winemakers by their labels," says Dr. Champlain Charest, owner/dream-meister of Bistro Champlain. "Now they come to me." And they do! In droves. From all over France, Italy, California and Canada, winemakers and vineyard owners make the pilgrimage to Charest's cellar in Sainte-Marguerite-du-Lac-Masson, to "the shrine" as Quebec's deputy premier, Bernard Landry, calls it. The 95-page wine list at Bistro Champlain represents 575 different classifications and 2,450 wines spread over 50 vintages.

Bistro Champlain

Bistro Champlain is in an 1864 general store in Sainte-Marguerite-du-Lac-Masson. Shelves that once sagged with dusty hardware and tinned goods have been replaced by the fabulous canvases of Jean-Paul Riopelle, Champlain Charest's great friend and internationally acclaimed Canadian painter. Two walls of the wine cellar at Bistro Champlain are dedicated to Pétrus and D'Yquem, among the most expensive, rare wines of the world. The balance of the cellar is filled primarily with Italian and Californian wines, with a small Canadian collection. Also aging gracefully are about 3,000 bottles of port. In 1997 Champlain opened the world's first cellar devoted solely to large-format bottles. The cave in a newly dug section beneath the bistro is filled with some of the world's finest, the backbone being more than a hundred bottles from Domaine Romanée-Conti in France. And, naturally, a Riopelle fills the end wall with colour.

In the casual atmosphere of the bistro, diners revel in fresh market cuisine. A lightly smoked trout salad is crowned with lamb's lettuce and dribbled with almond oil; foie gras is poached in orange-laced muscat wine; a thick caribou filet is grilled and served with a port sauce and shiitake mushrooms. Such cheeses as Oka, St. Agur, Ami du Chambertin, St. Nectaire and Ste. Honoré are available as a prelude to dessert or as a grand finale on their own.

161

Maple Syrup Crème Brûlée

This is the Bistro Champlain's ultimate comfort food. Laurentian maple syrup sweetens the rich custard, and maple sugar is burned on top. If you have a blowtorch, use it (I bought one especially for this recipe), but otherwise a preheated broiler will do — although the results are not quite so spectacular. If you don't have a source of maple sugar, substitute brown sugar. Spread it on a small baking pan and dry it in a warm oven before using.

1/2	vanilla bean or
	1 tsp. (5 mL) vanilla
2 cups (500 mL)	whipping cream (35%)
6	egg yolks
1/4 cup (50 mL)	maple syrup
1/4 cup (50 mL)	maple sugar
	Fresh seasonal fruit and
	mint leaves for garnish

✦ Slit vanilla bean lengthwise and scrape out seeds. Reserve bean for other uses. Combine seeds (or vanilla) and cream in a small saucepan. Heat gently till steaming, stirring frequently. Cool 10 minutes. Strain to remove seeds.

✦ In a medium bowl, whisk egg yolks and maple syrup until thoroughly blended. Stir in warm cream. Divide custard among eight 1/2-cup (125 mL) ramekins. Line a large baking pan with a paper towel or a dishcloth. Arrange ramekins on top. Add enough very hot water to come halfway up the sides of the ramekins. Bake in a preheated 300°F (150°C) oven 35 minutes or until custard is set but still creamy. Do not let the water boil. Refrigerate custards until chilled.

✦ Up to 1 hour before serving, sprinkle custards with maple sugar. Carefully broil or blowtorch until sugar is melted and darkly coloured. Watch to prevent scorching. Garnish with fresh fruit and fresh mint leaves. Serve immediately on a napkin-lined dessert plate. **Makes 8 servings.**

Above left: *Bistro Champlain wine cellar*
Above right: *Champlain Charest, Bistro Champlain*

Ultimate Maple Syrup Pie

This historical French-Canadian dessert was part of the food culture of les colons (settlers) and was known as sugar pie, tarte au sucre.

2	eggs
1 cup (250 mL)	brown sugar
1 cup (250 mL)	whipping cream (35%)
1/2 cup (125 mL)	maple syrup
1/2 tsp. (2 mL)	vanilla
1	9-inch (23 cm) pie shell (p. 81), baked and cooled Lightly sweetened whipped cream and/or toasted walnuts for garnish

✦ In a medium bowl, beat eggs lightly. Whisk in brown sugar, cream, maple syrup and vanilla. Beat long enough to dissolve the sugar crystals. Pour filling into pie shell and bake in a preheated 350°F (180°C) oven 40 to 45 minutes or until centre is just becoming firm. Let cool before serving. Serve topped with whipped cream and sprinkled with toasted walnuts. **Makes 8 servings.**

Wild Raspberry Maple Ice Cream

Throughout L'Estrie (the Eastern Townships) wild raspberries abound. Combine them with some of the finest maple syrup in the province and you have a dessert that reflects the tastes of the region with perfect simplicity.

4 cups (1 L)	raspberries (fresh or frozen and thawed)
2	eggs
1/2 cup (125 mL)	sugar
1 1/2 cups (375 mL)	half & half cream (10%)
1 cup (250 mL)	whipping cream (35%)
1/2 cup (125 mL)	maple syrup

✦ Mash raspberries thoroughly. Strain to remove seeds if desired. In a medium bowl, beat the eggs and sugar 4 to 5 minutes until thick and light yellow. Stir in the raspberry purée, half & half cream, whipping cream and maple syrup. Freeze in an ice-cream maker following manufacturer's instructions. **Makes about 4 cups (1 L).**

Pâtisserie

Pâtisserie de Gascogne on Sherbrooke Street in Montreal is a place of European elegance. Polished wood-framed mirrors reflect chocolate sculptures and classic cakes. Handmade truffles fill spun-sugar bowls; glazes sparkle and intensify the colours of fruit-embedded cream-filled tarts. Shards of bittersweet chocolate are stirred into warm milk to be served in demi-tasses with meltingly delicious meringues and buttery madeleines.

163

Maple Wine

In the region known as Bas Saint-Laurent, about 100 kilometres (60 miles) southeast of Rivière-de-Loup, you'll find the Érablière l'Éveil du Printemps, a small business specializing in traditional maple products and in a range of maple "wines." In the village of Auclair, visitors can sample and buy.

Wild Hazelnut Biscotti

Wild hazelnuts can be found across much of northern Quebec and Ontario. When ripe, the unhusked nuts must be dried then shelled, a laborious task but one, nonetheless, that Chef Roger Tremblay, a native of northern Quebec, does yearly. This is an adaptation of his recipe. Dip the crisp cookies into cappuccino, espresso, caffé latte, or just enjoy them with a glass of milk.

Maple liqueurs are being made under various brand names across the province. Any Societé d'alcools de Québec (SAQ) store has at least one. For this recipe you can substitute Frangelico, a hazelnut-flavoured digestif.

2	eggs
1 cup (250 mL)	sugar
2 tbsp. (25 mL)	Quebec maple liqueur
1/4 tsp. (1 mL)	vanilla
2 cups (500 mL)	all-purpose flour
1 1/4 tsp. (6 mL)	baking powder
1 cup (250 mL)	coarsely chopped roasted hazelnuts (p. 21)

✦ *In a medium bowl, lightly beat eggs, sugar, liqueur and vanilla until smoothly blended. In another bowl, stir together flour, baking powder and nuts. Add to egg mixture. Mix well, then knead together until smooth.*

✦ *Divide dough in half. Shape each half into a cylinder about 6 inches (15 cm) long. Place on a lightly greased baking sheet about 4 inches (10 cm) apart. Flatten loaves to 3 inches (8 cm) wide, leaving top slightly rounded. Bake in a preheated 350°F (180°C) oven 30 minutes or until light golden. Cool on a rack 15 minutes.*

✦ *Transfer to a lightly floured cutting board. Cut into 1/2-inch (1 cm) think slices. Arrange on baking sheet, cut side down. Bake 10 minutes. Turn slices over and bake 5 to 10 minutes longer or until golden and crisp. Cool on racks. Store in an air-tight container up to 2 weeks. **Makes about 30 biscotti.***

Ketchup aux Tomates Rouges

Across Canada you'll find this recipe in various guises. In my central Ontario region, we call it chili sauce. The Chow Chow (p. 203) from the south shore of Nova Scotia could easily be called Ketchup aux Tomates Vertes. In any case, these two relishes, delicious no matter what region in Canada you serve them, are traditionally eaten with the myriad tourtières or cipaille (p. 121) baked across French Canada.

6 quarts (6 L)	ripe tomatoes, peeled and sliced
3	large onions, minced
1/2 cup (125 mL)	coarse pickling salt
3 cups (750 mL)	finely diced celery
2	large sweet red peppers, diced
1 1/2 cups (375 mL)	cider vinegar
1 tsp. (5 mL)	crushed dried chilis
1/3 cup (75 mL)	mixed whole pickling spice, tied in a cheesecloth bag
4 cups (1 L)	brown sugar

✦ In a large bowl, combine tomatoes and onions. Sprinkle with salt. Cover and let stand at least 8 hours.

✦ Drain thoroughly and place in a large, heavy saucepan. Stir in celery, peppers, vinegar and chilis. Add spice bag. Cover and bring to a boil. Reduce heat and simmer, uncovered, 2 hours or until thickened. Stir often to prevent sticking. Add brown sugar. Stir and simmer over medium-low heat 25 minutes or until thickened again.

✦ Remove spice bag and ladle mixture into eight hot sterilized 2-cup (500 mL) jars, leaving 1/2-inch (1 cm) headspace at the top of each jar. Process in boiling-water bath 10 minutes. Let cool to room temperature. Store in a cool, dark place.
Makes eight 2-cup (500 mL) jars.

The Markets of Montreal

The markets of Montreal have flourished as part of the city's culinary culture since the 1800s. Here, you can quickly learn about the real products of Quebec. The first built, the Saint-Jacques Market, is now a seasonal market only. Atwater Market, located along the Lachine Canal, boasts one of the best cheese purveyors in the nation, Gilles Jourdenais's Fromagerie du Marché Atwater. Jean Talon Market, perhaps the most colourful, is set in the heart of Italian Montreal.

Chapter 5
Atlantic Canada

Newfoundland, with its vast territory of Labrador, is both wildly beautiful and unforgiving. In summer, the Great Northern Peninsula is one vast green expanse splashed with puddles and ponds, carpeted with peat bogs and slashed deeply by grand fjords. Wildflowers grow in profusion — fluffy white spires of Canada burnet, lilac pompoms of thrift, gaudy orange hawkweed and hot pink fireweed. Empty cars and pickup trucks line the roads, their owners out on the bogs harvesting bakeapples, the low-growing yellow fruit known in other parts of the world as cloudberries.

This is a sea-centred culture. From the North Atlantic over the centuries, Newfoundlanders have hauled tonnes of cod, a fish that until the recent collapse of the North Atlantic cod fisheries was the cornerstone of the region's economy as well as its cuisine. Since the 1500s and the days of the Basques, fishermen and women have caught, filleted, salted and dried fish along the cobblestone shores. The salt cod was then shipped east to France, Spain and England and south to the West Indies in exchange for rum and molasses. Salt cod also saw Newfoundlanders through the vilest winters. One of the most traditional of local foods is fish 'n' brewis, which is soaked salted fish combined with soaked hard bread and topped with scrunchions, bits of crisp fried salt pork.

Newfoundlanders have their own food, music and even their own vocabulary. "Come on over for a scoff and a scuff" is an invitation to a Newfoundland party. The scoff, or the meal, precedes the scuff, or the dance. The party might begin with thick split pea soup made with salted beef. There will be cod, either fried or au gratin, and perhaps a tureen of moose stew, seasoned liberally with winter savory, or a Jigg's dinner, a one-pot meal of boiled salt beef, root vegetables and pease pudding. And spring could never pass without a seal flipper pie. Desserts are often steamed puddings like figgy duff with molasses coady (spiced bread pudding with molasses-butter sauce) and, on special occasions, bakeapple (cloudberry) tarts and partridgeberry (lingonberry) pies.

Left: *Cultured scallops at Logy Bay Research Station, north of St. John's*
Above: *Don Hutchings with a bag of traditional vegetables, Whitbourne, Newfoundland*

The old cod fishery has given way to specialized fishing for tuna, herring, char, mackerel, turbot, red fish (ocean perch), lumpfish (for roe) and skate. Shellfish play a major new role in Newfoundland's wild harvest. Fishers haul in tonnes of snow crab. Icelandic and sea scallops, surf clams, shrimp, lobster, whelk, sea cucumber and green sea urchins are caught in varying amounts. Capelin, small fish that swim in huge schools, are shipped, either roe intact or lightly salted, as shishamo to Japan. Known simply as corned capelin in Newfoundland, they are delicious washed down with a bottle of Dominion beer. At Port au Choix, small shrimp are harvested; these sweet nuggets of pink cry out for a bit of butter and a hot skillet.

Nova Scotia

Although the Norse sailed the waters around Newfoundland in the tenth century, historians generally recognize the French-speaking Acadians who came to New France, now known as New Brunswick and Nova Scotia, in the very early 1600s as the first European settlers in Canada. In 1604 the first French expedition landed on St. Croix Island at the mouth of New Brunswick's St. Croix River. That winter the colony suffered so badly that the following year Samuel de Champlain selected a new site across the Bay of Fundy at Port Royal. There he founded North America's first feasting society, the Order of Good Cheer, to "keep our table joyous and well-provided."

Over the decades more French settlers arrived in the land they called Acadie. Today bright, star-splashed Acadian tricolour flags still wave in the ocean breezes throughout the Maritime provinces on the French Shore of Nova Scotia, on New Brunswick's northerly coastline, on southwestern Prince Edward Island and on Quebec's Magdalen Islands.

Acadian foods are plain and almost medieval in style. Much use is made of cod, eel, mackerel and herring. Herring roe is salted or served fresh. A stewlike dish called fricot pops up in many disguises but, in addition to the meat, always contains onions and potatoes. There is râpure, a baked casserole based primarily on grated potatoes, onions and some sort of meat. Poutine is another favourite. Literally it means "pudding" and comes in a number of sweet and savoury variations (and is quite different from the Québécois version, which, when properly made, requires blazing-hot french fries, lashings of steaming gravy and melting cheese curds). There are lots of rich pies made with lard-based pastry and filled with unlikely combinations like molasses and bits of crisp fried salt pork. Corn and root vegetables dominate the cuisine, but, particularly in the springtime, marsh plants such as samphire (Salicornia europaea) are harvested. And when the fishing boats come in there are fresh cod livers, which are preserved into a wonderful pâté and served to the luckiest of guests.

The first Scots came to the island we know as Cape Breton in 1621 and their heritage is obvious. Oatmeal is found in everything from bread and oatcakes to forach, a traditional wedding dish made with oatmeal, whipping cream and sugar.

On Nova Scotia's southeastern shore is a German settlement dating from 1753, when the British recruited a group of "foreign Protestants" to help counter the French and Catholic presence in Nova Scotia. Big Tancook Island in Mahone Bay is famous for its sauerkraut. Raising cabbages was the cornerstone of island life; the biggest heads were shipped to Europe on two-masted schooners, probably constructed in this, the ship-building centre of the Atlantic seaboard. Smaller cabbages were shredded, salted and sold in hundred-pound (45-kilogram) barrels.

Above: *Partridgeberries*

168

New Brunswick

In 1783 Loyalists poured northward by the thousands from the troubled New England states and collected near Shelburne, Nova Scotia, and in the lush Saint John River Valley in what is now New Brunswick. New England–style dishes such as Anadama or Yankee bread and Boston baked beans were added to Atlantic Canada's repertoire.

Defined by water, southern New Brunswick is criss-crossed by the languorous Saint John River. Is there a more vibrant green than on a sunny spring day by this river? Grazing cattle on its sandy banks are reflected in the mirrorlike water. Farmland is rich here, and rivers are often wild and full of life.

The province has two very different coasts. The Northumberland Strait on the northeast coast is warmer and shallower than the Bay of Fundy on the southeast. The rocky shores of Fundy seem to plummet at times into the tides. St. George and St. Andrews, large communities on the Fundy coast, are noted for their aquaculture. There the waters are cold, fast and deep.

The wild harvest is important in New Brunswick. It begins with the smelt run in early February, followed by maple syrup and trout season. Samphire greens are picked in tidal flats, while foragers trek along riverbanks to harvest thousands of kilograms of fiddleheads to grace the world's tables as well as their own. When the autumn leaves turn to burnished gold and frost begins to cover the meadows, the region becomes a mycologist's dream: chanterelles are everywhere.

Above: *Christina Deering holding lobsters at Quoddy Bay Fish Market, St. Andrews, New Brunswick*

Above: *Leonard Rayner, collecting Irish moss, near Miminegash, P.E.I.*

Prince Edward Island

Sweet lobster, world-famous blue mussels, briny Malpeque oysters and tonnes of red-earth-stained potatoes are all part of Prince Edward Island's culinary bounty. As part of the more recent developments, there are pond-raised Arctic char, aquacultured bay scallops and a farm that specializes in game such as wild boar. And in Charlottetown there is a full-fledged food technology centre at the University of Prince Edward Island.

Away from the city on the wide, wind-scoured beaches, clams squirt crossly at you when you step on them in the wet sand. Cream-coloured moon snails and spiralling periwinkles plough their tiny watery roads into the deeper water of the warm tidal pools. Furrowed fields that flow to the ocean are thick with oxeye daisies and in the early summer there are masses of multicoloured lupins.

Western Prince Edward Island (near Miminegash) is the harvesting centre of Irish moss. This seaweed, known commercially as carrageen, is used as a thickening agent in dozens of manufactured food products, but is still harvested in the age-old way. The moss is "glommed" from the surf after a storm by rakes pulled behind teams of horses. Boats are also used to harvest the moss beds that float close to shore. The moss is spread to dry in neat bands on the red-clay roadsides.

P.E.I. also has a small pocket of Acadian tradition. Near Mont-Carmel in the southwest, the community still cooks foods such as hominy corn soup, potato-barclam chowder and molasses cookies.

From the westerly end of the province it's only part of a day's drive to the wide, deserted sand beaches of Kings County, the home of major shellfish aquaculture. Most of the seed, the tiny free-floating shellfish embryos, is collected in St. Peter's Bay. Once attached, the "spat," as the embryos are called at this stage of development, are suspended on lines below white buoys into the nutrient-rich river estuaries.

Both shores of the Murray River estuary in eastern Prince Edward Island are dotted with brightly coloured floats marking aquafarms of blue mussels. Net "socks," each holding about 14 kilograms (30 pounds) of mussels, are suspended at intervals from 180-metre (600-foot) long lines. For 18 months, they flourish until harvested, plump and tender, to be processed and shipped around the globe. There is also an active lobster fishery. In late spring, when the shellfish is at its sweetest, lobster suppers are held by churches across the island.

If there is one word that would sum up, for me, the culinary character of Atlantic Canada, it would be *hospitable*. The kitchens of the region, with such a colourful culinary past, provide a welcome in the finest sense. Here the tables are set with largesse and great foods — from fricot to chowder — are shared with generous hearts.

Willie Krauch's Smoked Eel with Lemon Thyme Potato Pancakes and Dilled Sour Cream

The name Willie Krauch has been synonymous with fine hardwood-smoked salmon since 1956. In 1967 his fame was assured when Craig Claiborne wrote about him in *The New York Times*. But the small, rural Nova Scotian operation, near the dot on the map named Tangier, smokes other wonderful products, too. Every year three of his children (Willie passed away several years ago) process between 120,000 and 130,000 pounds (54,500 and 59,000 kg) of local mackerel and about 10,000 pounds (4,500 kg) of eel, fished locally for three to four weeks in the autumn.

1 cup (250 mL)	sour cream or crème fraîche
1/4 cup (50 mL)	minced fresh dill
2	large russet potatoes, peeled and grated
1	small onion, minced
2	eggs, lightly beaten
2 tbsp. (25 mL)	all-purpose flour
1 tsp. (5 mL)	finely chopped lemon thyme
1/2 tsp. (2 mL)	salt
1/4 tsp. (1 mL)	freshly ground pepper
1/4 cup (50 mL)	unsalted butter
1/2 – 3/4 lb. (250 – 375 g)	smoked eel
	Lemon thyme sprigs, dill and buckwheat sprouts (optional)

✦ Stir together sour cream and dill. Cover and refrigerate until needed. Place the grated potatoes in the centre of a tea towel and twist out excess moisture. Transfer to mixing bowl and combine with onion, eggs, flour, lemon thyme, salt and pepper.

✦ In a heavy skillet, melt a spoonful of butter over medium heat until it foams. Drop small mounds of potato mixture into the skillet, flattening and shaping into small circles with a spatula. Sauté until undersides are golden. Flip and continue to cook 4 to 5 minutes or until browned, pressing down from time to time. Keep warm in oven on cake rack. Repeat with remaining butter and potato mixture.

✦ Place pancakes on 3 or 4 warmed plates. Top with dilled sour cream, smoked eel and sprigs of lemon thyme, dill and buckwheat sprouts if desired. **Makes 3 to 4 servings.**

Taste of Nova Scotia

The "Taste of Nova Scotia" program showcases the province's long and diverse culinary history. Every time travellers see the "Taste" logo, they can be assured that at least some of the menu will reflect great local ingredients and often special dishes from the ethnic fabric of an individual region, be it Celtic from Cape Breton, Acadian from the French shore or German from Lunenburg.

173

Crispy Cornmeal-Breaded Oysters

Every fast food outlet in Atlantic Canada seems to sell breaded oysters — with fries, with salads or on a Soft Bread Roll (p. 194) as an oyster burger. They serve them with salsa, Chow Chow (p. 203) or Valerie's Version of Lady Ashburnham's Pickles (p. 205).

1 cup (250 mL)	cornmeal
1 cup (250 mL)	all-purpose flour
2 tsp. (10 mL)	turmeric
1 tsp. (5 mL)	medium curry powder
1 tsp. (5 mL)	salt
1/2 tsp. (2 mL)	cayenne
1/2 tsp. (2 mL)	fennel seeds, finely ground
1/2 tsp. (2 mL)	freshly ground black pepper
1/2 tsp. (2 mL)	coriander seeds, finely ground
24	shucked oysters
	Canola oil for frying
	Fennel sprigs for garnish

✦ In a medium mixing bowl, stir together cornmeal, flour, turmeric, curry powder, salt, cayenne, fennel seeds, pepper and coriander.

✦ Heat a non-stick skillet over medium heat and add enough oil to lightly cover the bottom. Dip oysters quickly into breading and transfer to hot pan. Sauté 2 to 3 minutes or until golden brown on both sides. Garnish with fennel sprigs. **Makes 6 servings.**

175

Left: *John Bil, Canadian oyster shucking champion in 1997*

Smoked Brook Trout Salad with Blueberry Vinaigrette

This recipe from the gracious Tattingstone Inn in Wolfville, Nova Scotia, has amazing colours and a tangy fruit flavour. The pickled blueberries are great to have on hand.

Blueberry Vinaigrette

1 1/2 cups (375 mL)	white wine vinegar
2 cups (500 mL)	wild blueberries
1	shallot, minced
1/4 tsp. (1 mL)	salt
1/4 tsp. (1 mL)	freshly ground black pepper
1 1/4 cups (300 mL)	vegetable oil

✦ In a small saucepan over medium heat, combine vinegar and 1 cup (250 mL) of the blueberries. Bring to a boil, reduce heat and simmer 5 minutes. Strain through a cheesecloth-lined sieve into a clean glass jar. (Vinegar can be kept in a cool, dark place for up to 1 month.)

✦ In a blender or a food processor, combine vinegar, shallot, salt and pepper. With machine running, gradually pour in oil until smooth. Pour into a bowl and stir in remaining 1 cup (250 mL) blueberries.

To Serve

8 cups (2 L)	mixed baby greens
4	fillets smoked trout
	Sweet red and green pepper rings
	Red onion rings
	Fresh blueberries

✦ Divide salad greens among 8 serving plates. Top each with a half fillet of trout, broken into pieces. Garnish with sweet pepper rings, onion rings and blueberries. Pour Blueberry Vinaigrette over top and serve immediately. **Makes 8 servings.**

Sea Parsley

Sea parsley, a relative of dulse, is beautiful to look at, with deeply curled burgundy leaves. Sea parsley is commercially grown only in tanks near Shelburne, Nova Scotia.

Fiddlehead Chowder Laced with Chili Oil

This fabulous chowder can be chunky and rustic or finely puréed and upscale. In either case, a drizzle of chili oil gives it an untraditional blast of flavour. Create your own oil using the following recipe or buy a bottle at any Asian food store.

The whole-wheat flour used is from the Speerville Mill in Debec, New Brunswick, but any other high-quality stone-ground flour may be substituted.

2 cups (500 mL)	cubed potatoes
4 cups (1 L)	chicken stock (p. 66)
2 tbsp. (25 mL)	unsalted butter
2	medium onions, finely minced
1/4 cup (50 mL)	Debec whole-wheat flour
1	300 g package
	frozen fiddleheads, thawed or
	2 cups (500 mL) steamed fiddleheads
2 tsp. (10 mL)	dried tarragon
	Salt and pepper to taste
1/2 cup (125 mL)	table cream (18%)
	Fresh tarragon sprigs for garnish
	Chili oil

✦ In a medium saucepan, cook potatoes in chicken stock about 15 minutes or until tender. In a large saucepan, melt all but 1 tsp. (5 mL) of the butter. Add onions; sauté over medium heat till transparent. Stir in flour; allow to cook and bubble 15 to 20 seconds, stirring. Stir in potatoes and stock; bring to a boil.

✦ Reserve a few whole fiddleheads for garnish and chop the rest finely. Add fiddleheads to soup with tarragon. Season with salt and pepper. Allow to cool 10 minutes. Purée and return to the saucepan. Simmer 5 to 10 minutes. Stir in cream and keep warm on low heat.

✦ In a small non-stick skillet, quickly sauté reserved fiddleheads in remaining butter about 1 minute or until heated through. Ladle chowder into 6 to 8 hot soup bowls and garnish with fiddleheads and fresh tarragon. Add a dash of Chili Oil to taste.
Makes 6 to 8 servings.

Chili Oil

1 cup (250 mL)	canola oil
1 tbsp. (15 mL)	crushed dried chilis

✦ Combine oil and crushed chilis in a small saucepan. Over very low heat, gently warm the oil. When just a little more than lukewarm, remove from heat. Pour into a glass jar and add the dried chilis. Refrigerate 6 to 8 hours before using. Strain if desired. Store, refrigerated, up to 1 week, or frozen up to 6 months.
Makes 1 cup (250 mL).

179

Tangled Garden

Tangled Garden, near Grand Pré, is a herb garden spiced with a cook's understanding of flavours and conceived with an artist's eye. Open to the public, the shop and the garden are a riot of colour. For your breakfast or afternoon tea, try their gooseberry–lemon balm jelly or strawberry lavender jelly. Use their hot chili oil with Fiddlehead Chowder or deglaze the pan in which you cooked pork tenderloin with their wonderful fennel vinegar.

Jerusalem Artichoke Soup

If you have a special, well-enclosed garden space, plant a few of these prolific tubers. You'll have them forever — and probably so will your neighbours. The Jerusalem artichoke *(Helianthus tuberosus)* is native to North America and its recorded history dates back to Champlain in 1603. They were dug and used across the continent by the First Nations as a raw or cooked vegetable.

This recipe was developed by Neil Baxter of the Stratford Chefs School for Northern Bounty, the first symposium on Canadian cuisine in 1993, as part of an opulent menu celebrating Champlain's Order of Good Cheer. The soup is often garnished with parsnip chips, thin slices of peeled parsnip that have been deep-fried.

2 tbsp. (25 mL)	unsalted butter
1	leek, white only, thinly sliced
1	stalk celery, thinly sliced
1	fennel bulb, thinly sliced
1 lb. (500 g)	Jerusalem artichokes, peeled and sliced
1	bouquet garni (1 bay leaf, 3 – 4 sprigs thyme and 2 – 3 parsley branches)
6 cups (1.5 L)	chicken stock (p. 66)
1/4 cup (50 mL)	whipping cream (35%)
	Salt and pepper to taste

✦ Melt butter in a large, heavy-bottomed saucepan over medium heat. Add leek, celery, fennel, artichokes, bouquet garni and chicken stock. Cover and bring to a boil; reduce heat and simmer 20 minutes or until artichokes are tender. Let cool 10 minutes. Purée in small batches until smooth. Return to soup pot; add cream; reheat gently. Season to taste with salt and pepper. Serve in warmed soup bowls. **Makes 6 to 8 servings.**

Lobscouse

In Newfoundland, a version of Lobscouse that contains mainly cabbage and is thickened with potatoes and turnips is called Flop.

This soup is even better the next day and is wonderful with fresh homemade bread.

1 lb. (500 g)	salt beef or ham
8 cups (2 L)	beef stock (p. 67)
5 cups (1.25L)	shredded cabbage
1	onion, sliced
2	bay leaves
3/4 cup (175 mL)	tomato juice
1	28-oz. (796 mL) can diced tomatoes
1 tbsp. (15 mL)	Worcestershire sauce
1 tsp. (5 mL)	hot pepper sauce
	Freshly ground pepper to taste

✦ In a large stock pot, combine salt beef and stock. Bring to a boil; reduce heat and simmer 15 minutes. Add cabbage, onion, bay leaves, tomato juice, tomatoes, Worcestershire sauce, hot pepper sauce and pepper. Simmer, covered, 1 1/2 hours or until cabbage is very tender. Discard bay leaves. Ladle into warmed soup bowls or refrigerate up to 3 days. **Makes 8 to 10 servings.**

181

St. John's

In St. John's, Newfoundland, the weather teases. Clouds scud over so swiftly that there can easily be three seasons in one day. The Cabot Tower on Signal Hill may bask in a spotlight of sunshine yet it'll be drippy on Duckworth Street. But the food wards off the worst weather. A boiled dinner with pease pudding warms away the foggy chills of even the dampest of days. And so does a "chocolate Sam," a steaming mug of hot chocolate laced with the darkest rum, a drink I learned about at Marble Mountain, the ski hill (a good one with tons of snow) near Cornerbrook.

Left: *Tangled Garden vinegars*

Grilled Digby Scallops, Barley Risotto and Roasted Turnip with Dried Tomato Sauce

At Digby Pines in Nova Scotia, Chef Claude AuCoin, the brother of Gerard AuCoin, who is the chef on the oil rig *Hibernia,* uses a "tian," or small metal ring, to cut perfect turnip rounds and to pile risotto onto the turnip in a precise tower, unmoulding just before serving. A tuna tin, cut out on both sides, would also work.

Dried Tomato Sauce

2/3 cup (150 mL)	sun-dried tomatoes in oil
1	shallot, chopped
1	clove garlic, minced
2	plum tomatoes, diced
2/3 cup (150 mL)	dry red wine
2 tbsp. (25 mL)	Canadian balsamic vinegar or high-quality cider vinegar
Pinch	cayenne
	Salt and freshly ground black pepper to taste

✦ Strain the tomatoes, reserving the oil. Chop the tomatoes. Heat the oil in a small skillet over medium heat. Add shallot and garlic; cook, stirring, about 3 minutes or until softened. Stir in sun-dried tomatoes, plum tomatoes, wine, vinegar and cayenne. Bring to a boil, reduce heat and simmer 20 minutes or until sun-dried tomatoes are softened. Purée in a blender; season with salt and pepper. Add a little water if sauce is too thick.

Barley Risotto

1/2 cup (125 mL)	pearl barley
2 tbsp. (25 mL)	canola oil
1	shallot, minced
1	small carrot, finely diced
1	clove garlic, minced
3 tbsp. (45 mL)	chopped fresh herbs (chives, parsley, thyme)
2 tbsp. (25 mL)	grated Parmesan cheese
	Salt and freshly ground pepper to taste
1/2	small turnip, peeled and cut in 1/2-inch (1 cm) slices

✦ Simmer barley in plenty of boiling salted water about 40 minutes or until tender. Drain and set aside. Heat all but 2 tsp. (10 mL) of the oil in a small skillet over medium heat. Add shallot and carrot; cook, stirring, about 5 minutes. Stir in garlic; cook 30 seconds. Add barley, herbs, Parmesan, salt and pepper.

✦ Place turnip rounds on a parchment-lined baking sheet; brush lightly with remaining oil. Bake in a preheated 350°F (180°C) oven, turning once, about 20 minutes or until browned on the outside and tender throughout.

183

Grilled Digby Scallops

32	medium to large Digby scallops
6	9-inch (23 cm) wooden skewers, soaked in cold water 30 minutes
2 tbsp. (25 mL)	canola oil
	Salt and freshly ground black pepper to taste

✦ Pierce scallops onto skewers; brush with oil and sprinkle with salt and pepper. Grill over medium-high heat, turning frequently, 5 minutes or until just firm to the touch and still soft in the centre.

To Serve

	Steamed asparagus
	Fresh herbs for garnish

✦ Spoon Dried Tomato Sauce on 4 serving plates to cover the bottom. Place a turnip round in the centre and top with a generous spoonful of Barley Risotto. Surround with Grilled Digby Scallops (removed from skewers). Surround with steamed asparagus and sprinkle with fresh herbs. **Makes 4 servings.**

Poached Salmon Chunks in Mayonnaise with Pickled Fiddleheads on Homemade Soft Rolls

This recipe was inspired by a lunch I enjoyed at Pond's Cottages on the legendary Miramichi River in New Brunswick. Everything, it seems, at Pond's is as close to homemade as you can get, including the delicious breads.

Pickled fiddleheads are available across Atlantic Canada under the brand name Scrumptious Delights. When Sandra Blackmore of Moncton, New Brunswick, decided to make them, it took her three years to perfect the recipe. The fiddleheads are picked on the banks of the Miramichi River and brined while they are perfectly fresh – that's the secret! The flavour Blackmore was attempting to capture was that of the traditional way of serving steamed fiddleheads – with a bit of butter and a splash of vinegar.

184

Poached Salmon Chunks

6 cups (1.5 L)	water
1 cup (250 mL)	dry white wine
2	stalks celery
1	bay leaf
6	whole peppercorns
2 lb. (1 kg)	salmon fillets

Mayonnaise

2	egg yolks
3 tbsp. (45 mL)	lemon juice
2 tsp. (10 mL)	Dijon mustard
1 tsp. (5 mL)	salt
1 cup (250 mL)	vegetable oil

8	Soft Bread Rolls (p. 194)
	Lettuce leaves, as needed
	Thin slices of red onion, as needed
1 cup (250 mL)	drained pickled fiddleheads

✦ For salmon, combine water, wine, celery, bay leaf and peppercorns in a Dutch oven. Bring to a boil, reduce heat and simmer 5 minutes. Reduce heat to low; add salmon and keep just below boiling point for 7 minutes or until fish is firm to touch and opaque throughout. Do not overcook. Remove from poaching liquid and cool completely. (Poaching liquid can be used as stock in soup.)

✦ To make mayonnaise, combine egg yolks, lemon juice, mustard and salt in a food processor. With machine running, gradually pour in oil to make a thick, smooth mayonnaise. Taste and adjust both salt and lemon juice.

✦ Break salmon into chunks; stir into mayonnaise. Cover and chill up to 24 hours before using.

✦ Make sandwiches of salmon, lettuce and red onion on soft bread rolls. Either add well-drained fiddleheads to the sandwich, or serve on the side. **Makes 8 servings.**

Aquaculture

Aquaculture farms float along Newfoundland's convoluted coastline. Sea scallops are cultured from wild "seed" in suspended net cages. They are sweet and ready for tables around the world after only two to three years and are shipped live, as are the province's yearly harvest of cultured blue mussels. Atlantic salmon, steelhead trout and some pan-sized Arctic char are being aquacultured as well.

Above: *Herring smokers on Grand Manan*

Steelhead Trout with Scallop Mousse in Phyllo Pastry

Bob Arniel is St. John's "Chef to Go." He is one of the most vocal supporters of great Newfoundland products. The trout comes from Bay d'Espoir, while the scallops are cultured in many locations around the province. He notes that if you don't have any scraps from filleting your own trout, buy an extra fillet.

Scallop Mousse

5 oz. (150 g)	scallops
3 oz. (75 g)	trout scraps from filleting (or 1 fillet, skinned)
1/3 cup (75 mL)	whipping cream (35%)
1	egg white
1 tbsp. (15 mL)	chopped fresh tarragon
	Salt and freshly ground black pepper to taste

✦ *Combine scallops and trout scraps in a food processor; process until just smooth. Add cream, egg white, tarragon, salt and pepper. Process until just combined. Transfer to a bowl, cover and chill thoroughly.*

Duxelles

2 tsp. (10 mL)	unsalted butter
1	shallot, minced
1 cup (250 mL)	minced mushrooms (about 4 oz./125 g)
1/4 cup (50 mL)	dry white wine

✦ *Melt butter in a skillet over medium heat. Add shallot and mushrooms; cook about 8 minutes or until mushrooms have released their liquid and it has evaporated. Add wine. Cook, stirring, until wine has completely evaporated.*

Trout

6	sheets phyllo pastry
1/4 cup (50 mL)	unsalted butter, melted
4	steelhead trout fillets (about 3 oz./75 g each), skinned
	Scallop mousse
	Duxelles

✦ *On a clean work surface, lay 1 sheet of phyllo, long end facing you. Brush lightly with melted butter. Repeat and layer with 2 more sheets. Cut each stack in half lengthwise. Place 1 fillet on each half.*

✦ *Top each fillet with 1/4 of the mousse, then 1/4 of the duxelle mixture. Brush exposed phyllo with butter. Fold over phyllo to enclose trout envelope-style and brush top with butter. Repeat with remaining ingredients. Place on a parchment-lined baking sheet. Bake in a preheated 350°F (180°C) oven for 15 minutes or until pastry is golden and filling is firm to the touch. Do not overcook. Meanwhile, make sauce.*

185

Sauce

1/4 cup (50 mL)	unsalted butter
1/4 cup (50 mL)	all-purpose flour
2 cups (500 mL)	fish stock (p. 189)
1/4 cup (50 mL)	dry white wine
3 tbsp. (45 mL)	chopped fresh tarragon
2 tbsp. (25 mL)	chopped chives
	Salt and freshly ground pepper to taste

✦ *Melt butter in a medium saucepan over medium heat. Stir in flour; cook, stirring, 1 minute or just until fragrant. Gradually whisk in stock; bring to a boil and cook 10 minutes. Stir in wine, tarragon, chives, salt and pepper.*

To Serve

2	large tomatoes, peeled, seeded and diced
	Fresh herbs

✦ *Place a phyllo bundle on each of 4 serving plates. Top with sauce and diced tomatoes. Garnish with fresh herbs. Makes 4 servings.*

Hibernia Halibut Parcels with Newfoundland Savory and Green Onion Stuffing with Dill Hollandaise

Halibut is usually delivered frozen to the oil rig Hibernia. The chefs defrost it slowly, then cut the fish into chunks about 2 inches (5 cm) thick. This recipe also works perfectly with thick cuts of Atlantic salmon. Chef Gerard Aucoin (pictured left) says that it is at its finest served with steamed vegetables or a fresh green salad.

1	egg, well beaten
1 tbsp. (15 mL)	milk
1 tsp. (5 mL)	unsalted butter
1/2 cup (125 mL)	chopped red onion
4	green onions, coarsely chopped
1/4 cup (50 mL)	sweet green pepper, coarsely chopped
1	clove garlic, chopped
1/2 tsp. (2 mL)	salt
1/4 tsp. (1 mL)	freshly ground pepper
4	halibut pieces (5 oz./150 g each)
1	411 g package
	frozen puff pastry, thawed
	Salt and freshly ground pepper to taste
1 tsp. (5 mL)	dried Newfoundland savory

✦ In a small bowl, beat egg and milk together; set aside. In a skillet, melt butter over low heat. Add red onion and cook, stirring occasionally, until transparent. Transfer to a food processor. Add green onions, green pepper, garlic, salt, pepper and 1 tbsp. (15 mL) of the eggwash. Process till finely chopped. With a very sharp knife, make a horizontal slit in each piece of halibut to create a deep pocket. Fill halibut pieces with stuffing; set aside.

✦ Roll out pastry on a lightly floured surface to 1/16-inch (2 mm) thickness. Brush with remaining eggwash. Cut in 4. Place 1 piece of halibut in centre of each piece of pastry. Sprinkle with salt, pepper and savory. Fold pastry over to make a neat package, pressing edges to seal. Transfer to a lightly oiled or parchment-lined baking sheet. With a sharp knife, cut 2 or 3 slits in top of each piece to allow steam to escape. Bake in a preheated 400°F (200°C) oven 40 minutes or until deep golden. Remove from oven and let stand 5 minutes before serving.

Dill Hollandaise

Although this classic sauce should be served as soon as it's made, it may be held for 10 to 15 minutes over warm water and whisked before serving.

3	egg yolks
1/4 cup (50 mL)	chopped fresh dill
4 tsp. (20 mL)	lemon juice
2 tsp. (10 mL)	water
1/2 tsp. (2 mL)	dry mustard
1/4 tsp. (1 mL)	salt
1/4 tsp. (1 mL)	cayenne
1/2 cup (125 mL)	unsalted butter, melted

✦ In a blender or food processor, combine egg yolks, dill, lemon juice, water, dry mustard, salt and cayenne. Blend at low speed 5 to 10 seconds. With machine running, gradually pour in half of melted butter. Increase speed to high; gradually pour in remaining butter. **Makes 1 cup (250 mL).**

To Serve

✦ Pour Dill Hollandaise on 4 warmed dinner plates. Top with halibut, sliced in two to expose stuffing. **Makes 4 generous servings.**

315 km. East of St. John's, Newfoundland

Life on board the oil rig Hibernia is active, work is heavy and crew members get very hungry. The cafeteria is open 24 hours and the food is delicious. Meals often include old-fashioned Newfoundland cabbage soup (sometimes called lobscouse), smoked salmon and wonderful seafood salads, cod tongues and cheeks, salt beef with pease pudding, fish 'n' brewis and, of course, potatoes. Great spuds are held in such high esteem that on a post in the kitchen is a list of 29 ways of cooking them. "Phil's potatoes" are mashed with bits of ham, green onion and sour cream, while "Cape Breton potatoes" are enriched with leeks and cream. The night we ate on board, the meal ended with bakeapple cheesecake, blueberry "sidewalks" (rich pastry rectangles topped with thickened blueberries), rhubarb tarts, fabulous date squares and the best molasses tea buns I've ever tasted.

The kitchens on board Hibernia are stainless and spotless with windows onto the ocean — and the fog. Life on board is not easy: Three weeks straight with no days off. It takes mental stamina. But, as pastry chef Joe Delaney teases, "It's the only job I've had that I've been paid to watch whales."

Shad

All along the Miramichi River in New Brunswick the deep pools and sections are named after those who live or have lived by the shore. The Kelly Channel is one such section, and it was at the Betts-Kelly Lodge that I had my first shad dinner. Shad, an ocean dweller like gaspereau, is not considered a choice fish. It's "bonier 'n a brush pile," but smoked, it's one of the tastiest fish I've eaten. Shad springtime-fresh from the river and baked stuffed with mashed potato, onion, bread and savory is a real New Brunswick tradition when served with pickled beets or relish. A bowl of steamed fiddleheads, picked from the shore where the fish was caught, can be sprinkled with vinegar, salt and pepper. There may be strawberry short-cake for dessert.

188

Maple-Roasted Salmon

This dish smells amazing as it cooks. It is adapted from a recipe by Executive Chef Tasos Markides of Fredericton's Sheraton Hotel.

1/4 cup (50 mL)	Jost Vineyard's Maréchal Foch or local dry red wine
1 cup (250 mL)	maple wood chips
4	sprigs fresh rosemary
4	sprigs lemon thyme
1 tbsp. (15 mL)	canola oil
1 tbsp. (15 mL)	maple syrup
1 tbsp. (15 mL)	maple vinegar (p. 151)
2 tsp. (10 mL)	brandy
1	Atlantic salmon fillet (8 – 10 oz./250 – 300 g), skinned
1 tbsp. (15 mL)	brown sugar

✦ *Pour wine over wood chips and let stand 6 to 8 hours.*

✦ *Wash rosemary and lemon thyme in very hot water to bring out the flavour. Combine 2 tsp. (10 mL) of the oil, maple syrup, maple vinegar and brandy. Pour over salmon; cover and refrigerate 1 hour.*

✦ *Arrange wood chips in a 10-inch (25 cm) cast-iron skillet or foil baking pan. Drizzle with remaining oil. Place on barbecue over high heat. Close lid and cook 5 minutes or until chips are just beginning to smoke. Remove skillet and top with rosemary and lemon thyme. Drain salmon and place on top of herbs and chips. Sprinkle with brown sugar. Return to barbecue, close lid and roast 7 minutes or until salmon is firm to the touch and opaque in the centre. The herbs will look almost charred and the wood will begin to smoke. Serve salmon hot, or chill it to use as a spectacular component on a green salad.* **Makes 2 servings.**

Above: *Traditional Shad dinner, Betts-Kelly Lodge on the Miramichi River, New Brunswick*

Lobster Oil

Lobster oil, one of the most innovative food products from Atlantic Canada, is being made by super-chef Stefan Czapalay. He's taken canola oil and infused it with lobster so that it is pungent with the flavours of the sea. His company, Canadian Cold Water, is based in Summerside, Prince Edward Island, as is his restaurant, Seasons in Thyme.

Dark Harbour Dulse

The west side of Grand Manan is rocky with precipitous cliffs. Eagles nest there. The shoreline is shaded until late in the morning. Dark Harbour dulse (Rhodymenia palmata), *the red rock-borne seaweed sold across Canada, is prized around the Maritimes for its quality.*

Fish Stock

Chef Bob Arniel stresses that white-fleshed fish is best for this recipe.

1/4 cup (50 mL)	unsalted butter
1 cup (250 mL)	chopped onion
1 cup (250 mL)	sliced mushrooms
1 lb. (500 g)	white-fleshed fish bones
1	bay leaf
1/2	bunch parsley
8	sprigs lemon balm
6	peppercorns
1/2 cup (125 mL)	dry white wine
4 cups (1 L)	cold water

✦ *In a large, heavy saucepan, melt butter over medium heat. Add onion and mushrooms; cook until softened, about 10 minutes. Add fish bones, bay leaf, parsley, lemon balm and peppercorns; cook 2 minutes.*

✦ *Add wine and water and bring to a simmer; do not boil. Simmer 30 minutes. Strain liquid through a fine sieve. Fish stock keeps 5 days refrigerated or 6 months frozen.* **Makes 4 cups (1 L).**

Salmon Burgers

This is not a fish cake but rather a light and flavourful free-form salmon patty that is wonderful on a Soft Bread Roll (p. 194) or on its own with a salad. There is only one trick, learned from the old French chefs who had their apprentices beat a similar salmon mixture over ice water for hours to ensure perfect quenelles. Freeze the fish for an hour, just long enough to develop ice crystals. A partially thawed piece of fish works well, too.

1	Atlantic salmon fillet (12 oz./375 g)
1	egg
2 tbsp. (25 mL)	chopped fresh dill, parsley or tarragon
1 tbsp. (15 mL)	sour cream or crème fraîche
1 tsp. (5 mL)	sea salt
1/4 tsp. (1 mL)	cayenne
1/2 cup (125 mL)	cornmeal
1/4 cup (50 mL)	canola oil
2	cloves garlic, sliced

✦ *Freeze the salmon 1 hour or long enough to ensure that some ice crystals are forming. Working quickly, skin salmon and cut into chunks. Place in a food processor. Add egg, herb, sour cream, salt and cayenne. Process till coarsely chopped.*

✦ *Place cornmeal in a shallow bowl. With your hands, lightly shape salmon mixture into 4 patties and coat them on both sides with cornmeal.*

✦ *In a large non-stick skillet, heat oil over medium-high heat. Transfer patties to oil; cook till golden. Flip; sprinkle garlic slices into the pan. When patties are browned, in 2 to 3 minutes, remove from pan, topping each with a bit of garlic.* **Makes 4 servings.**

189

Above: *Garth Neves collecting dulse on Grand Manan*

Baked Halibut with Tarragon Crust

This recipe is from the Amherst Shore Country Inn, on Nova Scotia's Sunrise Trail. The inn has been creating great comforting Maritime food since the 1980s.

1 cup (250 mL)	sour cream
3 tbsp. (45 mL)	chopped fresh tarragon
2 tsp. (10 mL)	minced green onion
1	clove garlic, minced
Dash	hot pepper sauce
Dash	Worcestershire sauce
	Freshly ground black pepper to taste
1 1/2 cups (375 mL)	fresh bread crumbs
1/2 cup (125 mL)	freshly grated Parmesan cheese
1/2 cup (125 mL)	shredded Swiss cheese
1/4 cup (50 mL)	chopped fresh parsley
2 lb. (1 kg)	skinless halibut fillets

✦ *In a bowl, combine sour cream, 1 tbsp. (15 mL) of the tarragon, green onion, garlic, hot pepper sauce, Worcestershire sauce and pepper. In a separate bowl, combine bread crumbs, Parmesan, Swiss cheese, parsley and remaining 2 tbsp. (25 mL) tarragon.*

✦ *Divide halibut into serving portions. Coat lightly in sour cream mixture, then in bread crumb mixture. Place on a parchment-lined baking sheet, leaving about 1 inch (2.5 cm) between fillets. Bake in a preheated 500°F (260°C) oven 12 minutes or until coating is golden and fish flakes easily with a fork. Serve immediately.*
Makes 4 to 6 servings.

To Market in Halifax

The rural community is in control of the Halifax City Market, and it shows. The products sold are what great markets across Canada are all about. Fabulous wild mushrooms set visiting chefs' mouths watering. Can they be shipped? How can I get them home? Money changes hands quickly and chanterelles from Nova Scotia soon are winging their way to Vancouver and Toronto. There's chèvre and goat's milk buttermilk; smoked fish, seasonal produce and great baking.

191

Normaway French Toast

Another Cape Breton way to use oats, golden and particularly delicious when awash with Nova Scotian maple syrup. I've been known to drive an hour for this great breakfast.

5	eggs
1/4 cup (50 mL)	milk
1 cup (250 mL)	old-fashioned or quick rolled oats
1/4 cup (50 mL)	brown sugar
1 tsp. (5 mL)	cinnamon
1 – 2 tbsp. (15 – 25 mL)	unsalted butter
6 – 8	slices Normaway Porridge Bread

✦ *Whisk eggs and milk together until frothy. In a separate dish, combine oats, sugar and cinnamon. Heat 1 to 2 tsp. (5 to 10 mL) butter in a non-stick skillet until foamy. Dip slices of bread into egg mixture, then coat with spiced oats. Fry, in batches, on both sides until golden. Serve with maple syrup.* **Makes 3 to 4 servings.**

Normaway Porridge Bread

For me Cape Breton means three things: songs, stories and salmon. The Normaway Inn, tucked among the hills of the Margaree Valley, has all three. Owner-innkeeper David MacDonald, himself a Cape Bretoner, generously shares his enthusiasm for the island's Scottish heritage. He holds ceilidhs, encourages evenings of story-telling and has access to at least seven salmon pools on a newly acquired 325-hectare (800-acre) property.

Few Scots would consider breakfast complete without a bowl of steaming oatmeal porridge. And no Scot would ever throw out the leftovers — hence this thrifty, and delicious, bread recipe. It's one of the best!

2 cups (500 mL)	cool cooked porridge
3/4 cup (175 mL)	canola oil
1/2 cup (125 mL)	brown sugar
1/2 cup (125 mL)	molasses
1 tbsp. (15 mL)	salt
2 cups (500 mL)	warm water
1 tbsp. (15 mL)	sugar
2 tbsp. (25 mL)	active dry yeast
10 – 11 cups (2.5 – 2.75 L)	white bread flour

✦ *In a mixing bowl, combine porridge, oil, brown sugar, molasses and salt. Stir thoroughly. There should be no lumps.*

✦ *Measure water into another large mixing bowl. Stir in sugar and sprinkle with yeast. Let sit 10 minutes or until foamy. Add porridge mixture, stirring to combine. Beat in half the flour, a cupful at a time, to make a smooth batter. Continue to beat 3 to 4 minutes. Cover and let rise until doubled, 1 to 1 1/2 hours.*

✦ *Stir in several additional cupfuls of flour. Turn out onto a floured surface and knead in remaining flour. Cover and let rise on the kneading surface 30 minutes. Divide dough into 4 pieces. Shape into loaves and place in 4 well-greased 9" x 5" (2 L) loaf pans. Let rise till doubled, about 1 1/2 hours. Bake in a preheated 350°F (180°C) oven 30 to 40 minutes or until deep golden.* **Makes 4 loaves.**

Ozzie's Lunch

Ozzie's Lunch, near St. Andrews, is famous. Rose Anne Waite, whose husband, Ozzie, passed away in 1974, serves road food at its best — deep-fried clams, lobster rolls, scallops and chips and homemade pies. Because she's a proud New Brunswicker she buys her lobster from Shediac, her scallops and shrimp from Grand Manan and her clams from Charlotte County just down the highway and uses local potatoes for her fries. A diner and a truck stop, the sparkling white building is ringed with shaded picnic tables. On Mother's Day, there's a two-hour wait. The big parking area is absolutely jammed and traffic slows on the road.

Just around the corner from Ozzie's is the tiny retail store of Oven Head Salmon Smokers. The words "fabulous," "addictive" and "outstanding" are scribbled in my notebook. Bay of Fundy salmon is brined then smoked for 40 hours over maple wood brought in especially from Quebec.

Soft Bread Rolls

You'll find homemade rolls stuffed with seafood throughout Atlantic Canada at fast food stands, at diners such as Ozzie's near St. Andrews and on the menus of upscale restaurants.

2 1/2 cups (625 mL)	lukewarm water
3/4 cup (175 mL)	sugar
2 tbsp. (25 mL)	active dry yeast
2	eggs, lightly beaten
1 1/2 tsp. (7 mL)	salt
3/4 cup (175 mL)	canola oil
7 – 8 cups (1.75 – 2 L)	all-purpose flour

✦ *In a large mixing bowl, combine 1/2 cup (125 mL) of the water with 2 tsp. (10 mL) of the sugar, stirring to dissolve. Sprinkle with yeast and let stand 10 minutes or until foamy. Whisk in remaining water and sugar, eggs, salt and oil. Beat in flour, a cupful at a time, to make a soft, sticky dough. Turn out onto a well-floured surface and knead 5 to 7 minutes or until smooth and very elastic. Place dough in a lightly greased bowl, turning to grease all over. Cover with greased waxed paper and a tea towel. Let rise in a warm place until doubled, 1 1/2 to 2 hours.*

✦ *Punch down dough and shape into 48 balls the size of golf balls. Place 2 inches (5 cm) apart on well-greased or parchment-lined baking sheets. Cover with a tea towel and let rise until doubled, about 1 1/2 hours.*

✦ *Bake in a preheated 375°F (190°C) oven 12 to 15 minutes or until golden brown and buns sound hollow when tapped on bottom.* **Makes about 4 dozen rolls.**

Anadama Bread

Although cornmeal-based bread can be found across the country, Anadama Bread is part of Atlantic Canada's food culture. In this updated version, molasses — preferably Crosby's — is essential.

1/2 cup (125 mL)	yellow cornmeal
2 cups (500 mL)	boiling water
1/2 cup (125 mL)	warm water
1 tsp. (5 mL)	sugar
2 tbsp. (25 mL)	active dry yeast
1/2 cup (125 mL)	fancy molasses, preferably Crosby's
1/3 cup (75 mL)	unsalted butter, softened
2 tsp. (10 mL)	salt
2 1/2 cups (625 mL)	whole-wheat flour
3 – 4 cups (750 mL – 1 L)	all-purpose or white bread flour
	Additional cornmeal

✦ In a large mixing bowl, cover cornmeal with boiling water. Stir and let stand 30 minutes or until lukewarm.

✦ In a medium bowl, combine warm water, sugar and yeast. Let puff 10 minutes. Stir into softened cornmeal. Beat in molasses, butter, salt and whole-wheat flour until mixture is smooth. Beat in remaining all-purpose flour, a cupful at a time, until dough is no longer sticky. Turn out onto a floured surface. Knead 4 to 6 minutes or until smooth and elastic, adding additional flour as needed.

✦ Place dough in a well-oiled mixing bowl, turning to coat. Cover and let rise until doubled, about 1 hour. Punch down; allow to rise 15 minutes longer. Cut dough in half and shape into loaves. Lightly oil two 9" x 5" (2 L) loaf pans and dust with cornmeal. Transfer loaves to pans, cover and let rise until doubled, 30 to 45 minutes. Bake in a preheated 375°F (190°C) oven 35 to 40 minutes or until well browned. **Makes 2 loaves.**

New Brunswick Cheese

Hallelujah! Another cheese-maker unafraid to use raw milk. Armadale Farms, more specifically Regina Duivenvoorden, specializes in gouda. Her hilltop property, just outside Sussex, overlooks her herd of Holsteins and a covered bridge, above. But, truly, it's her cheddar that is so memorable — biting yet smooth as silk. She sells her buttermilk, cheeses and butter at the Boyce Farmers' Market in Fredericton, at the smaller Moncton market and in a few health food stores.

195

Cape Breton Oatcakes

Many Cape Bretoners have a deep-rooted Scottish heritage. Their foods reflect that fact. These crisp cookies are served at breakfast or lunch or any time a snack is needed. Spread them with butter and spoon on apple butter or simply top them with cheese.

3 cups (750 mL)	quick-cooking rolled oats
1 1/2 cups (375 mL)	all-purpose flour
2/3 cup (150 mL)	sugar
1 tsp. (5 mL)	baking soda
1/2 tsp. (2 mL)	salt
1 cup (250 mL)	shortening or
	lard (the traditional ingredient)
1/4 cup (50 mL)	cold water

✦ *In a large bowl, stir together oats, flour, sugar, baking soda and salt until thoroughly combined. With a pastry blender or 2 knives, cut in the shortening until mixture is crumbly. Continue to mix by hand until it resembles fine crumbs. Sprinkle with cold water and stir until dough holds together.*

✦ *On an oat-covered or flour-dusted surface, roll oat dough until 1/4 inch (5 mm) thick. With a sharp knife, cut into 1- to 2-inch (2.5 to 5 cm) squares or triangles. Transfer to lightly greased baking sheets. Bake in a preheated 375°F (190°F) oven 12 to 14 minutes or until just beginning to turn golden and crisp.*
Makes 3 to 4 dozen oatcakes.

Newfoundland Berry Pudding with Dark Rum 'n' Butter Sauce

Partridgeberries *(Vaccinium vitis-idaea)*, also known as lingonberries, rock cranberries, lowbush cranberries and cow-berries, thrive all over Newfoundland and Labrador. In fact, they grow under all these other various identities in peat bogs, rocky tundra and barrens across northern Canada. They are brilliant red and tart when ripe. Saskatoon berries (serviceberries) or wild blueberries could be substituted in this recipe, but only partridgeberries will give you that distinct taste so loved in Newfoundland.

1/2 cup (125 mL)	unsalted butter, softened
1 1/2 cups (375 mL)	packed brown sugar
2	eggs
1/3 cup (75 mL)	all-purpose flour
1 tbsp. (15 mL)	baking powder
2 tsp. (10 mL)	cinnamon
1/4 tsp. (1 mL)	salt
3 cups (750 mL)	dry bread crumbs
1 cup (250 mL)	milk
3/4 cup (175 mL)	blueberries
3/4 cup (175 mL)	partridgeberries

Dark Rum 'n' Butter Sauce

1/2 cup (125 mL)	unsalted butter
1/2 cup (125 mL)	packed brown sugar
1 cup (250 mL)	whipping cream (35%)
1/4 cup (50 mL)	dark rum

✦ In a large bowl, beat butter and sugar until light and fluffy. Beat in eggs until smooth. In a separate bowl, stir together flour, baking powder, cinnamon, salt and bread crumbs. Gradually stir bread-crumb mixture into butter mixture alternately with milk to form a stiff dough. Fold in blueberries and partridgeberries.

✦ Spoon into a well-greased 6-cup (1.5 L) pudding mould. Cover with parchment, then foil. Place on a plate in a stock pot or Dutch oven. Fill with about 3 inches (8 cm) of water; bring water just to a simmer. Cover and steam about 1 1/2 hours or until cake tester inserted in centre comes out dry. Cool slightly before unmoulding. Meanwhile, prepare sauce.

✦ Melt butter in a medium saucepan over medium heat. Stir in sugar and bring to a boil, stirring constantly. Stir in cream and rum; simmer 2 minutes. Serve wedges of pudding with warm sauce poured over top. Refrigerate any leftover sauce. *Makes 6 servings.*

Bidgood's

A table filled with blue potatoes greeted me the first time I visited Bidgood's, the near-legendary store in the Goulds, a suburb of St. John's. Walking down the aisles of the supermarket is like viewing a compendium of real Newfoundland food, from pails of salt beef to partridge-berries. Across Canada, whenever the store's name is mentioned, displaced Newfoundlanders wax nostalgic.

Poutines à Trou

Anita Landry and I met years ago while she was promoting New Brunswick's great seafood. As Acadians, she and her family enjoy many traditions. Poutines à Trou is one such special dish. She writes, "This can be made year-round. However, in our family, Mother would make them especially at Christmastime with a kind of apple we grew and that seemed to be ready only at that time of year. This was the treat on Christmas morning and to lightly heat them in the oven of our wood stove made them taste even better. The saltiness of the pork with every bite is scrumptious. Some people enjoy cranberries mixed with the apples, adding four or five berries to the filling of each poutine."

If available, use Northern Spy apples or Gravenstein, the traditional apple of Atlantic Canada.

Dough

5 cups (1.25 L)	all-purpose flour
2 tsp. (10 mL)	cream of tartar
1 tsp. (5 mL)	baking soda
1 tsp. (5 mL)	salt
1/2 lb. (250 g)	cold shortening
1 3/4 cups (425 mL)	milk

Filling

5	large apples, peeled and diced
1 cup (250 mL)	raisins or cranberries
1/4 cup (50 mL)	finely diced salt pork

Syrup

1 1/4 cups (300 mL)	sugar
1 cup (250 mL)	water

◆ In a large bowl, stir together flour, cream of tartar, baking soda and salt. Using a pastry blender or your fingers, cut or rub in the shortening until mixture is the texture of coarse crumbs. With a wooden spoon and then your hands, work in milk, about 1/2 cup (125 mL) at a time, to form a stiff dough. Divide in half, wrap with plastic wrap and let rest while you prepare the filling.

◆ In a bowl, stir together apples and raisins. In a skillet over medium heat, cook salt pork just until crisp; pour off fat.

◆ Roll out 1 piece of dough to a 1/2-inch (1 cm) thick rectangle. Cut into 4 rough rectangles. Place about 2/3 cup (150 mL) of the apple mixture in centre of each rectangle and top with a few pieces of pork. Wet edges of dough with a little milk. At one short end, overlap corners to form a cone. Repeat at other short end, to bring the poutine into a rough round with an opening in the top. Place in a buttered 9" x 13" (4 L) casserole dish. Repeat with remaining ingredients. Bake in a preheated 400°F (200°C) oven 15 minutes.

◆ Meanwhile, make syrup. In small saucepan, bring water and sugar to a boil for 1 minute. Remove from heat. Pour about 1/3 of syrup into centres of poutines. Reduce heat to 350°F (180°C); bake another 35 to 40 minutes or until golden brown and apples are tender. Pour remaining syrup into poutines. *Makes 8 servings.*

198

Big Tancook Island

Today visiting Big Tancook Island (once renowned for its sauerkraut) is like entering a time warp. Family names have been around for 200 years. Cars need no licences and the roads are graded only when the mood hits. Potholes abound. Seed from the famous cabbages is still saved and every year planted after the first new moon in May. The pheasant-populated cabbage fields are fertilized with seaweed raked from the shale shores. The heads are big, and the tighter they are the better and heavier the sauerkraut. The shredded cabbage ferments for only two weeks before it's sold in pails.

Annapolis Valley Pear and Buttermilk Tart

This fabulous tart may be made all winter long using Bosc pears.

1 cup (250 mL)	sliced dried apricots
1/2 cup (125 mL)	apple cider
1 1/4 cups (300 mL)	all-purpose flour
1/4 cup (50 mL)	sugar
2/3 cup (150 mL)	chilled unsalted butter, cut in small cubes
3	large Bosc pears, peeled and thinly sliced
1/3 cup (75 mL)	buttermilk or unflavoured yogurt

Crumble Topping

3/4 cup (175 mL)	brown sugar
1/4 cup (50 mL)	butter, softened
2 tbsp. (25 mL)	all-purpose flour

Topping

1/2 cup (125 mL)	sour cream
1 tbsp. (15 mL)	brown sugar

✦ *In a small saucepan, combine apricots and cider. Cover; bring to a boil. Reduce heat and simmer 5 minutes. Remove from heat; let cool while preparing crust.*

✦ *In a food processor, combine flour and sugar. Add butter cubes and pulse till mixture looks like fine crumbs. Pat carefully into a 10-inch (25 cm) flan pan with removable bottom. Bake in a preheated 375°F (190°C) oven 15 minutes.*

✦ *Spoon apricots evenly over crust. Arrange pear slices on top. Drizzle with buttermilk. In a small bowl, mix sugar, butter and flour with a fork until blended. Crumble evenly over tart; return tart to oven. Bake an additional 45 minutes or until pears are tender and crust is deep golden brown. Let cool. Stir together sour cream and brown sugar. Refrigerate until needed.*

✦ *Top slices of pie with small spoonfuls of sweetened sour cream.* **Makes 8 servings.**

Nova Scotian Wine

At Jost Vineyards on the Northumberland Strait, Hans Christian Jost carries on his father's tradition by vinifying Seyval Blanc and Maréchal Foch to win numerous international medals. The company's ice wine, the only one produced to date in eastern Canada, is made with grapes bred at the college where viticultural research is carried out in Geisenheim, Germany. Farther south, Sainte Famille Wines has a small vineyard on the site of an Acadian village, La Paroise Sainte Famille de Pisiquit. Like Jost, their production includes Seyval Blanc and Maréchal Foch, Riesling and Vidal. The fruit wines of Telder-Berry are refreshing and unusual. Starting with a pick-your-own strawberry farm 15 years ago, the Telder family is now fermenting a large variety of Annapolis Valley fruit, from wild blueberries and cranberries to old-fashioned Gravenstein apples and pears.

Sand Cove Rhubarb and
Penfield Bog Cranberry Sorbet

Ross and Willa Mavis own the Inn on the Cove near
Saint John, New Brunswick. Ross roves the
Maritimes searching for new ingredients and then
cooks up a storm in their kitchen on his locally
broadcast program, *Tide's Table*.

1 3/4 cups (425 mL)	water
3/4 cup (175 mL)	sugar
2	sprigs fresh rosemary
5 cups (1.25 L)	chopped fresh rhubarb (1 lb./500 g)
2 cups (500 mL)	cranberries
Pinch	salt
1	envelope unflavoured gelatin
1	egg white (optional)
	Rosemary leaves for garnish

✦ *In a small saucepan over medium heat, combine 1 cup
(250 mL) of the water, sugar and rosemary sprigs. Bring to a
boil, reduce heat and simmer 5 minutes. Remove from heat,
cover and let stand 15 minutes. Strain, discarding rosemary.
In a large saucepan, combine rhubarb, cranberries, 1/2 cup
(125 mL) of the remaining water and salt. Bring to a boil,
reduce heat and simmer 7 minutes or until cranberries begin
to pop and rhubarb is softened. Remove from heat; stir in sugar
syrup. Sprinkle gelatin over remaining 1/4 cup (50 mL) water;
let stand 1 minute, then stir into hot rhubarb mixture. Cool
completely. If a slightly frothier sorbet is desired, beat egg
white to stiff peaks and fold gently into rhubarb mixture.*

✦ *Freeze in a 9" x 13" (4 L) baking dish or other casserole 1 to 2
hours or until almost firm. Using an electric mixer, beat well
until rhubarb is very creamy but chunks of cranberry remain.
Return to freezer 2 to 3 hours or until completely frozen. Before
serving, soften at room temperature 20 minutes. Garnish with
fresh rosemary leaves. **Makes 8 to 10 servings.***

Apple Schnaps

*From a traditional copper still outside the
tiny New Brunswick village of Baie-Verte,
Werner and Roswitha Rosswog (above)
produce Atlantic Canada's only apple
schnaps at Winegarden Estate. Proudly using
only New Brunswick fruit, they make a
proper eau-de-vie — dry and strong.*

201

Left: *Sour cherries in Annapolis valley*

St. John River Gingerbread

All along the St. John River, which meanders and twists its way from the forests of New Brunswick to the Bay of Fundy, small ferries criss-cross its ever-expanding width. Once there were old inns at these crossings where travellers could chase away the Maritime chill with a cup of tea and a slice of warm gingerbread blanketed with whipped cream.

1/2 cup (125 mL)	butter, softened
1/2 cup (125 mL)	sugar
1	egg
1 cup (250 mL)	molasses
2 1/2 cups (625 mL)	all-purpose flour
2 tsp. (10 mL)	baking soda
1 tsp. (5 mL)	cinnamon
1 tsp. (5 mL)	ground ginger
1/2 tsp. (2 mL)	ground cloves
1/2 tsp. (2 mL)	salt
1 cup (250 mL)	hot water
	Lightly sweetened whipped cream (optional)

✦ In a large bowl, cream butter, sugar and egg until light and lemon-coloured. Beat in molasses. In a separate bowl, sift or stir together flour, baking soda, cinnamon, ginger, cloves and salt. Blend with creamed mixture, stirring until no dry spots remain. Stir in the hot water, beating well.

✦ Pour into two 8-inch (20 cm) cake pans lined with waxed or parchment paper. Bake in a preheated 325°F (160°C) oven 30 to 35 minutes or until tester inserted in centre comes out clean. Slice into wedges and serve with lightly sweetened whipped cream. (For a special dessert, slice layers in half and fill with whipped cream and top with fresh peaches or applesauce.) *Makes 10 to 12 servings.*

Toutons

Golden and puffy, toutons were originally made on baking days with bits of leftover yeast dough. A real Newfoundland tradition, this delicious fried bread is best served piping hot with lots of molasses.

1/4 cup (50 mL)	skim milk
1/4 cup (50 mL)	shortening
1 tbsp. (15 mL)	salt
2 tsp. (10 mL)	sugar
3 cups (750 mL)	warm water
1 tbsp. (15 mL)	active dry yeast
6 cups (1.5 L)	all-purpose flour
	Canola oil for frying
	Molasses or maple syrup

✦ In a saucepan, combine milk, shortening, salt and 1 tsp. (5 mL) of the sugar. Heat until shortening melts. Let cool to lukewarm.

✦ In a small bowl, dissolve remaining 1 tsp. (5 mL) sugar in warm water, sprinkle yeast over top and let stand 10 minutes or until foamy.

✦ In a large mixing bowl, combine yeast mixture and milk mixture. Gradually beat in flour, 1 cup (250 mL) at a time, to make a soft, slightly sticky dough.

✦ Turn dough out onto a well-floured surface and knead until smooth and elastic, adding remaining flour as needed to keep dough smooth and to prevent it from sticking.

✦ Place dough in a lightly greased bowl, turning to grease all over. Cover with greased waxed paper and a tea towel. Let rise in a warm place until doubled, about 1 hour. Punch down dough and turn out onto a lightly floured board. Divide into 24 equal portions, roll into balls and flatten into 2-inch (5 cm) rounds.

✦ Heat 1/2 inch (1 cm) oil in a high-sided frying pan over medium heat and fry toutons, in batches, for 5 minutes on each side or until golden brown and insides are dry. Drain on paper towels and allow to cool slightly. Serve with molasses or maple syrup. *Makes 24 toutons.*

Purity

The Purity Factory in St. John's smells so good! In one large room partridgeberry-apple jam has just been cooked; in another they're pouring and pulling satin ribbons to make peppermint nobs. On the other side of the plant, they're baking old-fashioned British cream crackers. The employees can claim more than 1000 years of product knowledge among them, with the average work record being about 20 years. Baker Harvey Stringer has been there 25 years. Candy-maker Doug Evans, who when we visited was making banana kisses, began his on-the-job learning 30 years ago. This company is part of the heritage of Newfoundland food. Purity hard bread is used from Hibernia to the Great Northern Peninsula for fish 'n' brewis, while Purity syrups have long been the basis for drinks associated with "mumming," the New Year's Day custom during which neighbours appear in disguise at each other's homes.

Classic Rhubarb Chutney

The tradition of preserving is still very strong in Atlantic Canada. Clifford Matthews, co-owner and the man in the kitchen at Gowrie House in Sydney Mines, Cape Breton, shared this recipe. He recommends it with grilled chicken or pork tenderloin. I love it with cheese!

3/4 cup (175 mL)	sugar
1/2 cup (125 mL)	white wine vinegar
1/2 cup (125 mL)	apple cider
2	cloves garlic, sliced
1 1/2 tsp. (7 mL)	minced fresh ginger
1/2 tsp. (2 mL)	salt
1/8 tsp. (0.5 mL)	freshly ground black pepper
1/8 tsp. (0.5 mL)	ground allspice
1/8 tsp. (0.5 mL)	ground coriander
Pinch	each cinnamon and ground cloves
1/4 cup (50 mL)	sultana raisins
4 cups (1 L)	1/2-inch (1 cm) rhubarb slices
1	large peach, peeled and diced
1 cup (250 mL)	sliced strawberries
1/4 cup (50 mL)	minced red onion
1 1/2 tsp. (7 mL)	grainy mustard
1 tsp. (5 mL)	minced jalapeno pepper (optional)

✦ In a large saucepan, combine sugar, vinegar and cider; bring to a boil, stirring until sugar is dissolved. Stir in garlic, ginger, salt, pepper, allspice, coriander, cinnamon and cloves. Add raisins; simmer 5 minutes. Stir in rhubarb and peach; simmer 5 minutes. Place in large sieve set over a bowl to collect juices.

✦ Pour juices back into saucepan, bring to a boil and simmer briskly about 10 minutes or until reduced by about one-third. Stir in strawberries, onion, mustard and jalapeno pepper; cook 1 minute, stirring. Remove from heat and stir in reserved rhubarb mixture. Cool. Pour into sterilized jars and seal with new lids. Refrigerate up to 2 weeks. **Makes about 6 cups (1.5 L).**

Chow Chow

No Nova Scotian autumn would be complete without a batch of chow chow filling your house with spicy aromas of the harvest. This recipe has been handed down for generations in families and among friends in the Lunenburg/Mahone Bay area. Lynne Perry, the director of the province's South Shore Tourism Association, was given it by a neighbour and, as the tradition dictates, shared it with me.

8 quarts (8 L)	green tomatoes, finely diced
1/2 cup (125 mL)	pickling salt
5 lb. (2.2 kg)	onions, sliced
1/2 cup (125 mL)	mixed pickling spice
8 cups (2 L)	cider vinegar
3 lb. (1.5 kg)	brown sugar

✦ Place green tomato pieces in a large bowl. Sprinkle with salt; place a weighted plate on top and let stand overnight. Drain but don't rinse.

✦ In a stock pot, combine tomatoes and onions. Tie pickling spice in a piece of cheesecloth and place in the centre of tomatoes. Add vinegar to barely cover. Add sugar. Bring to a boil; reduce heat and simmer 4 hours or until tomatoes are very tender but still hold their shape.

✦ Pour into pint (500 mL) bottles and seal with new lids. Process in boiling-water bath 10 minutes. **Makes about twelve 16-oz. (500 mL) jars.**

203

David's Mincemeat

David O'Brien and I are culinary soulmates. We met when he, at the request of McCain Foods, did the legal work required to pull together Cuisine Canada in 1994. David is one of the best-travelled corporate lawyers in the nation. His knowledge of Canada, and in particular the Maritimes, is deep.

David started making mincemeat about 15 years ago when he did a stint in Newfoundland, and now, living in Woodstock, New Brunswick, he makes 80 L (80 quarts) every year to ship to friends from coast to coast. His entire house is permeated with the fragrances of Christmas for weeks before December 25.

3 lb. (1.5 kg)	regular ground beef
3 3/4 cups (925 mL)	demerara sugar
1 cup (250 mL)	Crosby's fancy molasses
5 lb. (2.2 kg)	apples, peeled and sliced
2 lb. (1 kg)	muscatel raisins (6 cups/1.5 L)
1 lb. (500 g)	currants (3 cups/750 mL)
1 lb. (500 g)	sultana raisins (3 cups/750 mL)
10 oz. (300 g)	candied mixed fruit (1 1/2 cups/375 mL)
10 oz. (300 g)	candied orange peel (1 1/2 cups/375 mL)
10 oz. (300 g)	candied citron (1 1/2 cups/375 mL)
8 oz. (250 g)	chopped pecans (2 cups/500 mL)
8 oz. (250 g)	chopped almonds (1 1/2 cups/375 mL)
1 tbsp. (15 mL)	salt
1 tbsp. (15 mL)	cinnamon
1 tbsp. (15 mL)	mace
1 tbsp. (15 mL)	ground cloves
3 1/2 cups (875 mL)	apple cider
2 1/4 cups (550 mL)	brandy

✦ In a large stock pot, combine all ingredients except brandy. Bring to a boil, reduce heat and simmer 1 1/2 hours or until apples are very tender and dark brown. Stir frequently to prevent sticking. Mix in brandy; pour into clean quart (1 L) jars and seal with new lids. Process in boiling-water bath 1 1/2 hours. Cool. *Makes about 8 quarts (8 L).*

Mincemeat Pie

✦ Roll out a bottom crust of your favourite pie pastry and place in 9-inch (23 cm) pie plate. Add 1 jar (4 cups/1 L) mincemeat, spreading it evenly. Top with top crust, crimp edges and make a few cuts in crust for vents. Brush with milk. Bake in a preheated 400°F (200°C) oven 10 minutes. Reduce heat to 350°F (180°C) and bake another 40 minutes or until crust is golden. For a lighter, taller pie, add 3 cups (750 mL) chopped apples, 1/4 cup (50 mL) brown sugar and 2 tbsp. (25 mL) lemon juice to mincemeat, piling filling high in pie plate. Cooking time may be 10 minutes longer. *Makes one 9-inch (23 cm) pie.*

Berry Wine

In November 1993, after years of waiting for a licence, Markland Cottage Winery opened, specializing in products made with Newfoundland and Labrador's huge crop of berries. Blueberries and partridgeberries are vinified both separately and in a combination named Barrens Blend. Their bakeapple (cloudberry) wine is the only one in the world.

Valerie's Version of Lady Ashburnham's Pickles

Maria "Rye" Anderson was a Fredericton telephone operator who married Capt. Tom Ashburnham, the black sheep of a titled English family. On the demise of his father, the fourth Earl of Ashburnham, and his four older brothers, young Tom became the Earl and his New Brunswick wife the Countess of Ashburnham. The new countess is said to have detested household chores and hence hired her sister to tend the kitchen and make her favourite pickles, jars of which were donated to charities.

Valerie Kidney, a fifth-generation New Brunswicker herself, shares her rendition. It is less chunky, not quite as thick and, I think, more delicious than the original.

12	6- to 8-inch (15 – 20 cm) cucumbers
1/2 cup (125 mL)	pickling salt
8 cups (2 L)	diced onions
1	sweet red pepper, minced
4 cups (1 L)	white vinegar
4 cups (1 L)	sugar
1/4 cup (50 mL)	all-purpose flour
2 tbsp. (25 mL)	dry mustard
2 tsp. (10 mL)	mustard seed
2 tsp. (10 mL)	celery seed
1 1/2 tsp. (7 mL)	turmeric

✦ Peel cucumbers. Chop finely, removing any large seeds. Transfer to a large bowl; sprinkle with salt and let stand overnight.

✦ Drain cucumbers and place in a large, heavy saucepan. Add onions, red pepper and vinegar. Bring to a boil, reduce heat and cook 10 minutes.

✦ In a separate bowl, thoroughly stir together sugar, flour, mustard, mustard seed, celery seed and turmeric. Stir dry ingredients into cucumber mixture. Continue to stir and cook until mixture returns to a boil. Simmer, uncovered, 4 to 5 minutes or until slightly thickened. Ladle into 1-cup (250 mL) sterilized jars and seal. Store in a cool, dark place. **Makes eighteen 1-cup (250 mL) jars.**

Saint John Fog

Innkeeper Margret Begner of Saint John, New Brunswick, enjoys this with her coffee, particularly in "terrible winter weather." Use only the freshest eggs and soft, supple vanilla beans. After scraping the seeds into the liqueur, plunge the outer bean into a pot of sugar to allow it to infuse for a few days. The vanilla sugar is particularly delicious when used in baking.

4	egg yolks
1 3/4 cups (425 mL)	icing sugar
1	vanilla bean
1 cup (250 mL)	half & half cream (10%)
1 cup (250 mL)	vodka

✦ In a large bowl, whisk egg yolks with sugar. With a sharp knife, slit the vanilla bean lengthwise and, using the tip of the blade, scrape the seeds into the egg mixture. Reserve the pod for other uses. Whisk the cream into the egg mixture, stirring to dissolve the sugar completely. Mix in the vodka. Transfer to a glass container or bottle; refrigerate 2 to 3 days to develop the flavours. Serve chilled. **Makes 2 1/2 cups (625 mL).**

205

There are certain facts that, although not particularly fashionable, must eventually be understood if this marvellous nation of ours is to flourish...no, if it is to survive.

We must begin to eat locally, regionally, nationally and only then internationally. Such a philosophy takes work and creativity and courage. It is very difficult to achieve. From our home and commercial kitchens we must learn to blast free and explore our local production, fitting it into our own ethnicity, encouraging our gardeners and farmers to grow what they can, sharing our knowledge and our tastes. This is the foundation of what Canada can become. This is our future.

Acknowledgements

Special thanks must go to my magnificent mom, to my daughters-in-law, Jackie and Szara, and to my super stepdad, the late Glenn MacDonald, for his wise counsel; and as always to the Morris family — tasters, testers and friends extraordinaire.

Thank you Denise and Anna and Eva, for the hand-holding and cajoling. And thank you to Shaun Oakey and to my truly dedicated team of recipe testers...Heather Epp, Jill Snider, Laura Buckley and Carolyn Gall.

Many thanks to The Canola Council of Canada and The Saskatchewan Canola Development Commission for supporting the testing of the recipes and thanks to Via Rail for helping with my travel.

I would also like to acknowledge Judy Love Rondeau of the Canadian Tourism Commission who had infinite faith in my dream and moved mountains to help us with this book on so many occasions.

My most sincere thanks to Valerie Kidney of New Brunswick for sharing recipes and great conversations; to Randy Brooks of Nova Scotia for so much encouragement over the years; to Carol Horne of Prince Edward Island and Diana Parsons of Newfoundland who helped to expedite our Hibernia trip. Hugs to Isabel Gil and Fair Gordon of Quebec who have helped me from the earliest stages of my career; to Richard Séguin of Quebec City who loves his city even more than I do; and to Gilles Bengle of Montreal who has helped me catch more than one plane when we lingered too long in a bistro or sugar shack. Thank you Tom Boyd — you are Ontario's finest! Thanks to my fishing buddy Colette Fontaine of Manitoba (mine was bigger!); my driving buddy, Nadine Howard of Saskatchewan; Cindy Burr of truly supernatural British Columbia; and Heather Day of Victoria who introduced me to the wonders of Rogers Chocolates.

Throughout my many pan-Canadian odysseys, there have been people who have influenced my career and my philosophy of food. Those who have had faith in me while I was tackling and wrestling with a very unusual career. They are my personal North Stars:

Jo Marie Powers, Carol Ferguson, Julia Aitken, Marie Nightingale, Elizabeth Baird, Stephen Smith, Rob McLaughlin, my dear friends Archie McLean and Maureen Read, Eric Peterson, Philippe Borel, Serge Simard, Werner Sapp, David Kent, Eve Johnson, Sharon Burke, Pierre Audette and Ann Desjardins, Bill Bennett and Marcy Beaton, Roger Dufau, Stephen Wong, Paul Raynor, Anne Lindsay, Nettie Cronish, Marilyn Crowley, Helen Kates, Sinclair and Frederique Philip, Champlain Charest and Monique Nadeau, Dr. Nancy and Bob Turner, Mitch Kostuch, David Gamble, Donald Ziraldo, Tom and Len Pennachetti, Helen Young, Paul Speck, Michael and Nobuyo Stadtländer, Tanya and Don MacLaurin, Robert and Liliane Gagnon, Dorothy Long, Larry and Margaret Dickenson.

Finally a huge thank-you goes to Raincoast Books who believed in this project from day one.

Canadian Tourism Commission

The Canadian Tourism Commission is an industry-government collaboration that promotes Canada domestically and internationally. Their website is terrific!

Tel: 877-8-CANADA (877-822-6232)
www.canadatourism.com

ViaRail

Via Rail is my favourite way of travelling in Canada. Their web site has schedules, new promotions, and information on crossing the country from Halifax to Vancouver.

888-VIARAIL (842-7245)
www.viarail.ca

Cuisine Canada

Cuisine Canada is a non-profit organization founded in 1994 to promote the regional cuisines of Canada. Its main activities include a conference – Northern Bounty, held every two years in a different region – and the Cuisine Canada national cookbook awards. Membership is open to anyone in the food and wine or related industries, including researchers, food scientists, nutritionists, food writers, chefs, restaurateurs, culinary historians, academics, hotel- and innkeepers, publishers and manufacturers. Each region holds events that are designed to strengthen the network of members.

877-828-7463
www.cuisinecanada.ca

For more specific information on wines and the wine growing regions in Canada, you may wish to contact the following:

B.C. Wine Institute

Suite 400, 601 West Broadway
Vancouver, B.C.
V5Z 4C2
800-811-9911
www.bcwine.com

Wine Council of Ontario

110 Hannover Drive, Suite B205
St. Catharines, Ontario
L2W 1A4
905-684-8070
www.wineroute.com

Fruit Wines Association of Canada

www.fruitwines.ca

Provincial Tourism Associations

British Columbia
800-663-6000
www.travel.bc.ca

Vancouver Island
250-754-3500
www.islands.bc.ca

Alberta
800-661-8888
www.discoveralberta.com

Saskatchewan
877-2ESCAPE (237-2273)
www.sasktourism.com

Manitoba
800-665-0040
www.gov.mb.ca/travel-manitoba

Ontario
800-668-2746
www.travelinx.com

Québec
800-363-7777
www.tourisme.gov.qc.ca

New Brunswick
800-561-0123
www.gov.nb.ca/tourism

Prince Edward Island
888-PEI-PLAY
www.peiplay.com

Nova Scotia
800-565-0000
www.explore.gov.ns.ca

Newfoundland and Labrador
800-563-6353
www.public.gov.nf.ca

Yukon
867-667-5340
www.touryukon.com

Northwest Territories
800-661-0788
www.nwttravel.nt.ca

For the past eighteen years I've developed a personal list of great dining experiences, some upscale, some rustic. Here are a few. In all of these you can taste the flavours of Canada.

British Columbia

Bishop's
2183 West 4th Avenue,
Vancouver V6K 1N7
604-738-2025
www.bishops.net

Chef Bernard's Café
1–4573 Chateau Boulevard,
Whistler V0N 1B4
604-932-7051

Diva at the Met
645 Howe Street,
Vancouver V6C 2Y9
604-602-7788
www.divamet.com

The Empress
721 Government Street,
Victoria V8W 1W5
250-384-8111
www.cphotels.ca

**Hainle Vineyards Estate Winery /
Amphora Bistro**
5355 Trepanier Bench Road,
Peachland V0H 1X0
250-767-2525 / 800-767-3109
www.hainle.com

Liliget Feast House
1724 Davie Street,
Vancouver V6G 1W2
604-681-7044

Lumière
2551 West Broadway,
Vancouver V6K 2E9
604-739-8185

Oceanwood Country Inn
630 Dinner Bay Road,
Mayne Island V0N 2J0
250-539-5074
www.oceanwood.com

Piccolo Mondo
850 Thurlow Street,
Vancouver V6E 1W2
604-688-1633

Sooke Harbour House
1528 Whiffen Spit Road,
Sooke V0S IN0
250-642-3421 / 800-889-9688
www.sooke-harbour.com

Spinnakers
308 Catherine Street,
Victoria V9A 3S8
250-384-6613
www.spinnakers.com

Tojo's Restaurant
202–777 West Broadway,
Vancouver V5Z 4J7
604-872-8050

The Wickaninnish Inn / Pointe Restaurant
Osprey Lane at Chesterman Beach,
Tofino V0R 2Z0
250-725-3100 / 800-333-4604
www.wickinn.com

Top: *Cranberry martini*

The Prairies

Calories Bakery & Restaurant
721 Broadway Avenue,
Saskatoon, Saskatchewan S7N 1B3
306-665-7991

Canadian Mountain Holidays
P.O. Box 1660,
Banff, Alberta T0L 0C0
410-762-7100 / 800-661-0252
www.cmhhike.com

North Knife Lake Lodge
North Knife Lake, Manitoba
Reservations through Webber's Lodges,
P.O. Box 304,
Churchill, Manitoba R0B 0E0
204-675-8875 / 800-665-0476
www.virtualnorth.com/webbers

Teatro
200 – 8th Avenue S.E.
Calgary, Alberta T2G 0K7
403-290-1012

River Café
Prince's Island Park,
Calgary, Alberta
403-261-7670
www.river-cafe.com

The Post Hotel
P.O. Box 69,
Lake Louise, Alberta T0L 1E0
403-522-3989 / 800-661-1586
www.posthotel.com

Tall Grass Prairie Bread Company
859 Westminster Avenue,
Winnipeg, Manitoba R3G 1B1
204-783-5097 (bakery)
204-779-4082 (office)

Ontario

Auberge de Pommier
4150 Yonge Street,
Toronto M2P 2C6
416-222-2220
www.toprestaurants.com/Toronto/Auberge

Britton House / Cook Not Mad
110 Clarence Street,
Gananoque K7G 2C7
613-382-4361

Eigennsen Farm
R.R.#2,
Singhampton N0C 1M0
519-922-3128

Hillebrand Estates Winery / Vineyard Café
1249 Niagara Stone Road,
Niagara-on-the-Lake L0S 1J0
905-468-7123
www.hillebrand.com

The Inn and Tennis Club
McKellar P0G 1C0
705-389-2171 (summer) / 416-245-5606 (off season)
www.manitou-online.com

Langdon Hall Country House Hotel
R.R.#33,
Cambridge N3H 4R8
519-740-2100 / 800-268-1898
www.countryinns.org/langdonhall

**On the Twenty Restaurant & Wine Bar /
Vintners Inn**
3836 Main Street, Jordan L0R 1S0
905-562-7313 (restaurant) / 905-562-5336 or
800-701-8074 (inn)
www.vintnersinn.on.ca

Vineland Estates Winery / Restaurant
R.R.#1, 3620 Moyer Road,
Vineland L0R 2C0
888-VINELAND (846-3526)
www.vineland.com

Québec

Auberge Chez Denis à François
404, chemin d'en Haut,
Havre-Aubert, Îles de la Madeleine G0B 1J0
418-937-2371
www.ilesdelamadeleine.com

Auberge Georgeville
71, chemin Channel,
Georgeville J0B 1T0
819-843-8683
www.fortune1000.ca/georgeville

Auberge Hatley
325 Virgin Hill,
North Hatley J0B 2C0
819-842-2451
www.northhatley.com

Auberge La P'tite Baie
187, route 199,
Havre-aux-Maisons, Îles de la Madeleine G0B 1K0
418-969-4073
www.ilesdelamadeleine.com

Bistro Champlain
75, chemin Masson,
Ste-Marguerite du Lac Masson J0T 1L0
450-228-4988
www.bistroachamplain.qc.ca

Le Château Frontenac
1, rue des Carrières,
Québec G1R 5J5
418-692-3861
www.cphotels.ca

Hovey Manor
Hovey Road,
North Hatley J0B 2C0
819-842-2421
www.manoirhovey.com

L'eau à la Bouche
3003 boul. Ste. Adèle,
Ste. Adèle J8B 2N6
450-229-2991

Laurie Raphael
117, Dalhousie,
Vieux-Port, Québec G1K 9C8
418-692-4555

La Marée Haute
25, chemin des Fumoirs,
Havre-Aubert, Îles de la Madeleine G0B 1J0
418-937-2492
www.ilesdelamadeleine.com

Le Passe Partout
3857, boul. Décarie,
Montréal H4A 3J6
514-487-7750 (restaurant) / 514-487-9887 (bakery)

La Table des Roy
1188, chemin Lavernière,
Étang-du-Nord, Îles de la Madeleine G0B 1E0
418-986-3004
www.ilesdelamadeleine.com

Unibroue / Fourquet Forchettes
80, Des Carrières,
Chambly J3L 2H6
450-658-7658
www.unibroue.com

Atlantic Canada

Amherst Shore Country Inn
R.R.#2,
Amherst, Nova Scotia B4H 3X9
902-667 4800 / 800-661-2724 (reservations)
www.ascinn.ns.ca

Chef to Go
2 Barnes Road,
St. John's, Newfoundland A1C 3Y2
709-754-2491
www.cheftogo.nf.ca

Dufferin Inn/San Martello Dining Room
357 Dufferin Row,
Saint John, New Brunswick E2M 2J7
506-635-5968
www.heritageinns.com/dufferininn

Gowrie House
139 Shore Road,
Sydney Mines, Nova Scotia B1V 1A6
902-544-1050

Inn on the Cove
1371 Sand Cove Road,
Saint John, New Brunswick E2M 4Z9
506-672-7799
www.innonthecove.com

Inn at Bay Fortune
Bay Fortune, Prince Edward Island C0A 2B6
902-687-3745 (summer) / 860-296-1348 (off season)
www.innatbayfortune.com

Inn at Spry Point
(sister property of the Inn at Bay Fortune)
Spry Point Road,
Souris, Prince Edward Island C0A 2B0
902-583-2400 (summer) / 806 296 1348 (off season)
www.innatsprypoint.com

Seasons in Thyme
644 Water Street E.,
Summerside, Prince Edward Island C1N 4J1
902-888-DINE
www.seasonsinthyme.com

Sheraton – Fredericton
225 Woodstock Road,
Fredericton, New Brunswick E3B 2H8
506-457-7000
www.sheraton.com

Tattingstone
434 Main Street,
Wolfville, Nova Scotia B0P 1X0
902-542-7696
www.valleyweb.com/tattingstoneinn

218

220

223